COMPLETE DEFENSE TO KING PAWN OPENINGS

COMPLETE DEFENSE TO KING PAWN OPENINGS

Eric Schiller

Cardoza Publishing

To the memory of Harry Golombek, Grandmaster,
International Arbiter, journalist, author and friend.

FIRST EDITION

Copyright © 1998 by Eric Schiller
- All Rights Reserved -

Library of Congress Catalogue Card No: 97-94716
ISBN: 0-940685-91-4

CARDOZA PUBLISHING
P.O. Box 1500 Cooper Station, New York, NY 10276
Phone (718)743-5229 • Fax (718)743-8284
Email: Cardozapub@aol.com
Web Site- www.cardozapub.com

Write for you free catalogue of gaming and chess books, equipment, software and computer games.

TABLE OF CONTENTS

INTRODUCTION

This powerful repertoire gives you a complete opening system against any King Pawn opening (1.e4), based on the very powerful and flexible Caro-Kann, the favorite weapon of many of the greatest chess players. It has been used extensively by amateurs and tournament players, as well as many World Champions, including Botvinnik, Petrosian and Anatoly Karpov, the current FIDE titleholder.

This book contains everything you need to know even if you have never played the Caro-Kann before or haven't even heard of it! Concepts are presented so that without memorizing any of the moves, you will still have a deep understanding of the strategies and tactics that will limit White's ability to obtain any significant opening edge, and allow you to seize the initiative and take control of the game.

You'll learn the main lines played by Grandmasters, and also all of the strange sidelines seen in amateur play. All White's options and strategies are explained in detail, and a plan is given for Black to combat them all. Analysis is up-to-date and backed by examples drawn from games of top stars. All of the latest theoretical opinions have been checked and evaluated, and the moves I recommend for Black should hold up even against the most experienced opponents.

Many repertoire books are just a jungle of variations with a labyrinth of lines and little discussion. Not so here. You'll get all the background you need, with explanations of critical ideas, and the move by move thinking of complete games by amateurs and top players alike so that you get a full picture of an opening, from the very first moves right through to the mate. This is important in the Caro-Kann since Black often has the edge once an endgame is reached.

This is the opening I have relied on for most of my career, and although I use other openings, the Caro-Kann is my favorite. I share a lot of my secrets with you in this book, even moves which have not yet been played and are kept in my electronic notebooks, in the hopes of making you a winner at the game of chess!

CARO-KANN DEFENSE

The Caro-Kann Defense is a solid defensive strategy that quickly plants a stake in the center of the board. It begins with the moves **1.e4 c6.**

The plan is to play 2...d5, no matter what White replies. The pawn at d5 will be supported by a pawn at c6, which, unlike a pawn at e6 as in the French Defense, does not block the entrance of the bishop at c8 into the game.

The Caro-Kann Defense, named for Horatio Caro and Marcus Kann, who were tournament players in the 19th century, appeals to patient players who relish fascinating endgame play. Even though it is one of the more popular defenses, the size of the repertoire is much smaller than in, say, the Sicilian Defense. Black gets to pare down the number of potential enemy strategies very quickly. The Caro-Kann also appeals to players with a strong fighting spirit. Tactics can dominate the middlegame, with long combinations involving temporary and permanent sacrifices.

The stronger the endgame skills, the better, since the Caro-Kann often leads to endgames which are difficult to win, or even draw (some of the time)! As you play the Caro-Kann your understanding of many endgames, especially those with rooks and minor pieces, will broaden and deepen, making you a better overall player.

Many great players have used the Caro-Kann Defense and you will meet some of them in the Heroes section. The roster is indeed impressive, including past and present World Champions such as Botvinnik, Spassky, and Karpov. Top challengers who regularly play the defense including World Championship Candidates Salo Flohr, Gata Kamsky, Bent Larsen, Yasser Seirawan, Jonathan Speelman, and Kevin Spraggett.

How to Study the Caro-Kann Defense

The Caro-Kann Defense is easy to learn because Black does not have to worry about handling fierce White attacks with many critical positions. In all, only a few types of structures can arise.

Positional understanding here is much more important than tactics. There are a few traps to avoid, but not nearly as many as in most other defenses to 1.e4. Therefore the opening is best studied from the middlegame outward. Start with the sections on typical tactics, just to observe the kinds of resources available to each side. Play through each of the illustrative games, ignoring at first most of the discussion of the first dozen moves or so. Observe the flow of the pieces, typical maneuvers, and tactical traps.

The next step is to examine the types of endgames you are likely to encounter. Just play through the longest games, including the ones in the notes to other games, and casually take note of the types of structures that are most frequently seen. The endgames are discussed in detail in the section on Pawn Structure.

Finally, go back and study the notes to the opening phase of each game. Learn your responses to each of White's strategies. Look at each diagram and try to decide which side has the advantage.

When you have done all of this, you will be ready to play the Caro-Kann Defense against any and all opposition.

OVERVIEW

    Some variations of the Caro-Kann Defense can be reached from many different openings, but as we are using it as a repertoire against 1.e4, we will concentrate on the normal move order.

    All of the lines in this book have been thoroughly tested and White cannot achieve more than a very minimal advantage. There are no openings that can absolutely guarantee an equal position for Black, since the advantage of the first move takes time to overcome. The opening repertoire provided in this book is as good as any alternative system, and offers a number of significant advantages. It is easy to learn, easy to play, and relies more on general ideas than on memorization of specific variations.

1.e4 c6.

With the first move, Black declares the intention of confronting White's e-pawn with 2...d5. There really isn't anything that White can do to prevent this, as White has only one piece, the pawn at e4, controlling the d5-square, and Black has the pawn at c6 and the support of the queen at d8.

White usually responds with 2.d4, taking more space in the center. There are a number of minor alternatives, the most significant of which is 2.c4, the **Accelerated Panov Attack,** which aims to destroy any Black pawn which dares to advance to d5. Nevertheless, Black can get away with that reply, so the plan is now often seen only as a way of reaching the regular Panov Attack, which we will meet later on.

Another plan is 2.Nc3, which can lead to the **Two Knights Variation,** transpose back into the main lines, or lead to strange offshoots such as the **Goldman Variation.** 2.Nf3 is also an invitation to the Two Knights, but can also involve the strange **Ulysses Gambit** after 2...d5; 3.d4!?

The timid move 2.d3 leads to a quiet maneuvering game. It is known as the **Indian Variation,** because White usually adopts an Indian formation with the fianchetto of the king's bishop at g2. White has other legal moves, but they are almost never seen. One example, **2.Ne2,** is illustrated in the Bronstein-Petrosian game in the Heroes chapter.

2.d4 d5.

Black has achieved the first goal of the opening—a solid stake in the center. The White pawn is under attack. Usually White defends the pawn by developing a knight at c3, but there are significant alternatives and transpositions.

These days, the most important alternative is 3.e5, the **Advance Variation**. Since about 1980 it has soared in popularity and is now of equal stature to the traditional 3.Nc3. Although the fixing of the pawn center takes some flexibility out of the position, White does secure an advantage in space. We will be avoiding all of the controversial main lines and selecting a little-known alternative strategy instead.

With 3.exd5 cxd5, White can either enter the **Panov Attack** with 4.c4, or play more quietly with other moves, in which case we are in the **Exchange Variation**. Both of these are common in tournament play and you should be well prepared to meet them. They require special positional handling, which we will discuss in the Basic Concepts chapter, in the section on pawn structure. Of somewhat less significance is the support of the center with 3.f3, known commonly as the **Fantasy Variation.**

The odd **Ulysses Gambit** can be played here by transposition via 3.Nf3 dxe4; 4.Ng5. The other transposition involves 3.Nd2, which will transpose to the main lines after 3...dxe4. White sometimes uses that move order to avoid the Gurgenidze System with 3.Nc3 g6, which in any case is not part of our repertoire.

Perhaps the lamest reply to the Caro-Kann is 3.Bd3, which is easily handled by 3...dxe4; 4.Bxe4 Nf6.

3.Nc3 dxe4.

Naturally White should recapture the pawn here, but sometimes players try to transpose to the Blackmar-Diemer Gambit with 4.f3. We will not allow this, but will keep the game in Caro-Kann paths belonging to the **Milner-Barry Gambit**. The sharp **Von Hennig Gambit** arises on 4.Bc4. It is very obscure, and not so easy to meet at the board if you are not properly prepared, so we will cover it, too.

4.Nxe4 Bf5.

Black has the initiative, for a brief moment, since the White knight is under attack and must move. Supporting the knight with 5.Bd3 has not proven popular, and the choice usually comes down to the normal retreat to g3 and the **Bronstein Variation** with 5.Nc5. That once had surprise value, but is now considered harmless.

5.Ng3 Bg6.

This is the main line of the Classical Caro-Kann. Black is ready to continue development, with the possibility of playing ...e6 since the bishop has already escaped from c8. The knights will be brought to d7 and f6, the other bishop can be developed at e7 or d6 as appropriate, and castling on either wing is possible.

That's just a brief overview of the Caro-Kann Defense, and there is much more to learn. We'll continue our study later with complete games illustrating all of the key ideas of the opening. Right now, let's concentrate on basic strategy and tactics.

STRATEGIC GOALS OF THE CARO-KANN

Black's goals in the Caro-Kann Defense are to contest the center and to develop without creating major weaknesses. First of all, Black will develop pieces as quickly as possible. As White's pawns advance further up the board they become possible liabilities in the endgame. Therefore Black should always keep in mind the technique of exchanging pieces, which not only reduces White's attacking possibilities but also leads to favorable endgames.

White should take control of the center immediately with 2.d4 and develop pieces as quickly as possible in order to gain control of space. There are two basic strategies: kingside attack and central breakthrough. We'll learn more about those in the section on Typical Strategies and Tactics.

PAWN STRUCTURE

Pawn structure is of paramount importance in all of the variations of the Caro-Kann. Each variation has its own particular structure, so we'll consider each of them in a separate section. The diagrams below show only the pawns.

Classical Structure

You can see at a glance why the Caro-Kann appeals to endgame players! White has a weak pawn at h5 and lacks an e-pawn to enable a central breakthrough. White has a little more space and mustn't be allowed to get the king to d6.

Advance Structure

The situation in this structure is quite different from the previous example. White's pawn on e5 guarantees a very substantial advantage is space. At the same time, however, the center can be undermined by ...f6 and ...c5.

Exchange Structure

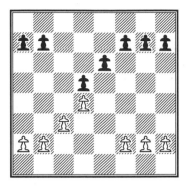

The semi-open c- and e-files define the contour of the middlegame and endgames in the Exchange Variation. White can take control of the center and advance the f-pawn to f5. Black can use a minority attack, advancing the b-pawn to b4, to weaken White's pawn structure. Those advances often provide the opponent with tactical opportunities, so they must be used very carefully.

Panov Structure

The endgame looks wonderful for Black if you strip away all the pieces! The isolated pawn at d4 is pathetically weak and in most cases the king and pawn endgame is a simple win for Black. Life is not so simple, however. Black has no presence in the center of the board, and White pieces will have great freedom to move about the board. The key to the normal Panov structure is piece placement. That is a subject for the next part of the book.

Before we leave the Panov pawn structure, there is one more important formation to consider. Sometimes White advances the c-pawn to c5 early in the game. This is the Advanced Panov structure.

Advanced Panov Structure

This structure usually works out well for Black if ...e5 can be played. That is not always easy to achieve, especially in our repertoire which stations a bishop at e6, blocking the pawn. We will see in the game Einarsson–Schiller, however, that there are plenty of resources for Black.

PIECE PLACEMENT

Where should your pieces be positioned for maximum efficiency in the Caro-Kann? This question cannot be answered generally, because each of the structures we saw in the last section requires a different answer. This time we'll put all the pieces on the board.

Classical Structure

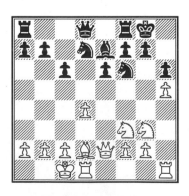

STRATEGIC GOALS OF THE CARO-KANN

King

The King should be castled on the kingside, usually after all the minor pieces have been developed, but before the rooks or queen move. You should leave it at g8, rather than sending it to the h-file, because in the endgame proximity to the center is important. You want to be able to get your king to d5 as quickly as possible.

Queen

The queen should not be developed until it can perform a genuinely useful function. The queen can be developed to a5, b6, c7. Try to exchange queens early to get to endgames where the d-pawn can be weak. One way to do this is with the maneuver ...Qd5-e4, when those squares are safe for occupation.

Rooks

Usually we want to station our rooks on open files, but here there aren't any. Black can use the semi-open d-file, which can become open if White plays Ne5 and Black exchanges and lures the d-pawn from d4 to e5. The role of the rooks in the Caro-Kann is generally to support pawn advances, especially from c6 to c5.

Bishops

In the Classical lines, the light squared bishop usually leaves the board pretty quickly. We want to keep our dark squared bishop, so that it can patrol critical dark squares, especially d6, c5, and e5. If White plays c3, then Black will have a better bishop in the endgame. Remember, the pawns guard the light squares, the bishop and knights are responsible for the dark squares.

Knights

In the Caro-Kann Defense, the Black knights are quickly placed on d7 and f6. The knight at d7 guards e5, and helps prepare the liberating advance of the c-pawn to c5. The knight at f6 keeps an eye on the key central squares e4 and d5. Black usually winds up with a knight in the endgame, and pure knight endings are quite common.

Pawns

Black has an excellent pawn structure, The only hole is at d6 and White has temporary control of e5. Otherwise there is nothing to worry about. The advance of White's g-pawn to g5 is a potential attacking threat, but it rarely can be used effectively.

The **a-pawn** can be advanced to a5 as part of a queenside attack, or to secure the b4-square. This is especially effective when White is castled on the queenside, which is usually the case.

The **b-pawn** can only advance at the cost of weakening c6. In rare cases, when White has placed a pawn or piece at c3, it can be used as an attacking weapon at b4. In exceptional cases the pawn goes to b5 to challenge a White pawn at c4, with the idea of freeing d5 for use by a knight.

The goal of the **c-pawn** is c5, where it can be exchanged for White's d-pawn. Then the c-file can be used for an attack.

The **d-pawn** is always absent in the Classical Caro-Kann.

The **e-pawn** advances to e6 and remains there for most of the game. It can play a significant role in the endgame. Sometimes Black will advance it to e5 to confront the White d-pawn.

Don't move the **f-pawn**! It must stay in place to defend the castled king. In some very rare cases ...f5 may be necessary, but keep in mind that the backward pawn at e6 will be very weak.

The **g-pawn** does not move unless forced to do so in reaction to a direct threat. In the endgame it may play a significant role, but in the middlegame any advance will weaken important dark squares.

With plenty of defense available on the kingside, pushing the **h-pawn** to h6 does not create a major weakness.. It eliminates back-rank threats by making a little breathing space for the king. In some cases, a knight uses the h7-square to pivot from f6 to g5.

Advance Structure

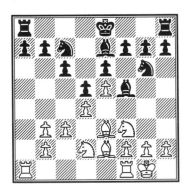

In a typical Advance subject, White has greater freedom of movement and better coordination of the minor pieces. The dark squared bishop is potentially bad, and Black has nothing to fear from direct attacks. In this endgame position, White enjoys pressure on the a-file but can only use a valuable rook to maintain control of it. Black can aim for ...c5 after castling on the kingside.

King

The King stays in the center for a while, but must inevitably castle to coordinate the rooks. Kingside castling is normal. Sometimes the king sits comfortably at d7, and Black should consider this possibility before castling. In the endgame, the king may wish to operate on the queenside.

Queen

White doesn't have any useful role for the queen, so often both queens are developed at b6. After the exchange, a true endgame may still be far away, as the rest of the army can remain on the board for a long time.

Rooks

In the endgame variation, White will keep one rook on the a-file and use the other one to support action in the center. With no open files, Black has no immediate plans for the rooks. As long as White has a rook at a1, a Black rook at a8 is useful. The other rook can come to c8, in support of an eventual advance of the c-pawn.

Bishops

The light squared bishop remains on the b1-h7 diagonal for most of the game. The dark squared bishop operates in the center, where all of the dark squares are important.

Knights

In this variation, the knights present an awkward problem. They do not find their way to the most natural squares. One winds up at c7, where it cannot support the advance of the c-pawn and even blocks a rook at c8. There is no easy way to reposition it to a more useful post. Yet it provides a great deal of support, covering b5, e6, and d5. If White plays c4, Black may be able to get the knight to d5 by playing ...dxc4 and ... b5.

Pawns

The **a-pawn** advances in the positions with the queens on the board, but in the endgame variation it should stay at a7, protected by the rook at a8. The advance to a6 may be forced in some positions, but going to a5 is risky unless you have potential control of a4 and a3.

The **b-pawn** stays in place until its advance will achieve some clear goal. If Black wants to play ...a6, the support of the b-pawn is essential. In some circumstances, the pawn will advance to b5 in support of ...c5, or to attack an enemy pawn at c4.

Getting your **c-pawn** to c5 is your key strategic goal. Then you can play ...cxd4 and White will have to accept either doubled and isolated b-pawns or a weak pawn at e5.

The **d-pawn** is rock solid. If White plays c4, you can consider capturing, since although it undoubles the pawns, it also gives you a juicy target at d4. Don't do this if White can quickly play d5!

The **e-pawn** isn't going anywhere.

The **f-pawn** can advance to f6 as part of a plan to destroy White's center. For this to work, you need pressure at c5 and e5, and the knight at c7 just isn't well placed to support this. Still if you feel the e-pawn will be safe at e6, even after your bishop at f5 is removed, then it is a plan worth considering.

The **g-pawn** is stuck in place, which is just as well, since moving it will only get you into trouble.

The **h-pawn** is best left alone unless you have some significant reason to advance it to h6 or f5. Sometimes you may do this to bring the bishop back to h7.

Exchange Structure

King

The King should be castled on the kingside as soon as possible. It would be most unsafe on the queenside, since White can easily blast open the c-file with c4.

Queen

The queen sometimes gets into the game at b6 or a5, but often it must rest, at least temporarily, at c8. This mere defensive role is not permanent, however. In major piece endgames the queen can move to c6 and exert her powerful influence on the queenside.

Rooks

The placement of the rooks is one of the trickiest questions in chess, and in the Caro-Kann both sides must wrestle with this difficult puzzle. It is clear that rooks should be on the c-, d-, and e-files as these files are either open or contain a weak target pawn. Unfortunately, each side has only two rooks, and three files are therefore one too many. The queen can help out, but often she is off on other errands. Careful study of the illustrative games will give you a good idea of the possibilities.

Bishops

Bishops are a pleasure to deal with in the Caro-Kann. Both bishops have an easy time developing.

The dark-squared bishop belongs at e7, and even if it has to capture a White pawn at c5 (a result of d4xc5) it often retreats to e7 when attacked. The c-file is no place for a bishop, since it can be attacked by Rc1, Qc2, Na4, or Ne4.

The bishop which starts the game at c8 is often known as a "bad" bishop in the Queen's Gambit Declined because 2...e6 locks limits its powers. In the Caro-Kann, however, the e-pawn is usually removed by an early central exchange, and the bishop can be stationed at e6, in defense of the center, or at g4, attacking either a knight at f3 or a pawn at e2. When supported by a queen at d7 or c8, the bishop can also go to h3 to attack an enemy bishop at g2. The bishop sometimes goes to f5, usually to attack a White knight at e4.

The light-squared bishop should only sit at e6 if the defense of the pawn at d5 is essential. This is usually the result of an error on Black's part, since passive defense is not part of the strategy of the Tarrasch. If the Black pawn has advanced from d5 to d4, however, then a bishop at e6 enjoys a wide perspective on both sides of the board and can be quite strong.

Knights

In the Exchange Variation, your Black knights are quickly placed on c6 and f6, and these are their best positions, keeping pressure at d4 and e4. The role of the knights is to control the center.

Pawns

You can advance the **a-pawn** up the board as long as you have sufficient support from your pieces. The aim of that strategy is to gain some space.

The **b-pawn** requires support to advance, and can weaken valuable squares on the c-file by doing so. Move it only if you can achieve some concrete strategic goal. For example, if you have a pawn at b5, you can play your knight to a5 and then c4.

There can be a **pawn at c6** if White exchanges knights there. In this case the pawn should advance to c5 as quickly as possible.

The **d-pawn** stays in place unless White plays c5, then you capture and move your knight to d5. In some rare circumstances, you might play ...Ne4 and if White captures, you will use the d-pawn to recapture.

The **e-pawn** is cemented in place and only your opponent can make it move. Even if White advances the f-pawn to f5, it is often wise to let the capture take place at e6. One strategy for Black is to try to attack the White center with ...f6, but that is very hard to achieve as the a2-g8 becomes very weak. The plan is better in an endgame when you have a king at d6.

The **g-pawn** does not move.

The **h-pawn** should stay where it is, unless there is a compelling reason to advance it to h6.

PANOV STRUCTURES

Relaxed Panov

Fractured Kingside Panov

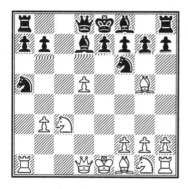

Gambit Panov

Advance Panov

There are four important Panov structures used in our repertoire. The first diagram shows what I call the Relaxed Panov structure. The second, which is a later development of the first, is the Fractured Kingside Panov. The third is the Gambit Panov structure. The final structure is the Advance Panov, characterized by a White pawn at c5. This strategy is comparatively rare in the lines we have chosen for Black, but one should be well prepared to meet it because it is easy to fall into a bad position.

Relaxed Panov

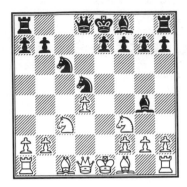

King

The king belongs safely castled on the kingside. Development is important, and you should try to move your king to safety. If the knight leaves c6, then checks on the a4-e8 diagonal can be annoying.

Queen

The queen tends to remain on the d-file, so that after an exchange of knights at d5, the queen can be used to recapture.

Rooks

The placement of the rooks must await White's castling decision. In any case it is useful to have a rook at c8. The other rook can go to e8 or d8 as needed.

Bishops

The light bishop usually exchanges itself for an enemy knight at f3 only when White must recapture with the g-pawn. Otherwise, if harrassed by the h-pawn, it retreats. The other bishop usually goes to e7, but may come to d6, b4, or capture a piece at c5.

Knights

Knights belong at c6 and d5 in this line. Keeping pressure on the isolated pawn at d4, and impeding the advance of that pawn, are high priorities for Black.

Fractured Kingside Panov

King
The king is already castled in this variation.

Queen
The queen again stays on the d-file, within sight of e5, but can sometimes shift to c7 and work on the dark squares.

Rooks
The c-file invites one rook, and the other often goes to e8, so that White cannot, with the exchange by a trick on the g-file in combination with a bishop at h6. Often Black can consider sacrificing the exchange in this case.

Bishop
The bishop needs to be available for defensive duties at f6 or f8, but if there is not much action on the g-file, can sometimes go to d6 to work on the f4-square.

Knights
The knights should operate on the queenside, and are a major component of the attacking force.

Gambit Panov

King

The king isn't going anywhere soon! Keeping the king safe is one of your most important strategic considerations in this line.

Queen

The queen must stay near home to guard the king, but can sometimes quickly take up an active post at b6.

Rooks

One rook goes to c8. The other has to find some roundabout method of entering the game. In out illustrative game, it never moves at all!

Bishops

The bishops will eventually see action on the queenside, but early in the game their roles are mostly defensive.

Knights

The knights often depart early in the game. Black, a pawn up, wants to exchange minor pieces whenever possible.

Advance Panov

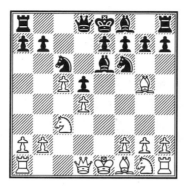

King
The king would like to seek shelter on the kingside, but in many lines this is not possible, so a prolonged stay in the center is possible.

Queen
The queen is part of the defensive team here and should not go out on excursions.

Rooks
The rooks tend to stay in place, unless Black castles.

Bishops
At some point the bishop on e6 will want to relocate, to f5 or g4 in most cases. The other bishop will get into the game after White exchanges the bishop at g5 for the knight at f6, which is often seen.

Knight
One knight will be used on the queenside, while the other is likely to be captured at f6. If White fails to capture, the knight can take up an active post at e4.

TYPICAL STRATEGIES AND TACTICS

In this section we examine typical strategic and tactical devices available to both sides. These patterns can often turn up in the early middlegame, so it is a good idea to pay close attention to these positions as well as those you encounter as you work your way through the illustrative games.

Only a small number of key ideas are shown here. Throughout the illustrative games and in the Heroes chapter you will meet additional important strategies and tactics that can serve as your middlegame weapons.

TACTICS FOR BLACK

Black is usually playing for an attack on the queenside if White castles there. A different form of queenside play is the minority attack, where you advance the b-pawn against a White pawn at c3. Finally, your most important weapon is a transition into a favorable endgame.

Queenside Attack

The standard queenside attack can take many forms, but the underlying idea is always the same. Create some weakness in the kingside pawn structure, then bring as many pieces as possible into the attack. Jon Speelman shows the spectacular side of the Caro-Kann by crashing through the queenside pawn barrier.

NIJBOER VS. SPEELMAN
London, 1992

White has just committed a terrible blunder, moving the bishop from b6 to c7. Although the Black king seems to be more exposed, it is White who is dead in the water. The bishop should have retreated to e3, at least cutting off the Black queen.

18...Bxc3!! This is no time to go on the defensive. There is a tactical refutation to 18...Kd7??; 19.Bxb8 Rxb8 in 20.Qxc6+!! Kxc6 and 21.Nd4+ Kd7; 22.Nxf3. **19.Bxb8 Bxb2+; 20.Kd2 d4; 21.Bc7 Rxa2; 22.Ke1 Qh1+; 23.Kd2 Bc3+. White resigned.**

Minority Attack

Black will often advance the b-pawn in situation where Black has a, b-, and d-pawns facing White pawns on all four queenside files. The idea is to weaken c3, and open up the b-file for use by rooks. In the following example, Black achieves this goal and uses the queenside infiltration as part of a kingside attack.

KUIJPERS VS. SIMAGIN
Moscow, 1963

Observe how Black carries out the plan with utmost efficiency, ignoring insignificant actions on the kingside. It is best to play straight through the moves to see the plan in action.

It is best to play straight through the moves to see the plan in action. **24...b4; 25.cxb4 axb4; 26.h5 bxa3; 27.bxa3 g5; 28.Qe5 Nxg4; 29.Qxg5 Nh6; 30.Kh1 Qc3; 31.Rad1 Kh8; 32.Qf4 Qxa3; 33.Rg1 Qe7; 34.Rg3 Qf6; 35.Qe3 Rb3; 36.Qe5 Qh4+; 37.Kg2 Ng4; 38.Qe2 Qh2+; 39.Kf3 f5; 40.Qf1 Ra2. White resigned.**

Transition into a Favorable Endgame

This theme will be seen over and over again throughout the book. Because White has often overextended, with a weak pawn at h5, for example, Black can aim for endgames in which that weakness can be exploited. Here is a recent example.

THIPSAY VS. NENASHEV
Calcutta, 1997

The pawn structure is a typical Classical Caro-Kann endgame. White's queenside majority of of no special value. The weakness of White's kingside becomes obvious after the exchange of queens.

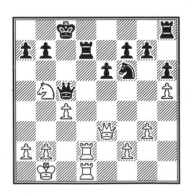

Black seized the opportunity to get into a favorable endgame. **24...Qxe3; 24.fxe3 Rxd2; 25.Rxd2 Kb8; 26.Rh2**. I don't care for this passive defense, as the h-pawn remains weak. It would have been wiser to offer the h-pawn immediately. Moving the king closer to the center at c2 might have been stronger. **26...Rd8; 27.Kc2 a6; 28.Nd4 Rc8; 29.Kd3 Rc5; 30.Nf3 Rf5.**

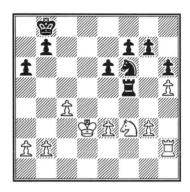

So the pawn falls anyway! **31.Ke2 Nxh5; 32.Rg2 Nf6; 33.g4 Ra5. 34.g5** generates a little counterplay. **35...Ne4; 35.gxh6 gxh6; 36.Rg8+ Ka7; 37.a3 Rf5; 38.Rh8 h5.** Now the win is inevitable. **39.b4 Nc3+; 40.Kf2 e5; 41.Kg2 Nd1; 42.e4 Rf4; 43.Nxe5 Ne3+; 44.Kg3 Rxe4; 45.Re8 h4+. White resigned.**

TACTICS FOR WHITE

There are three very important things to watch out for when you are playing Black in the Caro-Kann Defense. White will try to attack on the kingside, possibly making surprisingly effective use of the light squares. The center can be smashed open by the advance of the d-pawn, even if it involves a sacrifice, and you should be on the alert for that, too.

Kingside Attack

In our repertoire, the Black king almost always castles on the kingside. Even in the Classical Variation, which often sees queenside castling, we will be staying on the home flank. It is obvious that White will attempt to go after our king.

White can often sacrifice to break down our defensive pawn barrier. Here is a good example of a sacrifice that does not seem to have much support, at first, but which leads inevitably to victory.

DEFIRMIAN VS. BRUNNER
Biel, 1995

Black's kingside is defended by a rook and a bishop, but the position of the bishop is insecure. White moves away the knight, and then advances the h-pawn to attack it. The exit of the knight comes with a sacrificial flourish, and the bishop is soon trapped.

18.Nxg7! Kxg7; 19.h5 Bxd2+; 20.Rxd2 Bf5. 20...Bh7; 21.Bxd5 exd5; 22.Qf6+ Kg8; 23.Rh3 will win. **21.g4 Qc7.** 21...Bh7; 22.Bxd5 exd5; 23.Qf6+ Kg8; 24.g5! Qd8; 25.Qxh6 and the g-pawn will advance. **22.Re2 Ne7; 23.gxf5 Nxf5; 24.c3 Qe7; 25.Bc2 Qg5+; 26.Kb1 Kh8; 27.Re4 Ne7 28.Rhe1 Rg8; 29.Rf4 Rg7; 30.Rxf7** and White went on to win.

Another theme is the advance of the g-pawn, which can be sacrificed to create an open h-file, as in the next example. Judith Polgar, the greatest female player ever, smashes open the position.

J.POLGAR VS. KORCHNOI
Madrid, 1995

In positions such as this, White's attack is not easy to deal with. The knight on d5 is strong, but is not posted defensively, and rooks on the back rank are notoriously poor defenders. White smashes open the kingside in straightforward fashion.

22.g5 hxg5; 23.Rg4 f6; 24.exf6 gxf6. 24...Qxf6 runs into trouble with 25.Rxg5. **25.f4 e5.** Here Polgar captured the wrong pawn, at e5. She did win in the end, but would have won much more quickly with 26.fxg5 f5; 27.Rgg1 e4; 28.g6 f4; 29.h6 e3; 30.g7 etc.

Weakness of Kingside Light Squares

White often uses f5 and g6 as staging points for an attack, and the pawns at f7 and e6 are also subject to attacks and pins. The following excerpt shows an extreme example of exploitation for light square weaknesses. Notice that all of Black's pawns are in their normal, usually safe, positions.

BELYAVSKY VS. LARSEN
Tilburg, 1981

Black must not leave the king in the center too long, as it is not difficult for White to build a strong attack on a seemingly closed e-file. When White can attack with two knights, Black is often in serious danger. Knights can be sacrificed for important defensive pawns, and the open lines can be exploited by the heavy artillery.

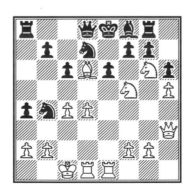

Except for the rook at d1, all White's pieces are on the attack. **19...fxg6.** 19...Bxd6 runs into 20.Nxd6#. **20.Rxe6+ Kf7; 21.hxg6+!! Kxe6; 22.Re1+ Ne5; 23.Bxe5. Black resigned**, rather than facing an ignominious mate. 23...Nd3+; 24.Kb1 Nxe5. (Or 24...Kd7; 25.Nxg7+ Ke7; 26.Qe6#.) 25.Rxe5+ Kf6; 26.Ng3 Qc8; 27.Qh5 Bd6; 28.Ne4#.

Central Breakthrough

Especially when Black has not castled, White will often be able to break through in the center with a timely advance of the d-pawn to d5. Even though Black has pawns at e6 and c6, this strategy can be effective because Black can ill-afford to open the e-file before castling. In this example, Black cannot castle because the rook has moved to g8 to guard the pawn. In general, this is a poor strategy but is sometimes required when something goes wrong early in the game.

KHALIFMAN VS. SEIRAWAN
Amsterdam, 1995

Black must watch the White d-pawn and d5-square at almost every turn. The common attacking method against a king in the center is to shove this pawn down Black's throat. Black is usually obliged to capture a pawn at d5, but this just opens up more lines, as here.

25.d5! cxd5. 25...Nxe5; 26.fxe5 Qe7; 27.d6 Qh4; 28.Qf3! Rd8; 29.Rg4! Qxh5; 30.d7+. The d-pawn provides all that is needed to win. Khalifman also refuted 25...Qc5 with 26.Qb3 Qb6. (26...Nxe5; 27.Qxb7 Rd8; 28.dxe6) 27.Qc3! Nxe5; 28.dxe6. **26.Nxd7 Qxd7.** 26...Kxd7; 27.cxd5 exd5; 28.Qf3 Kc6 (28...Kc7; 29.Rxd5). 29.Rd4! **27.cxd5 Rd8; 28.f5 e5; 29.Qxe5+ Qe7; 30.Qd4+- Kf8; 31.d6 Qf6; 32.Qc5 b6; 33.Qd5 Rh8; 34.d7 Qh4; 35.Rge1 Kg8; 36.Re8+ Kh7; 37.Qxf7 Rhxe8; 38.Qg6+. Black resigned.**

ILLUSTRATIVE GAMES AND ANALYSIS

You are now ready to explore the opening strategies in detail. In this part of the book, you will learn the theory of the Caro-Kann by examining instructive games in each of the key lines. It won't be necessary to memorize all the strategies shown: just concentrate on the ideas presented so that you have a basic understanding of the concepts behind the moves.

Throughout this chapter, we'll be looking at interesting games from a variety of players, which showcase the important concepts of the Caro-Kann.

The first time you go through the material, just follow the moves in **boldface** and ignore all the commentary. This will give you a feel for the flow of the game. Then do a second pass, reading the text commentaries but not paying too much attention to the subvariations. Finally, go through the game in detail, examining all the notes. Look at the final positions, where an evaluation is given. Make sure that you agree with, or at least understand, the reasons given for an advantage for one side or another.

Keep in mind that positions evaluated as equal are not necessarily drawn!

CLASSICAL VARIATION

We begin our examination of the theory of the Caro-Kann with the Classical Variation. Black observes the rules of development and gets the bishop into the game with tempo, attacking the White knight at e4, which is more or less forced into retreat. This buys enough time for Black to develop, and the advance of the e-pawn to e6 will no longer entomb the bishop at c8.

1.e4 c6; 2.d4 d5; 3.Nc3 dxe4; 4.Nxe4 Bf5.

MAIN LINE

1.e4 c6; 2.d4 d5; 3.Nd2 dxe4; 4.Nxe4 Bf5; 5.Ng3 Bg6; 6.h4 h6; 7.Nf3 Nd7; 8.h5 Bh7; 9.Bd3 Bxd3; 10.Qxd3 e6.

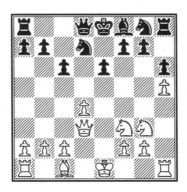

In the main lines, we adopt Eric Lobron's strategy of kingside castling followed by play on the queenside. Our king will be safe, and our pieces have plenty of mobility. White will castle queenside, and can then play on the kingside or in the center. Since direct kingside attacks are not usually successful, White will ordinarily try to organize play along the e-file, with knights coming to e4 and e5, supported by a rook or queen.

Lobron Variation

1.e4 c6; 2.d4 d5; 3.Nd2 dxe4; 4.Nxe4 Bf5; 5.Ng3 Bg6; 6.h4 h6; 7.Nf3 Nd7; 8.h5 Bh7; 9.Bd3 Bxd3; 10.Qxd3 e6; 11.Bd2 Ngf6; 12.0–0-0 Be7.

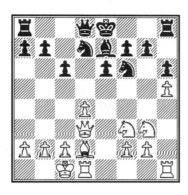

By placing our bishop at e7 we are declaring our intentions of castling on the kingside. White has already castled on the queenside. When the kings sit at opposite sides of the board, the general strategy is all-out attack. White's attack is usually based on knights in the center coordinating with an advance of the g-pawn to g4 and eventually to g5. Black operates on the c-file and a-file, thrusting pawns forward to open up lines. Sometimes the b-pawn takes part too. White has a choice of attacking formations. Before getting to those, however, we will look at a line where early endgames are the order of the day.

White Plays 13.Ne4

TISCHBIEREK VS. LOBRON
Hannover, 1991

1.e4 c6; 2.d4 d5; 3.Nd2 dxe4; 4.Nxe4 Bf5; 5.Ng3 Bg6; 6.h4 h6; 7.Nf3 Nd7; 8.h5 Bh7; 9.Bd3 Bxd3; 10.Qxd3 e6; 11.Bd2 Ngf6; 12.0–0-0 Be7; 13.Ne4.

White moves a knight to e4, and we exchange. **13...Nxe4; 14.Qxe4.** We bring our remaining knight to f6 to chase away the queen, and bring our own queen out, only to offer it in exchange. **14...Nf6; 15.Qe2.** 15.Qd3 Qd5; 16.Kb1 0-0; 17.Rde1 Ng4; 18.Re2 b5; 19.Rh3 Rfd8; 20.Ba5 Rdc8; 21.Rg3 Qxh5; 22.Ne5 b4 did not give White enough for the pawn in Perdomo-Lobron, New York Open, 1997. Instead, 17...c5; 18.Re5 Qd7 is a more solid alternative. White should not capture at c5 because after 19.dxc5 Qxd3; 20.cxd3 Ng4; 21.Re2 Bxc5, Black gets the pawn back with a superior position. **15...Qd5.**

Our queen attacks the pawn at a2, and White cannot allow us to take it. Whether White defends it with Kb1, or, as in the game, confronts our lady with an impudent c-pawn, we will swing the queen to e4, daring the enemy to exchange and enter an endgame. **16.c4 Qe4!; 17.Rde1.** Black wants to play ...Ng4 or ...Ne4, with pressure at f2. The alternatives are not impressive, for example Kavalek gives 17.Qf1 Ng4 and 17.Be3 Ng4; 18.Nd2 Qf5. More interesting is 17.Qxe4 Nxe4.

White already has problems. The pawn at f2 is weak and the pawn at d4 may need more support. Against 18.Be3 (18.Be1 Bf6; 19.Ne5 Rd8; 20.f3 Nd6; 21.Bf2 Bxe5; 22.dxe5 Nxc4 and in this position Black is again no worse, Armas - Tal, Germany, 1990.) 18...f5!? deserves consideration. White probably plays 19.Nd2 and, according to Armas, the chances are level. An alternative is 18...Nf6; 19.Ne5 Bd6; 20.f3 b5; 21.Kb1 bxc4; 22.Nxc4 Bg3; 23.Rh3 Bc7; 24.g4 Nd5; 25.Rhh1 Rb8; 26.Rd3 f6; 27.Rc1 Kd7; 28.Bd2 Rb7; 29.Ra3 Rhb8; 30.Rc2 Bb6 was agreed drawn in Leone-Frenklakh, World Junior (Women) 1997.

So, we return to the main line, and an exchange of queens. **17...Qxe2; 18.Rxe2.**

Black can castle here, or try an ambitious plan on the queenside. **18...b5!?** 18...0-0; 19.Ne5 Rfd8; 20.Bc3 Rac8 is one possibility, but White was tied down to the defense of his pawns in Ivanovic - Kavalek, Bugojno, 1982. Instead, 19.Bc3 brings about an interesting position. Black has several plans. Playing on the queenside, advancing either the a-pawn or the b-pawn, is ambitious. Black may bring the rook from f8 to d8 to put a little pressure on the d-file and centralize the rook, before undertaking any drastic action on the queenside. For example, 19...b5!?; 20.b3 bxc4; 21.bxc4 Rab8; 22.Ne5 Rb6; 23.g4 Rfb8; 24.Rd1 Ra6; 25.Rd3 is even. 19...a5 is also playable, as suggested by Faibisovich. There is another try, 19...Rfd8, which might be met by the interesting plan 20.Nd2!? b5; 21.b3 Rd7; 22.f3 to play on the kingside. 22...bxc4; 23.bxc4 c5; 24.dxc5 Bxc5; 25.g4 Rc8! Black has good counterplay on the c-file.

19.b3 0-0; 20.Kc2 Rfc8.

White's king is more exposed and White's pieces are not doing anything constructive. **21.c5.** Preventing Black from playing is...c5, but creating a backward pawn at d4. **21...Nd5.**

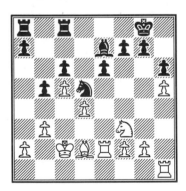

White has a poor position, and now desperately tries to get something going on the kingside. **22.g4 Bf6; 23.a3 a5.** The queenside cannot be closed here, because if either the a-pawn or b-pawn advances, the attacked Black pawn will move forward, sealing both files and controlling space. White's bishop will then be of limited use. **24.Rg1 a4; 25.b4 Ra7; 26.Re4 Rd7; 27.Bc1 Kh7; 28.Rd1 Rg8; 29.Rh1 Rgd8; 30.Rhe1 Kg8; 31.Bb2 Kh7; 32.Rd1 Ne7.** Black is still searching for a plan, while White marks time. **33.Rd2 Nd5; 34.Rd3 Kg8; 35.Rd2.**

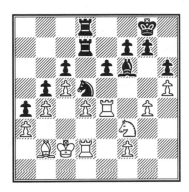

35...Bg5! Lobron finally gets the right idea! **36.Rd1?** (36.Nxg5 hxg5 would give Black some winning chances, thanks to the advantage of good knight against bad bishop. It is hard to find a constructive plan to exploit this because, there are not enough open lines for the rooks) **36...Nf6.** This wins a pawn, and the rest is easy.

37.Re2 Nxg4; 38.d5 (desperation) **38...Rxd5; 39.Rxd5 exd5; 40.Nd4 Rc8; 41.Nf5 g6; 42.hxg6 fxg6; 43.Ne7+ Bxe7; 44.Rxe7 Kf8; 45.Re6 Kf7; 46.Rd6 Re8; 47.Rxc6 Re2+; 48.Kb1 h5; 49.Rd6 Re6–+; 50.Rxd5 Nxf2; 51.Rd7+ Ke8; 52.Rb7 h4; 53.Rxb5 h3; 54.Rb8+ Kd7; 55.Rh8 Re1+; 56.Ka2 Re2.** White resigned.

White Plays 13.Rhe1 and Other Plans

HÜBNER VS. LARSEN
Tilburg, 1980
1.e4 c6; 2.d4 d5; 3.Nc3 dxe4; 4.Nxe4 Bf5; 5.Ng3 Bg6; 6.h4 h6; 7.Nf3 Nd7; 8.h5 Bh7; 9.Bd3 Bxd3; 10.Qxd3 e6; 11.Bd2 Ngf6; 12.0-0-0 Be7; 13.Rhe1.

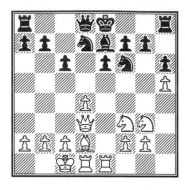

Moving the rook to the center indicates a desire to play in the center, instead of launching a kingside attack. White has completed development, and Black is still two tempi away. But there are no real targets, and Black need not hurry to castle. There are two other plans for White, concentrating on the queenside for the moment.

First, let's digress to the ultra-cautious 13.Kb1.

White anticipates Black's opening of the c-file with ...c5 and gets the king to safety. 13...c5! White's quiet move allows Black to resolve the central questions immediately. 14.dxc5 Nxc5; 15.Qb5+ Qd7; 16.Qxd7+ Ncxd7 gives Black an excellent and solid position. So, White is more likely to go for 14.Ne4 0–0; 15.dxc5 (15.Bc3!? b6; 16.Nxf6+ Nxf6 looks about even) 15...Nxc5; 16.Nxc5 Bxc5; 17.Qe2 Qb6. Black already has the initiative, and f2 is feeling the heat. 18.Ne5 Rfd8! Capturing at f2 is too dangerous, opening up the f-file for use by White's rooks. 19.g4 Bd4; 20.Nd3 Nd5. All of Black's pieces are getting into the act, while White's are badly placed. Not finding an effective defense, White decides to counterattack with 21.g5.

21...hxg5; 22.h6 (22.Bxg5?? loses instantly to 22...Nc3+) 22...g6; 23.h7+ Kh8. The Black king is now perfectly safe, and all endgames are winning for him, too. 24.c4 Nf4; 25.Bxf4 gxf4; 26.Ne5 Qc7; 27.Rxd4 Rxd4; 28.b3 Rad8; 29.Nf3 Qc5; 30.Nxd4 Qxd4. The return of the exchange secures an easy win. 31.Kc2 e5; 32.b4 f3; 33.Qxf3 Qxc4+; 34.Kb1 Qxb4+; 35.Ka1 Qd4+; 36.Kb1 Rd6. White resigned, Garma-Lobron, Novi Sad Olympiad, 1990.

The other alternative is 13.c4 0–0; 14.Bc3.

This is yet another line where an early c4 by White is not effective because Black, having castled short, can strike quickly on the queenside. 14...b5; 15.Ne5 (on 15.c5 Black plays 15...Nd5 and the knight can later get to b4. 15.cxb5? cxb5 and White is in bad shape, with Black commanding d5, the c-file, and threatening an advance of the b-pawn) 15...bxc4; 16.Qxc4 Nb6!; 17.Ba5. (17.Qxc6 Rc8; 18.Qb7 Nbd5; 19.Ne2 Ne4; 20.Rhf1 Ndxc3; 21.bxc3 Nxc3; 22.Nxc3 Rxc3+; 23.Kb2 Rc7.)

The White king is about to be attacked without mercy. 17...Nxc4; 18.Bxd8 Rfxd8; 19.Nxc4 Rd5.

After a few forced moves Black has many targets on both sides of the board, while White cannot easily get at the weakness at c6. 20.Ne3 Rg5. Black is a bit better, as ...c5 can be played to eliminate the only weakness. In the long run the bishop will be effective. Wheldon-Lobron, London, 1987.

Getting back the main game, White responds to the development of the rook by advancing the a-pawn. **13...a5.**

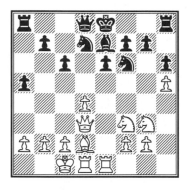

Black starts the queenside attack, and will castle on the next turn. Play in this variation can get very exciting with fierce battles on both flanks. **14.Qe2.** 14.c4 0–0; 15.Kb1 a4; 16.Qe2 Re8; 17.Ne5 Qb6; 18.Bc3 a3; 19.b3 Bb4; 20.Nxd7 Nxd7; 21.c5 Qa5 is better for Black, who can start cracking open the queenside with ...b6. Cullip-Ruxton, Edinburgh Open, 1989.

14...0–0. 14...a4 is also playable. 15.Ne5 0–0 may transpose to the main game, or can evolve differently, for example 16.f4 Nd5; 17.Nxd7 Qxd7; 18.c4 Nf6; 19.f5 a3 with a strong attack, even if White does not fall for 20.fxe6 Qxd4, 21.exf7+ Rxf7, 22.Bc3 Qf4+; 23.Qe3 axb2+. White resigned, Quinteros-Slipak, Buenos Aires, 1992.

15.Kb1. White may not have anything better, but this move permits Black to complete development and lay claim to full equality..

We should stop for a moment to consider the alternative line 15.Ne5 a4; 16.a3.

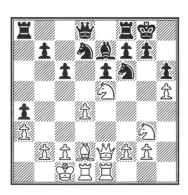

This line has more ambitions, and more risk. Black should take care to watch for a tactical trick at g6. 16...Nd5; 17.c4 N5b6 is very risky. Here is just a taste of the danger. 18.Ng6! fxg6; 19.Qxe6+ Kh8; 20.Qxe7 A1) 20...Rxf2; 21.hxg6 Rxg2; 22.Nf5 Rxg6; 23.c5 Nd5; 24.Qf7 Nf8; 25.Re7! b6. (25...Nxe7; 26.Nxe7 and what can Black do about mate at g8?) 26.Rh1! bxc5; 27.Bxh6 and mate is inevitable.; A2) 20...Nxc4; 21.Bxh6 Qxe7; 22.Rxe7 gxh6; 23.Rxd7 Rxf2; 24.hxg6 Rxg2; 25.g7+ Kh7; 26.Nf5 Nxb2; 27.Rh1 Nd3+; 28.Kb1 Rg6; 29.Nxh6! Rxh6; 30.g8Q+ Kxg8; 31.Rxh6 is a win for White. 16...Re8 is safest. Now the sacrifice of the knight at g6 is pointless, because the bishop is defended..

15...Qb6!?

Black concentrates maximum force on c5, so that the advance of the pawn can take place under favorable circumstances. **16.Ne5 a4.** 16...Qxd4? loses the knight at d7 after 17.Bc3! **17.c4?** White fails to sense the danger. 17.Nf5 exf5; 18.Nxd7 Nxd7; 19.Qxe7 Nf6 looks about even. The pawn at h5 is very weak, but White has the bishop and the open file. **17...a3; 18.b3 Qxd4.**

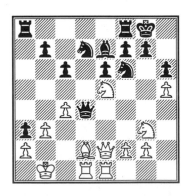

Now it is safe to take the pawn because of the threats at b2 and the pawn at h6 is taboo. **19.Bb4** (19.Bxh6? loses to 19...Qxe5; 20.Qxe5 Nxe5; 21.Rxe5 gxh6) **19...Qxe5; 20.Qxe5 Nxe5; 21.Bxe7 Rfe8; 22.Bb4**. After a series of forcing maneuvers, Black remains a pawn ahead.

22...Ned7; 23.Ne4 b6; 24.Nd6 Reb8; 25.f3 b5!; 26.Bc3 bxc4; 27.Nxc4 Nd5; 28.Bd2. Although Black has weakened his pawn structure slightly, his pieces are now active. **28...Nc5; 29.Ne5 Ra6; 30.Rc1 Rb5; 31.Rc4 Nf6; 32.g4 Nfd7; 33.Bc3.** 33.Nxd7 Nxd7; 34.Bc1 Ne5; 35.Rc3 Rd5, 36.Kc2 was the best defense.

33...Nb6; 34.Rce4 Nd5; 35.Bd2 f6; 36.Ng6. The knight cannot accomplish anything without assistance, but it is hard to bring the remaining forces into the attack.

36...e5. 36...Nxe4; 37.fxe4 Nb6 would have been more efficient, but there was probably considerable time pressure here. **37.Rc4 Nd3; 38.Ree4 c5.** Black keeps reducing the amount of space available to the White pieces. **39.Ra4 Rbb6.** 39...Rxa4; 40.Rxa4 would give White significant counterplay.

40.Rxa6 Rxa6; 41.Rc4. 41.Ra4 Rxa4; 42.bxa4 c4; 43.Kc2 Nc5; 44.a5 Kf7; 45.Bc1 Ne6; 46.Bxa3 Nd4+; 47.Kc1 Nxf3; 48.a6 Nc7; 49.a7 Nh2 will win for Black because the White knight cannot get to a useful square in time. 50.Bd6 Na8; 51.Kd2 Nxg4; 52.Kc3 Ke6; 53.Bf8 f5; 54.Kxc4 f4; 55.Bxg7 f3. Black wins.

41...Ra7; 42.Nh4 Nb6; 43.Rc3 Rd7; 44.Be3 Rd5.

Black's pieces are well-coordinated, while White's lack purpose. **45.Nf5 Kf7; 46.Ng3 Nd7; 47.Ne4 g6; 48.hxg6+ Kxg6; 49.Ng3 Ne1; 50.Bc1 Rd1; 51.Ne4!** Preparing to force more pieces off the board. **51...Nd3; 52.Kc2 Rxc1+; 53.Kxd3 Ra1!** 53...Rxc3+; 54.Kxc3 f5; 55.Nf2 provides more resistance.

54.Rc2 Rf1; 55.Ke3 Re1+; 56.Kd3 Rb1; 57.Nxc5 Nxc5+; 58.Rxc5 Rb2; 59.Rc2 f5!; 60.Rc6+ Kg5; 61.gxf5 h5!; 62.f6 Kg6! Larsen has always had a flair for rook endgames. Especially when rook pawns are involved! **63.Kc3 Rxa2; 64.Kb4 Kf7; 65.Ka4.**

65...Rf2; 66.Kxa3 Rxf3. This position is winning, because the Black pawns are faster.

67.Kb4 h4; 68.Rc8 Rf1; 69.Rc2 Kxf6; 70.Kc5 Kf5; 71.b4 h3; 72.b5 Rb1; 73.b6 Kf4; 74.Re2 e4; 75.Kd4 e3!; 76.Kc5. 76.Rxe3 Rb4+; 77.Kc5 Kxe3; 78.Kxb4 h2; 79.b7 h1Q; 80.b8Q Qb1+ and **Black wins. 76...Kf3; 77.Rh2 Kg3; 78.Re2 Rb3!; 79.Kc4 Rxb6; 80.Rxe3+ Kg2; 81.Re2+ Kf3.**

A book win for Black, so White resigned.

White Plays 13.Qe2

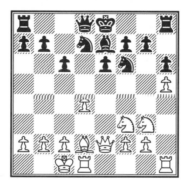

The most common strategy for White is to bring the queen to e2 and play on the e-file. I've decided to explore several approaches for Black here, because you may want to vary your repertoire, keeping your opponents a bit off balance. After all, this is the line which most books recommend for White, and if your opponents prepare, this is the variation which is most likely to appear on the board in the Classical Variation.

SISNIEGA VS. LOBRON
New York, 1988

1.e4 c6; 2.d4 d5; 3.Nd2 dxe4; 4.Nxe4 Bf5; 5.Ng3 Bg6; 6.h4 h6; 7.Nf3 Nd7; 8.h5 Bh7; 9.Bd3 Bxd3; 10.Qxd3 e6; 11.Bd2 Ngf6; 12.0–0–0 Be7; 13.Qe2 0–0.

Castling is thematic, and although there are alternatives, we should consider this the main line. White now must play on the e-file, either occupying e5 with the knight or bringing the rook from the flank to the center. **14.Ne5** is the main line, but we must step aside to consider an important alternative which can lead to sharp and complicated play. After 14.Rhe1 a5 White can try 15.Nf5?!

A bit reckless. But this sacrifice must be analyzed carefully, because there are more resources for White than appear at first glance. 15...Bb4! Taking the knight is too risky. (15...exf5; 16.Qxe7 Nxh5; 17.Nh4!) 15...Re8!?; 16.Nxh6+ gxh6; 17.Bxh6 Bf8; 18.Bg5 Be7; 19.Ne5 Nxe5; 20.dxe5 Nd5; 21.Qg4!? Bxg5+; 22.f4 is an interesting double-piece sacrifice, but Black has adequate resources. 22...f5; 23.exf6 Qxf6; 24.fxg5 Qf4+; 25.Qxf4 Nxf4 with an extra piece for two pawns. This line might be a practical alternative to the text. 16.Nxh6+. In for a penny, in for a pound! 16...gxh6; 17.c3 Re8; 18.cxb4. Otherwise the retreating Black bishop will defend the kingside from f8. 18...axb4; 19.Ne5 Rxa2; 20.Bxh6 b3!; 21.Nxd7?

Instead of simply recapturing, Burger brings the game to a quick conclusion with a brilliant stroke. 21...Qa5! White resigned in Glatt-Burger, Budapest, 1982, but there remained questions to be answered after 22.Nxf6+! Kh8; 23.Bg7+! Kxg7; 24.Nxe8+ Kf8; 25.Qe4 Ra1+; 26.Qb1 Rxb1+; 27.Kxb1. Black will win the knight at e8, and the pawn at b2, yet with two rooks and a flying h-pawn, the endgame is not so easy. A logical continuation is 27...Qa2+; 28.Kc1 Qa1+; 29.Kd2 Qxb2+; 30.Ke3 Qc3+; 31.Ke4 Kxe8; 32.h6 Qc2+; 33.Ke3 Qc3+. (33...Qg6; 34.Rh1 Qxg2; 35.h7. White wins!) 34.Ke2 Qc2+; 35.Ke3 and draws.

In any case, let's get back to the game after 14.Ne5.

14...Rc8. I am not convinced that this move is best. It is probably appropriate for Black to play 14...c5 right away, before White can coordinate his pieces. 15.dxc5 Nxc5!

Black can go to work on the queenside quickly. 16.Ng4 (16.Bxh6 Qa5; 16.Kb1 Qb6; 17.Be3 Rfd8; 18.c4 a5; 19.f4 Qc7; 20.Bd4 Rd6; 21.Bxc5 Qxc5; 22.Rxd6 Bxd6; 23.Rd1 Rc8; 24.a3 Bxe5; 25.fxe5 Nh7 is better for Black. There are too many pawn weaknesses in White's position. 26.Rd7 b6; 27.Qf3 Ng5; 28.Qb7 Qxc4; 29.Qxb6 Ne4; 30.Qe3 Qc2+. White resigned, Fercec-Tukmakov, Kastel Stari, 1997) 16...Qc7; 17.Kb1 Rfd8; 18.Bc3 Nxg4; 19.Qxg4 Bf8.

Black is a little bit better. The kingside is defended by the bishop at f8, and the knight at g3 is not in a position to attack. White goes dreadfully wrong on the next move. 20.a3? (20.Rhe1 Rxd1+; 21.Rxd1 Rd8; 22.Rxd8 Qxd8; 23.Bd4 would have kept the game level.) 20...b5; 21.Qe2 Qc6; 22.f3?! Rxd1+; 23.Rxd1 a5. Black's attack is formidable. White should now acquiesce to the advance of Black's b-pawn, since trying to prevent it proves futile. 24.Qd2? b4! The pawn sacrifice opens up the a-file. 25.axb4 axb4; 26.Bxb4 Qa6; 27.Ba3 Na4; 28.Qd4 Bxa3; 29.bxa3 Qb5+; 30.Qb4 Nc3+. White resigned, Xie Jun-Brunner, Bern (match), 1995.

End of digression. **15.Rhe1 b5; 16.Kb1**.

A more cautious alternative to the ultra-sharp 16.Nf5!?, seen by transposition in the Heidrich-Lobron game in the Heroes Chapter. **16...b4; 17.f4 Nd5**. The powerful knight on d5 brings Black equality. **18.Ne4 f5!?** An important decision, which takes away the outpost at e4, but weakens e6 in the process..

18...c5! is best, for example :

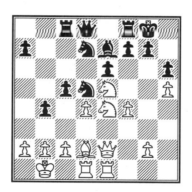

19.dxc5 Nxc5; 20.Nxc5 Bxc5; 21.g4 Qc7! Any attempt at direct attack by White will be turned back. 22.g5 Bd6!; 23.gxh6 gxh6! (23...Qxc2+; 24.Ka1 gxh6; 25.Nxf7 Rxf7; 26.Rc1 Bf8; 27.Qxe6 Qxd2; 28.Rg1+ Kh8; 29.Rxc8 Qxf4; 30.Qxd5 Qf1+; 31.Qd1. Black should lose this endgame.) 24.Rg1+ Kh8; 25.Qd3 Rfd8; 26.Qb3 Bc5, where 27.Rg2? runs into 27...Ne3!; 28.Rdg1 Nxg2; 29.Rxg2 Rg8 and Black is enroute to victory.

Suppose that White exchanges knights instead? 19.Nxd7 Qxd7; 20.dxc5 Qc7; 21.g4 Bxc5; 22.g5 (22.Nxc5 Qxc5; 23.Bc1 Rc7; 24.g5 hxg5; 25.fxg5 Rfc8; 26.Rd2 loses to 26...Nc3+!!; 27.bxc3 bxc3; 28.Rdd1

Rb7+ 29.Ka1 Qb4 and mate follows) 22...Nxf4; 23.Bxf4 Qxf4; 24.gxh6 Qxh6; 25.Rd7 Bb6 looks clearly better for Black.

After 18...f5, our game continues with **19.Nf2**.

Here Black plays aggressively. **19...Bh4!?** 19...Nxe5; 20.Qxe5 Rf6; may be a playable alternative. 21.Nd3 (21.g4 Bd6!; 22.Qe2 Bxf4; 23.Bxf4 Nxf4; 24.Qf3 Nd5; 25.Nd3 gives White some play for the pawn, but Black can also enjoy a lively game. 25...f4; 26.Re4 a5; 27.Rg1 a4; 28.Nc5 a3; 29.g5 hxg5; 30.Rxg5 axb2; 31.Kxb2 Nc3; 32.Qg2 Qa5! Even after 33.Rxg7+ Kh8 Black's king is safer than White's. A sample finish: 34.Kc1 Nxa2+; 35.Kd1 f3!; 36.Qg5 Nc3+; 37.Kd2 Nxe4+; 38.Nxe4 Qxg5+; 39.Rxg5 f2! Black wins) 21...a5 is perhaps nothing special for White. **20.Ned3!** The weakness at e6 is exposed. **20...Qe7**. The pin at f2 does not keep White from going after e6. **21.Qxe6+ Qxe6; 22.Rxe6 N7f6.**

The standard weakness at h5 gives Black some compensation. White knows that almost any endgame with knights on the board can be very difficult. Black's weak pawn at f5 is a big liability, however, and there are still plenty of rooks on the board to use the open e-file. **23.Rh1 Bxf2, 24.Nxf2 a5.** White suffers from a need to defend the h-pawn. The knight at f6 has more involvement in the game than the rook at h1. A plausible alternative is 24...Rfe8; 25.Re5 Nd7; 26.Rxe8+ Rxe8; 27.Nd3 Re2; 28.Bxb4 Rxg2; 29.c4 Ne3; 30.b3 Nc2; 31.Ne1 Nxe1; 32.Rxe1 Nf6.

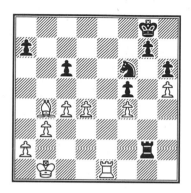

A typical Caro-Kann endgame. Black has sacrificed a pawn, knowing that the pawn at h5 is vulnerable and can only be defended by a rook. So although White now enjoys the open e-file, he has to give it up to save the h-pawn. **33.Rh1** (33.Re5 Nxh5; 34.Rxf5 Ng3; 35.Ra5 h5; 36.Rxa7 h4; 37.Rc7 h3. Black wins) **33...Kf7** with about equal chances.

   25.Re5 Nd7; 26.Ree1 c5; 27.dxc5 Rxc5; 28.Nd3 Rc7.

Black still has three forms of compensation—the weakness of the pawn at e6 and the limited scope of the bishop d2 and, perhaps most importantly, much more active pieces. **29.Re2 Rfc8; 30.Rc1 Rc4; 31.Ne5 Nxe5; 32.Rxe5 Rd4.** 32...Nxf4; 33.Rxf5 Ne2; 34.Re1

Ng3; 35.Rf3 Nxh5 gives Black more winning chances than White. **33.Re2 Nxf4; 34.Bxf4 Rxf4; 35.Re5.**

This rook endgame should by all rights end in a draw, and it does. **35...Ra8; 36.c3 bxc3; 37.Rxc3 a4; 38.Rf3 Rg4!; 39.Rexf5 Rxg2; 40.Rf2 Rg1+; 41.Rf1 Rxf1+; 42.Rxf1 Ra5; 43.Rh1 g5; 44.hxg6 Kg7; 45.b4 Rf5; 46.Kb2 Rf3; 47.Rg1 h5; 48.Rg5 h4; 49.b5 h3; 50.b6 a3+; 51.Kc2 Rf6; 52.Rh5 Rxb6.** Drawn.

White plays 9.Bf4

KUPREICHIK VS. LOBRON
Ljubljana, 1989

This variation is similar to the main lines except for the position of the bishop at f4. Both sides will continue with standard plans. White will castle queenside, and Black will settle on the other flank.

1.e4 c6; 2.Nc3 d5; 3.d4 dxe4; 4.Nxe4 Bf5; 5.Ng3 Bg6; 6.h4 h6; 7.Nf3 Nd7; 8.h5 Bh7; 9.Bf4.

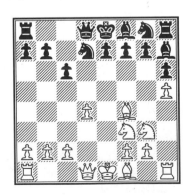

9...Ngf6; 10.Bd3 Bxd3; 11.Qxd3 e6; 12.0–0–0. 12.Qb3 is an odd diversion, seen in Alexandru-Schiller, ICC, 1997. 12...Qb6; 13.0–0 Be7; 14.Rfe1 0–0; 15.c3 Nd5; 16.Bd2 Qxb; 3 17.axb3 Bd6; 18.Ne4 Bc7; 19.c4 N5f6; 20.Ba5 Bf4; 21.Bb4 Rfb8; 22.Bd6 Bxd6; 23.Nxd6 Nxh5. Black had an extra pawn. **12...Be7; 13.Kb1.** There are several alternatives which must be examined. We will consider 13.Ne5, 13.Ne4 and 13.c4. Of course, White can also combine these strategies.

An active plan is 13.Ne5 0–0 and now White has several tries. We'll start with 14.c4.

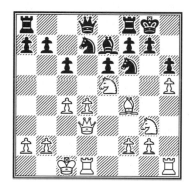

This is a logical continuation, and Black will have to play very carefully, or perhaps very recklessly, to maintain good chances. 14...Nxe5 is worth testing. 15.dxe5 (15.Bxe5 Ng4) 15...Qc7 is recommended by Kasparov & Shakarov.

The exchanging plan 14.Nxd7 Qxd7 can be followed by 15.Be5, where I think Ng4!?, which is still unplayed is probably best.

We can return to the idea seen in our main game if White tries 14.Kb1.

14...Nxe5; 15.Bxe5 Ng4; 16.Qe2 Nxe5; 17.dxe5 Qc7. White has some pressure here, with a promising outpost at d6 and temporary control of the d-file. But at the same time he has to worry about the weak pawns at e5 and h5. 18.f4 Rad8; 19.Rdf1. White trades the d-file for attacking potential on the kingside, but Black's position is solid, and there is no need for concern. 19...Qa5; 20.Ne4 Rd4!; 21.c3 Rd7. The rook is driven back, but doubling will still be possible, and now there is a slight crack in the kingside pawn structure. 22.g4 Rfd8; 23.Rh3 Qa4! Taking advantage of the fact that d1 is now under-defended. 24.b3 Qb5. An interesting decision. Black calculates that despite the small weaknesses, White's queenside is solid enough to withstand any attack, while the Black king is less secure. 25.Qxb5 cxb5; 26.Kc2.

The menacing kingside pawns are now a liability in the endgame. 26...b4 ; 27.Rg3 bxc3; 28.Rxc3 Bb4; 29.Re3 Rd4; 30.Re2 was agreed drawn in Zapata-Garcia Palermo, Bayamo, 1983.

Finally, let's consider 14.Qe2, which can be met by the expansionist 14...a5.

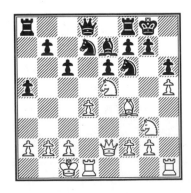

15.c4?! (15.Rhe1 looks much more promising) 15...a4 16.Kb1 a3 17.b3 Ra6 18.Qf3 Qc8 19.Rhe1 Rd8 20.Qe3 c5 21.Nxd7 Rxd7 was drawn in Timman-Lobron, Plovdiv 1983.

So, having examined the lines arising from 13.Ne5, we turn to an alternative knight move: 13.Ne4.

Black can achieve a reasonable game by exchanging knights here. 13...Nxe4; 14.Qxe4 Nf6 is the obvious and natural move. 15.Qd3 (15.Qe2 Qd5; 16.Kb1 is evaluated as better for White by Karpov—a remark which Kasparov & Shakarov quote, but do not comment on. This received a test (via transposition) in our main game, transposing to the relevant position after 16...0-0) 15...Qd5!; 16.c4 Qe4 is dead even.

Another plan is the rapid advance of the c-pawn. 13.c4!? b5!?; 14.c5! Even though this concedes the d5 square, the only way to avoid this would be to play 14.b3?!, which would be too weakening on the queenside. (14.cxb5? cxb5; 15.Qxb5 lets Black castle with a much better game.) 14...0-0; 15.Kb1! The idea is to allow the bishop to retreat to c1 and allow a knight to occupy f4. 15...a5!; 16.Bc1 a4; 17.Ne2 Qb8! From this post the queen can be useful both on the b-file and long diagonal.

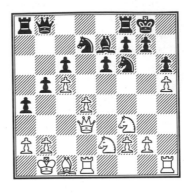

Now White played 18.g4?! A premature, and somewhat panicky response. (Better is 18.Nf4! Rd8; 19.Qc2 b4; 20.Qc4 Nd5; 21.Nxd5 exd5; 22.Qd3 and there is no way to continue the queenside attack, so White can launch his own offensive on the kingside.) 18...Nxg4; 19.Rdg1.

19...f5! Although the pawns at c6 and e6 will be very weak, it is important to seal the kingside and keep control of central squares, including e4. 20.Nf4! (20.Rg2 a3!?; 21.b3 e5!) 20...Rf7! Once again Black must avoid temptation at f2. 21.Qe2 Nf8! would have been a more effective defense. 22.Nxe6 Bf6; 23.Nxf8 Qxf8; 24.Qe6?! One can well understand the appeal of this move, which attacks two loose pawns and creates a pin on the e-file. Black has a magic solution. 24...Qc8 with a clearly superior position.

Returning to the game, it is time for Black to castle. **13...0-0.**

This is the newer approach from Lobron, one of the most successful employers of the Classical Caro-Kann, who knows when to push his a-pawn! **14.Ne4 Nxe4; 15.Qxe4 Nf6; 16.Qe2.** We now have a line similar to that which arises after 13.Ne4, which is not a promising line for White, though Karpov seems to think that White has an advantage here, if Black plays his queen to d5.

16...Qd5. Evidently, Lobron disagrees. **17.Ne5 Qe4!** This queen maneuver lies at the heart of many of Black's games. In the endgame Black's chances are quite good, because the pawn at h5 is generally a liability. **18.Qd2.** 18.Qxe4 Nxe4 does not give White anything - see Thorsteins - Lobron, Reykjavik, 1984. 18...Nd5. Lobron deftly exploits the d5-square. **19.Bg3 Rfd8; 20.Rde1 Qf5.**

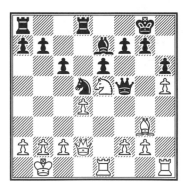

Black has achieved full equality. **21.Nd3 Rac8; 22.Be5 c5.** The thematic advance has been well-prepared. **23.dxc5 f6!** Less clear is 23...Bxc5; 24.Nxc5 Rxc5; 25.g4!? **24.g4 Qf3.** 24...Qxg4 would be very risky. 25.Reg1 Qb4; 26.Qxh6 Bf8; 27.Bd6. **25.Bd4 Qxg4.** But now there is a gain of tempo involved. **26.Be3 Qf5; 27.Bxh6!?**

Is this sacrifice necessary, correct, or simply optimistic? **27...gxh6; 28.Qxh6 Kf7; 29.Qc1.** The retreat is motivated by the fact that Black is getting ready to attack by moving his knight and then sacrificing the exchange on d3. Clearly Kupreichik did not evaluate the position correctly when he went in for the sacrifice.

29...Bxc5; 30.Reg1 Bd6! Overprotecting f4 and opening the c-file which can be useful if the rooks stay on the board. **31.h6 Rg8; 32.Qd1 Rxg1; 33.Rxg1 Rg8; 34.Rh1 Rh8; 35.Rh5 Qe4; 36.a3 Bf8–+; 37.Qd2 b6; 38.f3 Qg6; 39.Qh2 Rxh6; 40.Rxh6 Qxh6; 41.Qb8 Qh1+; 42.Ka2 Qxf3; 43.Qxa7+ Be7; 44.Qa4 Ne3; 45.Qh4 Nxc2; 46.Nf4 Nd4.** White resigned.

CONSERVATIVE VARIATION

HORT VS. LARSEN
Buenos Aires, 1980

1.e4 c6; 2.d4 d5; 3.Nd2 dxe4; 4.Nxe4 Bf5; 5.Ng3 Bg6; 6.h4 h6; 7.Nf3 Nd7; 8.Bd3 Bxd3; 9.Qxd3 e6.

This is similar to the main lines, except that the pawn is at h4 instead of h5. The difference is significant in several ways. To begin with, the pawn at h4 is not as weak as when it is further advanced. The pawn controls g5, so that White can more quickly get in g4-g5, accelerating the kingside attack. From Black's perspective, the pawn at h4 does commit White to queenside castling, allowing Black to choose an appropriate defense. In our repertoire we will castle kingside, as we do with the main lines. You should remember that the pawn at h4 can advance to h5, but not with gain of tempo as in the main lines. Nevertheless, if Black plays too slowly, White may be able to afford that luxury if the attacking strategy demands it.

10.Bd2. 10.Bf4 is sometimes seen, with the idea of steering the game into the queenside castling lines after 10...Qa5+; 11.Bd2 Qc7. 10...Be7 was originally suggested by Kasparov. Surely the Lobron Variation with kingside castling is even better with the pawn still at h4!? 11.Ne4 Nb6; 12.Be5 Nf6; 13.Nfd2 Nbd5; 14.a3 Rg8.

The odd position of the rook is seen elsewhere in the Classical lines. Black must now castle queenside, but White's forces are not well placed, and the Black knight may be able to use the h5-square. 15.c4 Nxe4; 16.Nxe4 Nf6. (16...Qa5+ comes into consideration, though forcing the king to f1 does not seem like much of an achievement.) 17.b4 Nxe4; 18.Qxe4.

Black is certainly no worse here. The White pawn at d4 is weak, as is the one at h4. The king is safe, as White can't afford to advance the f-pawn and weaken the e1–h4 diagonal. Moritz-Luft, Bundesliga, 1994. 18...Bf6. (18...a5! is strong, in my opinion. 19.b5 Rc8! and lines are opening on the queenside, exposing White's weaknesses.) 19.Rd1 Bxe5; 20.dxe5 Qc7; 21.0-0 Rd8 would have been a bit better for White if rooks were exchanged at d8, after which the advance of the b-pawn would loosen up the queenside.

Two other moves fail to achieve anything for White. 10.Be3 Ngf6; 11.0-0-0 Qc7; 12.Kb1 Nd5; 13.c4 Nxe3; 14.Qxe3 was agreed drawn in Rajamaki-Mannisto, Kankaanpaa, 1989. Kingside castling is not often seen, and when it is played, tends not to achieve much success. 10.0-0 Ngf6; 11.Re1 Be7; 12.Bd2 0-0; 13.c4 Bd6; 14.Ne4 Nxe4; 15.Qxe4 Nf6 gave Black a solid game in von Freyman-Iljin Zhenevsky, Moscow Soviet Championship, 1924.

Having completed our examination of the sidelines, let's return to the main game, where 10.Bd2 is countered by **10...Ngf6.**

11.0–0–0. 11.0–0 Be7; 12.c4 0–0; 13.b4 was introduced in Jonker-Kalisvaart, Junior tournament, 1997. Black should play 13...Rc8; 14.Rfd1 b5; 15.cxb5 cxb5; 16.Qxb5 Nd5 and Black will regain the pawn, either at b4 or h4. 11.c4 Be7; 12.Bc3 0–0; 13.Rd1 b5 provided sufficient counter-play in Roder-Danielsen, Copenhagen 1994.

11...Be7; 12.Kb1. 12.Ne4 Nxe4; 13.Qxe4 Nf6; 14.Qe2 Qd5 is fine for Black. Compare this to the Main Line with 13.Ne4. 12.Rhe1 0–0; 13.Ne4 c5. (13...Nxc4; 14.Qxe4 Nf6; 15.Qe2 Qd5; 16.Kb1 Qh5. Black has a good game. You will play ...Rfd8 and work on the queenside.) 14.dxc5 Nxc5; 15.Qxd8 Rfxd8; 16.Nxf6+ Bxf6; 17.Be3 Na4; 18.Bd4 Bxd4; 19.Rxd4 Rxd4; 20.Nxd4. The chances in the endgame are even. Juarez Flores-Lobron, Manila Interzonal, 1990.

12...c5!; 13.Rhe1 0–0; 14.Ne4. 14.c4 cxd4; 15.Nxd4 Nc5; 16.Qe3 Qb6 gives Black good queenside counterplay. The pseudo-sacrifice at f5 is nothing special. 17.Ngf5 exf5; 18.Nxf5 (18.Qxe7 Rae8! traps the enemy queen.) 18...Bd8; 19.Qg3 Nh5; 20.Qf3 Qg6 provides the kingside with more than enough defense. **14...Rc8; 15.dxc5 Nxc5; 16.Nxf6+ Bxf6; 17.Qxd8 Rfxd8.**

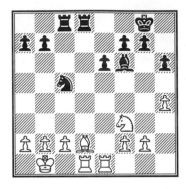

Black is certainly no worse here. The pressure at h4 gives Black a little better game than usual. **18.Be3 Rxd1+; 19.Rxd1 a6; 20.c3 Kf8; 21.g4 Be7; 22.Ne5 Ke8.** A small trap, since the h-pawn is poison. 22...Bxh4??; 23.Bxc5+ Rxc5; 24.Nd7+ Ke7; 25.Nxc5 Bxf2; 26.Nxb7 is an easy win for White. **23.h5 Ne4; 24.f3 Nd6; 25.Kc2 b5; 26.b3 Bf6; 27.Rxd6 Bxe5.**

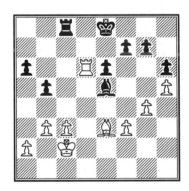

The endgame is slightly in Black's favor, because the c-pawn is weak. **28.Rd3?!** Logical, but it would have been better to exchange pawns. 28.Rxa6 Bxc3; 29.a4 Bd4+; 30.Kd3 Bxe3; 31.Kxe3 would have led to a rook endgame in which Black would have an extra pawn but White has serious counterplay. **28...Ke7; 29.a4?!** 29.f4 Bd6; 30.Kd2 was necessary. It is hard to see how Black could win from that position. **29...bxa4; 30.bxa4 Bd6; 31.Bb6.** 31.Kb3 e5; 32.c4 Rb8+; 33.Kc3 Rb1; 34.c5 Bc7; 35.c6 Bd6 was better, since 36.Bc5, intending to advance the c-pawn, loses to 36...Rc1+. **31...e5; 32.Ba5?!**

32.a5!? Ke6; 33.Kb3 Bc5; 34.Bxc5 Rxc5; 35.Kb4 Rb5+; 36.Ka4 is suggested by Chekhov, but deserves further analysis of the sharp 36...Rd5!? If the rook leaves the d-file for e3, Black takes the initiative with ...f5! That leaves 37.Rxd5 Kxd5.

We have a pure king and pawn endgame in which White's pawns are very weak. Because the endgame is instructive and the pawn structure can arise in many Caro-Kann variations, I present one endgame possibility. You are encouraged to explore it further! 38.Kb4 g5. White cannot capture en passant because that gives Black a potential outside passed pawn on the h-file.

39.Kb3 Kc5; 40.c4 Kd4; 41.Kb4 f6! forces the king to retreat. If the c-pawn advances, then it is lost after Black moves the king to d5 and White is in zugzwang. 42.Kb3 e4; 43.fxe4 Kxe4; 44.c5. Forced, or else Black advances the f-pawn and wins. 44...Kd5; 45.Kb4 Ke6; 46.Kc4 Ke5; 47.c6 Kd6; 48.Kd4 Kxc6; 49.Ke4 Kd6; 50.Kf5 Ke7; 51.Kg6 Ke6; 52.Kxh6 Kf7; 53.Kh7 f5; 54.h6 (54.gxf5 g4 and Black wins) 54...fxg4; 55.Kh8 g3; 56.h7! Black cannot advance the pawn further because of stalemate! 56...Kg6; 57.Kg8 g2; 58.h8Q g1Q; 59.Qh7+ Kf6 and we reach a highly theoretical queen and pawn endgame.

White faces a difficult defense, because the king is in a hopeless position on the far edge of the board. The endgame is not simple, and it is more difficult to play as White. Black will advance the g-pawn to g6, and White will not want to capture because of the danger of a passed h-pawn later on. Black can later capture at h5, opening up the g-file, which can be used by the rook. Meanwhile, White's c-pawn is not going anywhere.

Let's get back to the game, after 32.Ba5?! has been played.

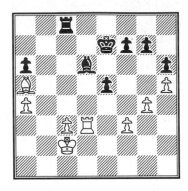

32...Ke6; 33.Kb3 g6; 34.Bb4 Bc7; 35.c4 Rb8! Black drives the enemy king to the distant a-file, and only then switches to the kingside. **36.Ka3.** 36.Kc3? is not on because of 36...e4!; 37.fxe4 Be5+; 38.Kb3 a5, as pointed out by Chekhov. **36...gxh5; 37.gxh5 Rg8; 38.Bd2 f5.**

Now White commits the final, decisive error. **39.Kb4?!** 39.Bxh6 Rh8; 40.Bd2 Rxh5; 41.Kb3 Rh3; 42.Kc2 Rh4!; 43.Kb3 e4; 44.fxe4 fxe4; 45.Re3 Bb6; 46.Rg3 would make Black's task much more difficult, perhaps even impossible. **39...Rg3; 40.Rb3.** Now it is too late for 40.Bxh6 because Black has 40...e4! 41.Re3 Rxf3; 42.Rxf3 exf3; 43.Be3 Bg3; 44.h6 Kf7 and Black wins, as the variation, again by Chekhov, ends with Black advancing the pawn to c2, winning the enemy bishop, and then promoting the f-pawn: 45.c5 f2; 46.Bxf2 Bxf2; 47.c6 Bb6; 48.Kc4 Kg6; 49.Kd5 Kxh6; 50.Ke5 Kg5 etc.

40...f4! This excellent move cuts off the White bishop and sets up threats of ...e4. **41.Be1 Rh3; 42.Bf2.**

Now ...e4 is no longer a threat, because White blockades the f-pawn, but there is a new danger. **42...Kd6!; 43.c5+ Kc6.** The king blockades the c-pawn, which is stuck in place. Meanwhile, the h-pawn falls. **44.Kc4 Rxh5; 45.Kd3 Rh2; 46.Ke2 Rh1; 47.Be1 h5; 48.Kf2** and **White resigned**, because the advance of the h-pawn is inevitable.

TAL ATTACK

There are several ways to handle the positions arising after an early Bc4, and in this game we will concentrate on the plan for White which involves a combination of an advance of the h-pawn with the development of the knight at e2. This system was adopted by Tal in his games at the 1960 World Championship Match against Botvinnik. He also played it later in his career.

TAL VS. VUKIC
Bugojno, 1978

1.e4 c6; 2.d4 d5; 3.Nd2 dxe4; 4.Nxe4 Bf5; 5.Ng3 Bg6; 6.Bc4 e6; 7.N1e2 Nf6; 8.h4. 8.0–0 is discussed in Van der Wiel-Seirawan, in the Heroes chapter. **8...h6.**

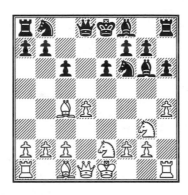

White continues to concentrate on the bishop at g6. The question now is how best to take advantage of the f4-square. There are three logical plans. White can bring the knight there with a direct attack against the bishop. This is, by far, the most popular move. Placing the bishop on that square makes less sense, but it does control a lot of dark squares. Finally, stationing a pawn on the square makes no sense at all, unless a rapid advance to the f5-square is planned.

9.Nf4. The knight can also reach this square via h3. The expansionist plan 9.f4 Bd6; 10.h5 Bh7; 11.Bd3 Bxd3; 12.Qxd3 Nbd7; 13.Bd2 Qc7; 14.0–0–0 0–0–0; 15.Ne4 Nxe4; 16.Qxe4 Rhe8 is good for Black, since the pawn at f4 is merely awkward. White certainly does not want to open the e-file! The game Gurgenidze-Podgayets, Soviet Championship 1968, was eventually won by Black.

9...Bh7.

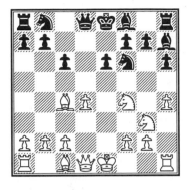

I have met many Caro-Kann players who don't seem to be well prepared in this system, and that is a dangerous situation. Indeed, while I find that I can play the main lines of the Lobron Variation with little memorization, here the play can be very sharp and Black must know the lines in order to emerge safely from the opening. White has a great deal of pressure at e6. Black must find a way to develop without allowing the demolition of the pawn structure by a timely sacrifice there. In the principal continuation in the present game, we will see such a sacrifice from Mikhail Tal, but will show how defense is possible. We will concentrate on the variation with immediate castling, **10.0–0,** but must first consider an enterprising alternative.

10.Qe2 leaves the d-pawn weak but puts pressure on the e-file.

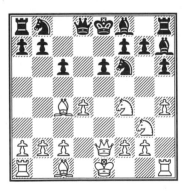

Keres claimed this was a strong and elastic continuation. Kasparov is not so sure. He analyzes 10...Bd6, where 11.Bxe6? is a typical sacrifice, but after 11...0-0! White is in trouble on the e-file. Protecting the pawn does not confer any advantage to White either. 11.Be3

Nbd7; 12.Ngh5 Nxh5; 13.Nxh5 Rg8! is another illustration of the ...Rg8 theme. 14.g4 Qc7; 15.g5 Bg6!; 16.0-0-0 0-0-0; 17.Ng3 hxg5; 18.Bxg5 Bf4+; 19.Bxf4 Qxf4+; 20.Qe3 Qh6; 21.Bd3 Bxd3; 22.Rxd3 Nb6. After the exchange of queens Black had the better endgame, thanks to the weakness of the kingside pawn, Tal-Botvinnik, 5th match game, World Championship,1960.

11.c3 is also possible, but after 11...0-0 and Keres had to admit that White's attack should not succeed.

Let's also consider the advance of the c-pawn at the tenth turn. 10.c3 Nbd7; 11.Qe2 Qe7!; 12.0-0.

Black has a surprising resource here. 12...g5!; 13.hxg5 hxg5; 14.Nh3 g4; 15.Ng5 Bg6; 16.f4 gxf3; 17.Qxf3 Bh6; 18.Bf4 Nd5! (18...0-0-0?? allows 19.Qxc6+ bxc6; 20.Ba6#.) 19.Bxd5 Bxg5; 20.Be4 Rh4!; 21.Bxg5 Qxg5; 22.Bxg6 Qxg6; 23.Rae1 0-0-0 and Black broke through on the kingside, Aronin-Kasparian, Sochi, 1952.

One last plan for White was effectively dealt with by Botvinnik. 10.Bb3 Bd6; 11.Nfh5 Rg8; 12.Bf4 Bxf4; 13.Nxf4 Nbd7; 14.Qd2 Qc7; 15.0-0-0 0-0-0 gave Black a fine game in Ciocaltea-Botvinnik, Tel Aviv Olympiad, 1964.

So, we return to the simple 10.0-0. Black answers **10...Bd6.**

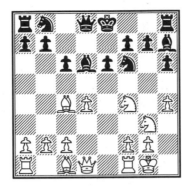

White has a slight edge in development, but Black has only one weakness—e6. Though the square is protected by a pawn at f7, White can aim a lot of firepower in that direction. There are several candidate moves here, but the most interesting one is the immediate sacrifice of the knight at e6.

11.Nxe6. 11.Re1 Bxf4; 12.Bxf4 0–0; 13.Be5 Nbd7; 14.Bb3 was seen in Angelov-Serafimov, Bulgarian Championship, 1992. I think Black should play 14...Nxe5; 15.dxe5 Nd5. I don't see a White attack succeeding, for example: 16.Qg4 Qe7; 17.Rad1 Rad8; 18.Nh5 Bg6; 19.Nxg7 Kxg7; 20.h5 Qg5; 21.Qxg5 hxg5; 22.hxg6 Kxg6 with an endgame that is likely to be drawn.

11.Bb3 is too quiet to cause any trouble. 11...0–0; 12.Re1 Nd5; 13.Nxd5 cxd5; 14.Qg4 Qf6; 15.Nh5 Qg6; 16.Qxg6 Bxg6; 17.Nf4 Bf5; 18.Be3 Nc6 is marginally better for Black, because the White bishop at e3 is useless, Zippitsch-Zagarovsky, Postal, 1971.

11.Ngh5 is certainly a mistake. 11...0–0; 12.Re1 Re8; 13.c3 Nbd7; 14.Bd2 e5 frees Black's game and illustrates the general strategy that should be applied in such situations. 15.Qb3 Rf8; 16.dxe5 Nxe5; 17.Rad1 Nxh5; 18.Nxh5 Qxh4; 19.Bf4 Nxc4; 20.Qxc4 Bb8! White was in trouble in Bellon-Seirawan, Las Palmas, 1981.

11...fxe6; 12.Bxe6.

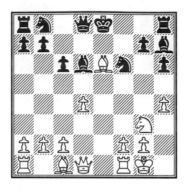

What does White have for the piece? There is compensation in the form of two pawns, the inability of the Black king to castle, weaknesses on the light squares on the kingside, and the initiative.

12...Qc7. Black must get the queen and knight developed and the king must head to the queenside as quickly as possible. The correct strategy is shown in the present game. It is interesting that Tal repeated this line, which he used against Botvinnik in their 1960 title match. **13.Nh5.** Tal had previously played 13.Re1, in the match against Botvinnik in 1960. That game is presented in the Heroes chapter. **13...Rf8; 14.c4 Bg6.** Black chases the knight back. Because White must react to the threat, this does not interfere with the need to get castled. **15.Ng3 Nbd7; 16.c5.** White forces the powerful dark-squared bishop from the board, but at the cost of crippling the kingside pawn structure and creating a big hole at d5.

16...Bxg3; 17.fxg3 Nd5; 18.Re1. 18.Rxf8+ Nxf8; 19.Bxd5 cxd5; 20.Bf4 Qd7; 21.Qe2+ Be4 does not give White enough for the piece. **18...0-0-0; 19.Qg4 Bf7; 20.Bxd5 Bxd5; 21.Bf4.**

White has to work to justify the piece here, and the dark squares are about the only available resource. Black will eventually lose the g-pawn, but that just opens up a line toward the enemy king.

21...h5!? 21...Qa5; 22.Qxg7 Qb4!? is another interesting line, even though White gets to obliterate the remaining kingside pawn. 23.Rad1 (23.Bxh6 Qxb2! leads to a forced mate!) 23...Qxb2; 24.Rd2 Qc3; 25.Qxh6 Rf6; 26.Qg5 Rdf8 looks pretty ugly for White. 27.Bd6 (27.h5?? loses to 27...Rxf4!; 28.gxf4 Qxd2) 27...Rh8; 28.Qe3 Qxe3+; 29.Rxe3 escapes to an endgame, but after 29...Bc4; 30.Kh2 Rf1, Black still has an attack.

22.Qg5? 22.Bxc7 hxg4; 23.Bxd8 Kxd8; 24.Re3 would have been considerably stronger, and White is probably no worse. **22...Qa5!; 23.Re2 Qa4; 24.Rd2 Rde8; 25.Qxg7 Qc4; 26.Qg6 Re2.**

Black takes the initiative by invading the seventh rank. **27.Qd6.** This seems to present an awesome threat at c7, but Black has anticipated this and responds with a forcing variation.

27...Rxf4!; 28.Qxf4 Bxg2.

White has two pawns and a rook for two minor pieces, but one must take into account the weakness of the light squares on the kingside.

29.b3 Qe6; 30.Rxe2 Qxe2; 31.Qf2 Qxf2+; 32.Kxf2 Bh3. Black cannot lose this endgame, as it is easy to station the minor pieces at d5 and g4, and protect everything. White's extra pawns are both backward.

33.Re1 Kd8. 33...Nf6; 34.Re7 Nd5; 35.Rh7 Bg4 would have been a quicker draw, so one presumes Black was either trying to win or was in time trouble. **34.Kf3 Nf8; 35.Re5 Bg4+; 36.Ke4 Nh7; 37.Kf4 Kd7; 38.d5!** Black should have blockaded this square earlier. **38...cxd5; 39.Rxd5+ Kc6; 40.Ke5 Nf8; 41.b4 Nd7+; 42.Kd4 Kb5.**

Black is using the king as a blockader, and this is sufficient to hold the draw. **43.a3 Nb8; 44.Rg5 Nc6+; 45.Kc3 a5; 46.Rg7 axb4+; 47.axb4 Nd8; 48.Rh7 b6; 49.cxb6 Kxb6; 50.Kc4 Nc6; 51.Rg7 Be2+; 52.Kc3 Bf3; 53.Rg6 Bd1; 54.Rg5 Be2; 55.Rc5 Bg4; 56.Rc4 Ne7. Draw agreed.**

KASPARIAN VS. MAKAGONOV
Leningrad, 1938
1.e4 c6; 2.d4 d5; 3.Nc3 dxe4; 4.Nxe4 Bf5; 5.Ng3 Bg6; 6.Nh3 Nd7; 7.Nf4 Ngf6; 8.Bc4.

This move order is not accurate, because Black can react immediately in the center. White should insert h4, forcing ...h6, earlier, as in the Tal-Botvinnik game in the heroes chapter.

8...e5!; 9.Nxg6. 9.dxe5 Qa5+; 10.Bd2 Qxe5+; 11 Nge2 Bc5; 12.0–0 0-0-0; 13.Ng3 Qd4; 14.Bd3 Rhe8. Black may be able to take the poisoned pawn and live. 15.b4 Bxb4; 16.c3 Bxc3; 17.Nge2 Bxa1; 18.Nxd4 Bxd4; 19.Qc2 was drawn in Keres-Kasparian, Moscow, 1952. Somewhat more complicated is 9.Qe2 Qe7; 10.dxe5 Qxe5; 11.Be3 Bb4+; 12.c3 Bc5; 13.Bxc5 Qxe2+; 14.Bxe2 Nxc5; 15.0–0–0.

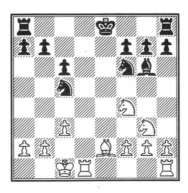

This is a logical endgame continuation. White has nothing to work with, except that the Black king is still in the center. 15...Nce4. (15...Rd8; 16.f3 Rxd1+; 17.Rxd1 Ke7; 18.Re1 Kd7; 19.h4 h6; 20.Nxg6 fxg6; 21.Bc4 b5 22.Bf1 was marginally better for White in Ljubojevic-

Portisch, Tilburg, 1978.) 16.Rhe1 Nxg3; 17.Nxg6 hxg6; 18.hxg3 0–0; 19.Bf3 Rfe8 was no worse for Black in Van Wieringen-Hoekstra, Postal 1991.

So, White captures at g6 and we recapture toward the center. **9...hxg6.**

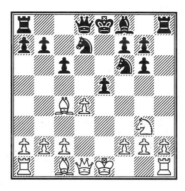

Black does not mind the doubled pawns, as the h-file can be useful and the kingside squares are now thoroughly protected. **10.Qe2.** 10.dxe5 Qa5+; 11.Bd2 Qxe5+; 12.Qe2 (this position is evaluated as better for White by Trifunovic, but experience has not validated this judgment) 12...Qxe2+; 13.Bxe2 Bc5; 14.0–0 0–0–0; 15.Rad1 Rde8; 16.Bc3 Rh4 was agreed drawn in Tompa-Fette, Hamburg 1990.

10.0–0 is logical, and it is surprising it has taken so long to appear in tournament play.

Black has three logical candidate moves. 10...Nb6; 11.dxe5 Qxd1; 12.Rxd1 Nxc4; 13.exf6 gxf6; 14.Re1+ Kd7; 15.Bf4 is surely better for White. 10...Bd6; 11.Re1 Qc7; 12.Bg5 gave White a little pressure in Socko-Bagheri, World Junior Championship, 1997.

So let's look at 10...exd4; 11.Re1+ Be7; 12.Qe2. This is the only sensible line. If the queen captures at d4, then Black swings the knight to b6 with equality. Does White have enough for the pawn here? Perhaps. 12...Nb6; 13.Bb3 a5. Black can also try 13...Kf8!? This transposes below to Jocks-Fette. 14.a3 a4; 15.Ba2 Qd7; 16.Bf4 c5 and I don't think White has anything better than 17.Qxe7+ Qxe7; 18.Bd6 Nbd5; 19.Bxc5 Qe6; 20.Rxe6+ fxe6; 21.Bxd4 Rc8 when there is reasonable compensation for the exchange, but no more.

In any case, White often prefers to move the queen to the e-file, while the d-pawn is off limits because of the pin on the e-file. Black naturally breaks the pin with **10...Be7.**

Here White can head for an endgame, as in the continuation of our game, or try an enterprising pawn sacrifice similar to that seen in the note to the last move. Again, White can castle and sacrifice the d-pawn. **11.dxe5.**

An important alternative is the thematic gambit continuation 11.0–0 exd4; 12.Re1 Nb6; 13.Bb3 Kf8!?

Black gives up the right to castle, but the rook can enter the game from h4 if needed. Now the bishop is no longer pinned. This may be the best plan against the pawn sacrifice, whether played at move ten or move eleven. 14.Bg5 Nfd5; 15.Bxe7+ Qxe7; 16.Qd3 Qh4!?; 17.h3 Nf6. (17...Nf4; 18.Qd2 c5; 19.Re4 Nxh3+; 20.gxh3 Qxh3; 21.Qg5! and the vulnerability of c5 puts Black at a disadvantage.) 18.Rad1 Rd8; 19.c3 Rd7; 20.cxd4 looks dangerous for Black, because White can play Ne4. 20...Qf4; 21.Ne4 Rh5; 22.Qc2 Qc7; 23.Nc5 Re7; 24.Nd3 Nbd5; 25.Re5 Rexe5; 26.dxe5 Ne8; 27.Qc5+. Black resigned. Jocks-Fette, Hamburg, 1990. 16...Qf6 is less ambitious, but a lot safer. 17.Re4 c5; 18.Rae1 can be met by 18...Qc6.

After the capture at e5, the play takes on a forcing character. **11...Qa5+; 12.Bd2 Qxe5; 13.0-0-0 Qxe2; 14.Bxe2 Bc5.**

The attack on the f-pawn provides enough time to deal with the problems of the position. **15.f4 Kf8.** 15...Bf2 strikes me as superior. Black can go into the endgame with knights against bishop as long as the king can be extricated from the center, or a few pieces can be exchanged so that the king is not subject to direct attack.

16.Bf3 Re8; 17.Kb1 Nb6; 18.f5. This move is not easy to meet, but certainly capturing at f5 would have been better than allowing the creation of a serious weakness at g6. **18...Nbd5?!; 19.fxg6 fxg6; 20.Bxd5.** Why give up the bishop? 20.h3 would have maintained a serious advantage. **20...Nxd5; 21.c4 Nf6; 22.Bg5 Kf7; 23.h3.** Too late. Black doubles rooks on the e-file and equalizes. **23...Re5; 24.Bf4 Re7; 25.Rhf1 Rhe8; 26.Kc2 Re6; 27.Rf3 Re1; 28.Bd2 R1e6; 29.Bc3 Re3; 30.Rdf1 Rxf3; 31.Rxf3 a6; 32.Kd3 Rd8+; 33.Ke2 Re8+; 34.Kd3. Draw agreed.**

MARSHALL ATTACK
1.e4 c6; 2.d4 d5; 3.Nc3 dxe4; 4.Nxe4 Bf5; 5.Ng3 Bg6; 6.f4

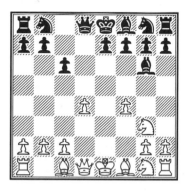

Amazingly, this fairly obvious candidate move is not even mentioned in the 1997 edition of ECO, though it was discussed in the 1984 volume. Black obtains a decent position by playing normal developing moves, after dealing with the threat of f5.

MARSHALL VS. CAPABLANCA
New York, 1927
1.e4 c6!; 2.d4 d5; 3.Nc3 dxe4; 4.Nxe4 Bf5; 5.Ng3 Bg6; 6.f4 e6.

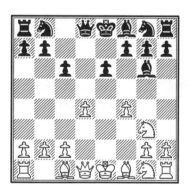

Black obviously must deal with the threat of f5.

7.Nf3. 7.h4 h5 leads nowhere for White, according to analysis by Trifunovic, which runs 8.Nf3 Nd7; 9.Bc4 Be7; 10.0-0 Qc7. It is too dangerous to go pawn grabbing, because White will get in f5. 11.Ne2 0-0-0; 12.c3 with equal chances. **7...Bd6.** White has many plans here. Some can transpose to other variations, for example: if h4 and ...h6 are included. There are three independent lines. White can develop the bishop to c4 or e2, or can advance the c-pawn to c3. **8.Bd3.** White offers an exchange of bishops. It is best to let White capture, if desired, then the h-file will be open. The main thing is to keep sufficient control of f5. 8.c3 is harmless. 8...Ne7; 9.Bd3 Nd7; 10.Ne4 Qc7; 11.Ne5 (Mrdja-Astolfi, Cannes, 1990) should be met not by the weakening advance of the f-pawn, but with castling, for example: 11...0–0: 12.Nxd6 Qxd6: 13.Bxg6 hxg6.

Transposing to the systems with a bishop at c4 is also possible, though Black can pursue some independent paths: 8.Bc4 Ne7; 9.Qe2 (9.0–0 Nd7; 10.Ne5 Nf6; 11.c3 Qc7; 12.Qe2 0–0; 13.Be3 c5; 14.dxc5 Bxc5; 15.Bxc5 Qxc5+; 16.Kh1 Rad8; 17.Nxg6 hxg6; 18.Bb3 Nf5 was drawn in Stoltz-Flohr, Bled, 1931) 9...Nd7; 10.Ne5 Qc7; 11.Ne4 Bxe4; 12.Qxe4 Nf6; 13.Qe2 Nfd5; 14.Bd2 0–0; 15.Bb3 f6; 16.c4 fxe5; 17.fxe5 Bb4; 18.cxd5 Bxd2+; 19.Qxd2 cxd5. A draw was agreed, but there was still plenty of potential play for both sides in Nowarra-Roensch, Schwerin, 1969.

8...Ne7; 9.0–0. Sooner or later Black will castle, develop the knight at d7, and exchange bishops at d3. Black can choose the order. I think I'd capture immediately, not giving White the chance to play Ne4. Still, even the slowest plan is fine, as seen in this game. **9...Nd7; 10.Kh1.** 10.Ne4 is logical, but after 10...Bxe4; 11.Bxe4 Qb6; 12.c4 Nf6!, Duckstein-Muller, Amsterdam, 1966, Black has time to retreat the queen.

10...Qc7; 11.Ne5 Rd8!; 12.Qe2 Bxd3; 13.Nxd3 0–0.

Black has a solid position and is ready to advance the c-pawn, which should achieve equality. **14.Bd2 c5; 15.Ne4.** 15.dxc5 Nxc5; 16.Nxc5 Bxc5; 17.Rad1 Bd6 is just equal. **15...Nf5!** Black wants d4 for the knight! **16.dxc5.** 16.Nxd6 allows the intermezzo 16...Nxd4! **16...Nxc5; 17.Ndxc5 Bxc5; 18.Bc3 Bd4!**

This is an awkward move to meet. The Black knight occupies an excellent post, and it is Black who is playing for a win. **19.Rad1 Bxc3; 20.Nxc3 Rxd1; 21.Nxd1 Rd8.** Black does not fall for 21...Nd4?; 22.Qe4! Nxc2; 23.Nc3 Na3; 24.Rc1 Nc4; 25.Nb5 although the position after 25...Nd6!; 26.Rxc7 Nxe4; 27.Nxa7 Rd8; 28.g3 Nd6 is not so bad. **22.Nc3 Qb6.** Capablanca heads for a favorable endgame. If he had wanted to stay in the middlegame, he might have tried 22...h6, keeping the queen at c7 to prevent Rd1, which would leave the f-pawn undefended. **23.Rd1! Rxd1+; 24.Nxd1 Qb4.**

Queen and knight endgames are almost always tricky, and frequently arise in the Caro-Kann. This position is instructive. There is more danger than meets the eye. **25.Qf2?** 25.g3 was necessary, when 25...Nd4 can be countered by 26.Qd3! **25...h5; 26.a3 Qd6; 27.Nc3 Qd4!** Capablanca understands that the knight endgame is advantageous. **28.Qxd4.** White cannot avoid the exchange of queens. 28.Kg1 Kf8 lets Black centralize the king before exchanging queens.

28...Nxd4; 29.Ne4 Nxc2; 30.Nd6 Ne3!

The exchange of pawns on the queenside just accentuates White's advantage. **31.a4.** 31.Nxb7 Nc4 is bad for White. **31...Nd5; 32.Nxb7?** The queenside majority will not compensate for the central pawns. White should have defended the f-pawn. **32...Nxf4; 33.b4 Nd5; 34.b5 Nc3; 35.Na5.** 35.Nc5 may have been what Marshall had in mind, but 35...Kf8!; 36.Kg1 Ke7; 37.Kf2 Kd6 wins another pawn. **35...Nxa4; 36.Nc6 Kf8; 37.Nxa7 Ke7.**

Black threatens to walk over and collect the b-pawn, after which the extra kingside pawns will be enough to win. **38.Nc6+ Kd6; 39.Kg1 f6; 40.Kf2 e5; 41.Nd8 Kd7!** The g-pawn will not fall! **42.Nb7 Kc7; 43.Na5 Nc3.** The rest is technical. **44.Kf3 Nxb5; 45.Ke4 Nd6+; 46.Kd5 Kd7; 47.Nc6 Nc8; 48.Nb8+ Ke7; 49.Nc6+ Kf7; 50.Nd8+ Ke8. White resigned.**

F4 ATTACK

1.e4 c6; 2.d4 d5; 3.Nc3 dxe4; 4.Nxe4 Bf5; 5.Ng3 Bg6; 6.h4 h6; 7.f4

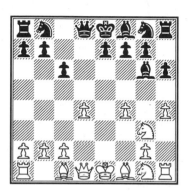

The odd three pawn attack is aimed directly at the bishop at g6, but usually Black manages to exchange this bishop for its counterpart, so it is not effective. White's pawns look ugly. This reflects their underlying weakness. Note that Black is not behind in development. These are some of the reasons that the attack is not popular these days.

KAMINSKI VS. KORTCHNOI
Polanica Zdroj, 1992
1.e4 c6; 2.d4 d5; 3.Nc3 dxe4; 4.Nxe4 Bf5; 5.Ng3 Bg6; 6.h4 h6; 7.f4 e6; 8.Nf3 Nd7

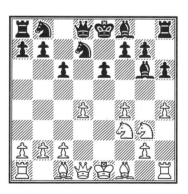

9.h5. White drives the bishop back, but as usual the pawn is a bit overextended and can be weak in the endgame. 9.Bd3 Bxd3; 10.Qxd3 Ngf6; 11.0-0 Qc7; 12.c3 Bd6; 13.Ne5 0-0; 14.Bd2 c5; 15.Ne2 cxd4;

16.cxd4 Nd5 is clearly better for Black. The White pawns just look silly, Boer-Dobai, Open, 1997. **9...Bh7; 10.Bd3 Bxd3; 11.Qxd3 Qc7.**

Black stands well. All critical squares are under control and castling will be possible in either direction.

12.Bd2. 12.Ne5!? is suggested by Korchnoi. 12...c5! is his recommended reply, and he evaluates the position as unclear. (12...Ngf6 is my suggestion. I think Black is fine.) 12.0-0 0-0-0; 13.Qe2 Ngf6; 14.c4 c5; 15.b4 is an enterprising, but ultimately flawed plan. 15...cxd4; 16.a3 was seen in Goldenberg-Leriche, Open, 1997. The correct reply is the advance of the d-pawn, for example: 16...d3; 17.Qxd3 Nxh5!; 18.Nxh5 Nf6; 19.Qe3 Nxh5; 20.Qxa7 Ng3; 21.Qa8+ Qb8; 22.Qxb8+ Kxb8 with a roughly level game.

12...0-0-0. Against this formation, Black should definitely castle on the queenside. **13.Qe2 Ngf6.** Black should continue to develop normally. **14.0-0-0.** 14.Ne5! is more challenging. 14...Nxe5; 15.dxe5 (15.fxe5? loses to 15...Rxd4) 15...Nd5 (15...Nd7; 16.0-0-0 Be7; 17.Be3 Kb8 is a safe alternative from Sindik-Hunt, Staffordshire Centenary, 1997.) 16.0-0-0. Korchnoi claims that White is better here. Still, 16...Bc5; 17.Ne4 Be7 is not so bad for Black.

14...Bd6; 15.Ne5 Rhf8.

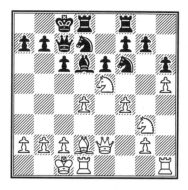

This position has been reached several times. White has several fairly obvious plans, but none of them confer any advantage. White can take an immediate decision regarding the role of the rook at h1, or can defer that and play on the queenside.

16.Rhf1 is the latest try, but it doesn't seem to have much of an effect. 16.Kb1!? c5; 17.c3 is another Korchnoi suggestion, but I am not so impressed after 17...Nb6 followed by ...Nbd5. 16.c4 should be met by 16...c5. Now White can improve the position of the bishop with 17.Bc3 but Black can counter with 17...Nb6; 18.dxc5 Bxc5; 19.b3 Nbd7; 20.Kb1 Nxe5; 21.fxe5 Nd7; 22.Ne4 Be7 and White has nothing tangible, Sax-Rodriguez, Biel Interzonal, 1985. 16.Rhe1 c5; 17.dxc5 Nxc5; 18.Kb1 Kb8 leads to a quieter positional struggle. 19.Bc1 Rfe8; 20.Rd4 Nd5 led to a tense position in Marjanovic-Haik, Marseille, 1986.

16...c5; 17.Nc4 Nb6. 17...cxd4; 18.Nxd6+ Qxd6; 19.Be3 is uncomfortable for Black. **18.Nxd6+ Rxd6; 19.dxc5.** White must be careful. 19.Be3? allows 19...c4; 20.f5 Nbd5 and Black has the advantage. **19...Qxc5; 20.Be3 Rxd1+; 21.Rxd1 Qc7; 22.Bxb6 Qxb6.**

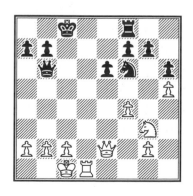

Black is at least equal here. In the long run, White's kingside pawns are weak. **23.Ne4 Nd5; 24.g3 Rd8; 25.Qd3?!** 25.Qc4+ Kb8; 26.Qc5 would invite a transition to an endgame with plenty of play. While I agree with Korchnoi that the chances are equal, I would be quite comfortable playing Black. 25.c4!? Qe3+; 26.Qxe3 Nxe3; 27.Rxd8+ Kxd8; 28.Nd6 Ke7; 29.c5 Nf1 is evaluated by Korchnoi as unclear. Yes, that is what most pure knight endgames are! It is important to remember that "equal" does not mean drawn. I think it quite likely that in a practical game one side or the other would win this ending. I don't know if either player is more likely to win from this position, but would not expect a draw. Let's extend the endgame analysis just a little bit. 30.g4 Ne3; 31.Nxb7 Nxg4; 32.c6 Nf6.

Here it is clear that Black will have the outside passed pawn and the better winning chances. This is just one line, there are many others that could be presented in this apparently simple endgame!

25...Rd7; 26.Qd4 Qxd4; 27.Rxd4 b6.

Once again, the weakness of the pawn at h5 provides Black with all the necessary play. **28.c4 Ne3; 29.Nd6+ Kb8?!** 29...Kc7 was a better try, according to Korchnoi, who gives further. 30.Nb5+ Kc6; 31.Rxd7 Kxd7; 32.Nxa7 Nf1; 33.g4 Ne3; 34.g5 Ng2 with advantage to Black.

30.b3?! White returns the favor. The correct plan was to retreat the rook to d2, then play Ne4, which gets rooks off the board. Korchnoi presents some interesting analysis of the position. I quote just one line: 30.Rd2 Nf1; 31.Rd3 Kc7; 32.Ne8+ Kd8; 33.Nd6 Ke7; 34.Nc8+ Ke8; 35.Nd6+ Kf8; 36.g4 Ng3; 37.Kc2 Ne2; 38.Nb5 with equal chances. **30...Ng4; 31.b4 Nf6; 32.c5 bxc5; 33.bxc5 Kc7.**

Black is clearly better, because the White c-pawn is blockaded and the h-pawn is still surrounded by air.

34.Ra4 Kc6; 35.Ra5! Nxh5; 36.Nc8 Rc7; 37.Nxa7+ Kb7; 38.Kd2 Kb8; 39.Nb5 Rxc5; 40.a4 Nxg3; 41.Ra6 Ne4+; 42.Ke3! Nc3; 43.Nd6 Nd5+; 44.Kd4 Rc1; 45.Nxf7 Nxf4; 46.Ke5 Nd3+; 47.Kd6 e5.

White must play with precision, or else fall to Black's extra pawns. There was still a way to draw, but White missed it.

48.Rb6+? 48.Nxe5! Nxe5; 49.Kxe5 leads to a very well-studied endgame position, which is known to be a draw with best play. Here is one possibility, from Korchnoi. 49...Rg1; 50.Kf4 h5; 51.Kf3 h4; 52.Kf2 Rg4; 53.Kf3 Rg3+; 54.Kf2 g5; 55.Rg6 Kb7; 56.a5 Ka7; 57.a6 Rg4; 58.Kf3 Rg1; 59.Kf2 Rg3; 60.Rf6 Rg4; 61.Kf3 Ra4; 62.Rg6 and Black cannot make progress.

48...Ka7; 49.Rb5 e4; 50.Ne5 Nxe5; 51.Rxe5 Rg1; 52.Rxe4 Rg5–+; 53.Rb4 Ka6; 54.Kc6 Rg6+; 55.Kd5 Ka5; 56.Rh4 Rg5+; 57.Ke6 h5; 58.Rf4 g6; 59.Kf7 Rg4; 60.Rf1 Kxa4. White resigned.

YANOFSKY ATTACK

1.e4 c6; 2.d4 d5; 3.Nc3 dxe4; 4.Nxe4 Bf5; 5.Ng3 Bg6; 6.Nf3 Nd7; 7.Bd3.

White usually gains space on the kingside with 7.h4 h6 and often 8.h5 Bh7 before offering this logical exchange. White elimates Black's most powerful piece by direct means. Nevertheless, the variation has fallen from favor, since it is not necessary to capture at d3, as it is when Black has already played ...h6.

YANOFSKY - GOLOMBEK
Hastings, 1951

Long and complex endgames, particularly those with knights and queens, are typical in the Caro-Kann. Here is an example of a marathon that lasts more than a hundred moves. This game takes you through several endgames to an amazing, if somewhat tragic, finish.

1.e4 c6; 2.d4 d5; 3.Nc3 dxe4; 4.Nxe4 Bf5; 5.Ng3 Bg6; 6.Nf3 Nd7; 7.Bd3 Ngf6; 8.0–0 e6.

9.Re1. If White is going to castle on the kingside, then the rook clearly belongs at e1, since it has nothing to do at f1. The advance of the f-pawn is not a significant theme in this variation. Nevertheless, there are many alternatives to consider.

9.Qe2 Qc7; 10.c4 Bxd3; 11.Qxd3 Bd6; 12.Bd2 is one logical line.

This is a typically classical approach. Black can castle in either direction. Since our repertoire uses mostly kingside castling, we'll move in that direction. 12...0-0; 13.Bc3. White's plan is to overprotect e5, and perhaps later uncover the long diagonal with a timely advance of the d-pawn. 13...Rfe8; 14.Rfe1 Rad8; 15.Ne4 Nxe4; 16.Qxe4 Be7; 17.Re3 Bf6 is a very solid position for Black, Schwartzman-Fenoglio, Mar del Plata, 1934.

9.b3 represents another way to place the bishop on the a1–h8 diagonal. 9...Be7; 10.Bb2 0-0; 11.c4 Qc7; 12.Re1 was seen in Gromer-Cortlever, Buenos Aires, 1939. Black should now exchange at d3, rather than letting White exchange at g6.

9.Bg5 Be7; 10.c4 0-0; 11.Bxg6 hxg6; 12.Qe2 Re8! Black equalizes by freeing the f8 square for use by a minor piece and preparing for an eventual advance of the e-pawn. White can prevent that plan by occupying e5 with a knight. As we see, however, this plan does not achieve any tangible results. 13.Rad1 Nh5; 14.Bxe7 Nxg3; 15.hxg3 Qxe7; 16.Ne5 Nxe5; 17.dxe5 Rad8; 18.Rxd8 Rxd8; 19.Rd1 was agreed drawn in Yanofsky-Matanovic, Winnipeg, 1967.

9.c4 Be7 has not led to any success for White.

There are three distinct plans, depending on what White has in mind for the dark-squared bishop. 10.Bxg6 (10.Bf4 Bxd3; 11.Qxd3 0–0 is just equal. 10.b3 Bxd3; 11.Qxd3 0–0; 12.Bb2 a5; 13.Rad1 a4; 14.Rfe1 axb3; 15.axb3 Bb4 gave Black a good game in Honfi-Bilek, Hungarian Championship 1955) 10...hxg6; 11.Qe2 Qc7; 12.Rd1 (12.Bd2 0–0; 13.Rfe1 b5 is interesting, for example 14.cxb5 cxb5; 15.Rac1 Qb7 and in the long run the isolated pawn may prove to be weak) 12...0–0; 13.d5 cxd5; 14.cxd5 Nc5; 15.b4 Nxd5; 16.Rxd5 exd5; 17.bxc5 Bf6; 18.Rb1 Qxc5 brought Black equality in Matulovic-Hort, Vinkovci, 1968.

The immediate exchange at g6 is of course another candidate plan. 9.Bxg6 hxg6.

The structure resulting from the capture at g6 is important and can arise in many lines. Black has nothing to fear from this exchange, and can continue development in comfort. 10.Re1 (10.c4 Qc7; 11.Re1 Be7; 12.Qe2 0–0; 13.Bd2 a5; 14.Ng5 c5; 15.dxc5 Nxc5; 16.Bc3 Rfd8; led to a quick draw in Tolush-Lundquist, Postal World Championship, 1962.) 10...Bd6 (10...Be7; 11.Bg5 Qb6 is a sensible alternative. Black can then castle in either direction.) 11.Qe2 0–0; 12.Bg5 Qc7; 13.a3 Rfe8; 14.Ne5 Nf8 might have been a bit better for White if the bishop captured the knight at f6, Hartoch-Dunkelblum, Amsterdam, 1962.

Finally, 9.Be3 Bd6; 10.Ng5 Qc7; 11.c4 Bxd3; 12.Qxd3 h6; 13.Nh3 c5; 14.Rad1 cxd4; 15.Bxd4 Ne5; 16.Bxe5 Bxe5 gave Black the more active game in Pamiljens-Suesman, New England Open, 1963.

With that out of the way, we return to the position after 9.Re1, where Black should play **9...Be7.**

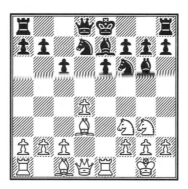

White again has a huge number of plans here! Still, if you know the correct squares for your pieces you can navigate the maze easily. **10.Bg5** will be taken as the main line.

10.c4 aims to takes space on the Queenside and center and deprives Black's Knight of the d5 square. Note that the Bishop on c1 will move after d5 is covered. OK, but somewhat passive is 10.c3. White needs to be active in the opening. 10...Qc7.

Once more, White has a choice of plans. Let's start with the fianchetto on the queenside. 11.b3 Bxd3; 12.Qxd3 0–0; 13.Bb2 Rad8; 14.Qc2 (14.Qe2 Rfe8; 15.Red1 Bd6; 16.Ne5 c5; 17.Nxd7 Nxd7; 18.dxc5 Bxg3; 19.hxg3 Nxc5 led to an eventual draw in Trifunovic-Golombek, Cheltenham, 1951) 14...Rfe8; 15.Re2 Nf8; 16.Ne5 Ng6; 17.Rf1 c5; 18.dxc5 Bxc5; 19.Qc1 Bd4; 20.Bxd4 Rxd4; 21.Nxg6 hxg6; 22.Rd1 Red8; 23.Red2 Rxd2; 24.Rxd2 b6; 25.h3 Rxd2; 26.Qxd2 leads to a queen and knight endgame, in which the better player is likely to find a tactic somewhere, though objectively the position is level. Unzicker-Honlinger, Bad Pyrmont, 1949.

11.Bg5 leads to typical play after 11...0–0; 12.Bxg6 hxg6; 13.Qe2 Rfe8; 14.Ne5 Bb4; 15.Red1 Bd6; 16.Bf4 Rad8 got interesting after 17.b4 Bxb4; 18.Nxg6 Qa5, but after 19.Ne5 c5; 20.Rab1 cxd4; 21.Rxd4 Bc3. Black was already a little better in Vasilchuk-Petrosian, Soviet Junior Championship, 1945.

10.Qe2 Bxd3; 11.Qxd3 0–0 gives Black no cause for concern.

White cannot expect to achieve anything in this position. 12.Bg5 (12.b3 c5; 13.Bb2 cxd4; 14.Bxd4 Bc5; 15.Rad1 Qb6; 16.c4 Rad8 did not bring White anything in Thomas-Reilly, Margate, 1935. 12.Ng5 Re8; 13.N5e4 Nf8; 14.Nxf6+ Bxf6; 15.Be3 Qc7; 16.Ne4 Be7 also failed to provide any advantage for White in Kajev-Kasparian, Kiev; 1940) 12...h6; 13.Bd2 c5; 14.dxc5 Bxc5; 15.b4 Be7; 16.c4 Nb6; 17.Qb3 Qc7 gave Black good counterplay in Yates-Bogoljubow, Hastings, 1922.

10.Ne5 Bxd3; 11.Nxd3 0–0; 12.Bg5 Nd5; 13.Bd2 Qb6; 14.c3 c5; 15.c4 Nc7; 16.dxc5 Nxc5; 17.Be3 Rfd8; 18.Bxc5 Bxc5; 19.Ne4 Bd4 is already better for Black, and in fact the game did not last long. 20.Qc2 e5; 21.Nc3 Qg6; 22.Rac1?? White resigned before losing both knights for one bishop, Michel-Ross, Bad Elster, 1939.

10.c3 Bxd3; 11.Qxd3 0–0; 12.Qe2 Re8; 13.Bg5 Qc7; 14.Rad1 h6 brought Black equality in Sorensen-Regedzinski, Buenos Aires, 1939. 10.b3 Bb4; 11.Bd2 Be7; 12.Qe2 Bxd3; 13.Qxd3 0–0 makes the advance of the b-pawn look irrelevant, Niephaus-O'Kelly De Galway, Heidelberg, 1949.

10.Ng5 Bxd3; 11.Qxd3 0–0; 12.c3 c5; 13.Bf4 h6; 14.Nh3 cxd4; 15.cxd4 Nd5 gave Black the better pawn structure in Giam-Thiellement, Lugano Olympiad, 1968. 10.Bxg6 hxg6 transposes to the note on the bishop exchange at move 9.

Last, and perhaps least, 10.a4 0–0; 11.c3 c5; 12.a5 Qc7; 13.Qe2 was played in Kagan-Hübner, Lucerne, 1979. Liberzon suggests 13...a6 as the equalizer.

Placing the bishop at g5 on move ten at least gives White some pressure at f6, and as we have seen, the move is often part of White's strategy. Black responds by castling. **10...0–0**

Here White may as well capture at g6, as there doesn't seem to be any better plan. **11.Bxg6.** 11.Qe2 Bxd3; 12.Qxd3 c5; 13.Ne4 Nxe4; 14.Bxe7 can lead to fireworks. 14...Nxf2; 15.Qxh7+ Kxh7; 16.Bxd8 Nh3+; 17.gxh3 Raxd8; 18.Rad1 cxd4 and Black had the advantage in the endgame, Broadbent-Golombek, England, 1947.

11...hxg6; 12.c3. 12.Qd3 c5; 13.Rad1 cxd4; 14.Qxd4 Qa5; 15.Qh4 Rfd8; 16.a3 Nf8; 17.Ne4 Rxd1; 18.Rxd1 Rd8 covered all the key defensive squares in Broadbent-Golombek, British Championship, 1946. 12.c4 Rc8; 13.Qe2 c5; 14.Red1 Qc7; 15.Rac1 Rfd8 was solid for Black in Darga-Donner, Bled, 1961.

12...c5; 13.Qe2. 13.Qb3 Qc7; 14.Rad1 Rfe8; 15.Qc4 Nb6; 16.Qe2 Rad8; 17.dxc5 Bxc5; 18.Rxd8 Rxd8; 19.Ne4 Be7 gave Black no problems in Ufimtsev-Makagonov, Leningrad, 1947. **13...cxd4; 14.Nxd4 Re8.**

White enjoys an advantage in space, but has nothing concrete. The next phase of the game is just maneuvering, and the only real change is that the bishops leave the board.

15.Nf3 Qb6; 16.Rad1 Rad8; 17.Qc2 Nf8; 18.Be3 Bc5; 19.Bxc5 Qxc5; 20.Qb3 Qc7; 21.h3 Nd5; 22.Rd4 Nb6; 23.Red1.

Now Black forces a pair of rooks from the board, and then a pair of knights depart.

23...e5; 24.R4d2 Rxd2; 25.Rxd2 Nfd7; 26.Re2 Qc6; 27.Ne4 Nc4; 28.Ned2 Ndb6; 29.Nxc4 Nxc4; 30.Nd2 Nd6; 31.Nf3 Nc4; 32.Nd2 Nd6; 33.Nf3 Nc4. Both sides have been buying a little time toward time control. **34.Qd1 Qc7; 35.Qe1 f6; 36.Qb1 Qf7; 37.Qd1 Nb6; 38.Qb3 Qxb3; 39.axb3 Kf7; 40.Kf1 Re7.**

At time control, the position is dead even. There are many adventures yet to come, however, and some endgame lessons to be learned.

41.Rd2 g5; 42.Ne1 Ke6; 43.Nd3 Rc7; 44.Nb4 Nd7; 45.Nd5 Rc6; 46.Ne3 g6; 47.Ke2 Ra6; 48.Nc4 Rc6; 49.Na5 Rc7; 50.b4 b6; 51.Nb3 Rc6; 52.Rd1 f5; 53.Nd2 Nf6; 54.Nf3 g4. Finally one of the pawns makes it past the central meridian! Yanofsky was headed for a second-place finish, while Golombek was looking at a share of last place, so both players had plenty of incentive to play for a win.

55.hxg4 Nxg4; 56.Rd8 Rc7; 57.Rg8 Kf7. The Black king cannot advance, so it retreats to annoy the White rook. **58.Rh8.** The game could have ended in a draw if White had chosen to move the rook between d8 and g8, with the Black king shuffling between e7 and f7. **58...Kg7; 59.Rd8 e4.** This lets the White knight into the game, but Black didn't have a superior alternative.

60.Nd4 Kf7; 61.Nb5 Re7; 62.Ra8 Ne5.

Finally things get interesting. White wins the a-pawn, but that pawn is not of great significance as White had a potentially passed c-pawn in any case.

63.Rxa7 Rxa7l; 64.Nxa7 Ke6. The pure knight endgame is very tactical, and it is easy to go wrong. **65.b3.** 65.Nc8! looks much stronger. **65...Nd3; 66.g3.** Black threatened ...Nf4+-d5, protecting b6 and attacking c3. **66...g5; 67.Nc8 Nc1+; 68.Ke3 Na2.** 68...Nxb3; 69.Nxb6 is very bad for Black. **69.c4?** This looks good, but it isn't as efficient as 69.Kd2 f4; 70.gxf4 gxf4; 71.Nxb6 e3+; 72.fxe3 fxe3+; 73.Kxe3 Nxc3; 74.Kd4, which should have been played.

69...Nxb4; 70.Nxb6 Ke5.

White has two connected passed pawns, but they are not easy to advance. **71.Nd7+ Ke6; 72.Nc5+ Ke5; 73.f4+ exf3; 74.Kxf3 Nc2.** White's king must remain in the center to defend against the advance of Black's pawns, so it is not easy to advance the queenside ones.

75.Ke2 f4! Black must eliminate White's last kingside pawn before dealing with the queenside. **76.gxf4+ Kxf4.** Black moves the king farther away from the queenside pawns, but that can be remedied later. The main thing is to keep the g-pawn far away from the White forces, so that one of the pieces will have to go and deal with it eventually. Or, as we see in the game, it can find its way forward to the promotion square.

77.Kd2 Nd4; 78.Kd3 Nc6; 79.Ne6+ Kg4; 80.Ke4 Na5.

White can preserve the pawn with Nd4, but chooses to give up the g-pawn to get the c-pawn going. This lack of patience proves costly. The game must have been adjourned at least once already, but it is not clear whether the players spent time analyzing this endgame.

81.c5? Nxb3; 82.c6 Na5; 83.c7 Nc4! Perhaps White missed this. Now if White queens then ...Nd6+ draws immediately. **84.Kd5 Nb6+; 85.Kc6 Nc8; 86.Kd7 Nb6+; 87.Kc6 Nc8; 88.Kb7 Ne7; 89.Nd4.** The threat of Nc6 seems terminal, but Black has another checking defense, based on ...Nf5-d6+.

89...Kf4; 90.Nc6 Nf5; 91.Kb8 Nd6; 92.Nd4.

White seems so close to the goal, just one move away from Nb5! But Black has a pawn too.

92...g4!; 93.Nb5 g3!; 94.Nxd6 g2; 95.c8Q g1Q; 96.Qf5+ Kg3; 97.Ne4+ Kg2; 98.Qg4+. After nearly a hundred moves, and who knows how many hours of play, Golombek now blunders away the game. **98...Kh2??** 98...Kf1; 99.Qf3+ Ke1 would have drawn.

99.Qh4+ Kg2; 100.Qg3+ Kh1; 101.Qh3+ Qh2+; 102.Ng3+. Black resigned, because of the 102...Kg1; 103.Qf1#.

BRONSTEIN VARIATION

1.e4 c6; 2.d4 d5; 3.Nc3 dxe4; 4.Nxe4 Bf5; 5.Nc5

The variation with 5.Nc5 is rarely seen because the knight can be easily chased away. Bronstein and Fischer dabbled with it for a while. Its limited early success was due primarily to attempts to refute the opening, instead of simply settling for a comfortable game after driving back the bishop.

BRONSTEIN VS. PETROSIAN
Moscow, 1966

1.e4 c6; 2.d4 d5; 3.Nc3 dxe4; 4.Nxe4 Bf5; 5.Nc5 b6; 6.Nb3. 6.Na6 was Bobby Fischer's preference, but it was not really tested. 6...Nxa6; 7.Bxa6 Qc7. (After 7...Qd5! I think Black is already better.) 8.Qf3 b5; 9.Bd2 Qb6; 10.Qxf5 e6; 11.Qd3 Qxa6; 12.a4 Nf6; 13.Nf3 Be7; 14.0–0 gave White a small advantage in Fischer-de Gruchy, Montreal, 1964.

6...e6. Here White has many different moves, but sooner or later the knight is likely to come to f3, and it might as well do so immediately.

7.Nf3. 7.Bd3 Bg6. (7...Bxd3; 8.Qxd3 Bd6; 9.Nf3 Nf6 is a solid alternative.) 8.Ne2 Bd6; 9.Bf4 Qc7; 10.Bg3 Ne7; 11.Qd2 Nd7; 12.0-0 0-0; 13.Nf4 Bxd3; 14.Nxd3 Nf5 was agreed drawn in Van der Werf-Dorenberg, Dieren, 1990.

There are two other plans, but they are not very interesting. 7.Bf4 Bd6; 8.Bg3 Nf6; 9.Bd3 Bg6. (9...Bxd3; 10.Qxd3 a5 looks good, too.) 10.Ne2 Qc7; 11.c3 Nbd7; 12.Bxd6 Qxd6; 13.Ng3 0-0; 14.Bxg6 hxg6; held no danger for Black in Meyer-Skozinski, Germany, 1990. 7.Be3 Nf6; 8.Bd3 Bxd3; 9.Qxd3 Be7; 10.Nf3 Nbd7; 11.0-0 0-0; 12.Rfd1 Qc8; 13.Qe2 Re8; 14.Ne5 Nxe5; 15.dxe5 Nd5; 16.c4 Nxe3; 17.Qxe3 Qc7; 18.Rd3 Rad8; 19.Rad1 Rxd3; 20.Rxd3 Rd8; 21.Rxd8+ Qxd8 led to a draw in Lutzke-Lange, Germany, 1993. **7...Bd6.**

White does not have many plans here. Exchanging bishops at d3 doesn't make much sense, so the bishop either has to be fianchettoed, which is logical because the pawn at c6 is weak, or just slowly develop.

8.g3. 8.Be2 Nd7; 9.0–0 h6; 10.Nbd2 Ngf6; 11.Nc4 Be7; 12.Bf4 0–0; 13.Qd2 c5; 14.Rad1 Nd5 was fine for Black in Dolmadjan-Dzanev, Pernik, 1992. **8...Ne7; 9.Bg2 h6; 10.0–0 0–0; 11.Qe2 Nd7.**

Black has every reason to be satisfied with the position. All of the critical squares are defended. The White knight at b3 is out of play and can be attacked by an advance of the a-pawn. **12.c3.** 12.Ne5 Qc7 13.Re1 Nd5 gave Black a solid game in Lopez-Walker, Postal, 1988.

12...Rc8; 13.Nbd2 Bg4; 14.h3 Bh5; 15.Nc4 Bb8; 16.b4 b5! The pawn at c6 is well defended, and White cannot take advantage of the hole at c5. Black will quickly occupy d5 with a knight. **17.Na5 Nd5; 18.Bd2 Re8; 19.c4.** White has no other constructive plan, but Black is already taking over.

19...bxc4; 20.Nxc4 e5!; 21.dxe5 Nxe5; 22.Ncxe5 Bxe5; 23.Rae1. A draw was agreed here, and that is a reasonable result, since after 23...Bd6; 24.Qxe8+ Qxe8; 25.Rxe8+ Rxe8; 26.a3 c5; 27.Re1 Rxe1+; 28.Nxe1. Black has no time to take the b-pawn because the knight at d5 is under attack.

THE RICHTER GAMBIT

MCCOY VS. WAL
California, 1972
1.e4 c6; 2.d4 d5; 3.Nc3 dxe4; 4.Nxe4 Bf5; 5.Bd3

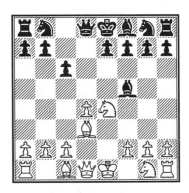

White hopes Black will eat the d-pawn and fall way behind in development, but Black has a simple equalizing plan. **5...Nd7; 6.Nf3.** 6.Qe2 sets a trap, and you should play 6...e6; 7.Nd6+ Bxd6; 8.Bxf5 Qa5+; 9.Bd2 Qxf5, which was fine for Black in Adamson-Mantia, Columbus, 1963. Pleased to avoid 6...Ngf6; 7.Nd6# as in Duffy-Burg, Dayton, 1973 and other games.

6...Ngf6; 7.Qe2. 7.Nxf6+ Nxf6; 8.0–0 Bg4; 9.Be3 e6; 10.c4 Be7; 11.h3 Bh5 is no problem for Black. A great attacking master offered a pawn sacrifice here, but it has never faced the necessary test, as Black chose to decline. 12.b4!? 0–0. (12...Bxf3; 13.Qxf3 Bxb4; 14.Rab1 Qe7; 15.Rb3 0–0 should be explored.) 13.Rb1 e5? A difficult move to understand. 14.dxe5 Bxf3; 15.gxf3 Nh5; 16.f4 g6; 17.Be2 Ng7; 18.Qxd8 Raxd8; 19.Rfd1 Nf5; 20.Bxa7 Ra8 was Richter-Vogt, Berlin Championship, 1937. White could have established a decisive advantage with 21.Bc5 Bxc5; 22.bxc5 Rxa2; 23.Bg4.

7...Nxe4; 8.Bxe4 Bxe4; 9.Qxe4 Nf6; 10.Qd3.

White has achieved nothing in the opening and Black has an excellent Caro-Kann position. Black can play the standard plan of ...e6, followed by ...Bd6, or ...Be7 and kingside castling, or adopt a fianchetto formation as in the game.

10...g6; 11.Bg5 Bg7; 12.0-0 0-0; 13.Rfe1 e6. I would prefer 13...Qd6 here. **14.Qb3 Qa5; 15.Qxb7?**

This is a reckless move. White should have just moved a rook to d1. **15...Rab8!; 16.Qxc6 Rxb2.** The invasion of the seventh rank is a powerful strategic weapon.

17.Ne5 Rxa2; 18.Rac1 Nd5. There is a worthwhile alternative here. 18...Ng4 exploits the pin along the fifth rank. 19.Bf4 Nxe5; 20.Bxe5 Bxe5; 21.dxe5 Rd8 is likely to be a draw in the end, but Black has the better game.

19.Nd7. White might try 19.c4! Nb4; 20.Qd6, where 20...Nd3! is another plan to take advantage of the loose bishop at g5. After 21.Nxd3 Qxg5; 22.d5 Rd8; 23.Qc7 Rd2. Black has good counterplay.

19...Nb4!; 20.Qc4 Rxc2; 21.Ra1? Suicide. 21...Qxa1!; 22.Rxa1 Rxc4; 23.Nxf8 Kxf8; 24.Rxa7 Bxd4; 25.Ra8+ Kg7; 26.h3 Rc2. White resigned.

VON HENNIG GAMBIT
1.e4 c6; 2.d4 d5; 3.Nc3 dxe4; 4.Bc4

This is not especially unorthodox, and, like the Blackmar-Diemer gambit into which it can transpose, the Von Hennig Gambit is included here mostly because it is perceived to be an unorthodox opening. In fact, it is a classical gambit.

SCHILLER VS. FRENKLAKH
San Mateo, 1996
I have sometimes coached Jennie Frenklakh, one of America's most promising young women players. So, knowing she would play the Caro-Kann, but not wanting to use one of the lines we had studied together, I decided on using this gambit, which was brought to my attention by Gabe Kahane, one of my students with a strong inclination toward aggressive play. This game illustrates an interesting, but often overlooked facet of gambit play. It is generally thought that the defender is the one under pressure to play accurately, but in reality there is also some pressure on the gambiteer to make the most of the investment.

1.e4 c6; 2.d4 d5; 3.Nc3 dxe4; 4.Bc4 Nf6; 5.f3 exf3. 5...b5 is a rather wild line, but it has some appeal, and I have used it myself. 6.Bb3 e6; 7.Bg5 e3; 8.Nge2 Be7; 9.Bxe3 Nbd7; 10.0–0 0–0 is about even, Van Schaardenburg-Boersma, Groningen, 1989, or 7.fxe4 b4; 8.Nce2 Nxe4; 9.Nf3 Nd7; 10.Qd3 Nd6; 11.0–0 Qb6; 12.c3 Be7; 13.Ng5 Nf6; 14.Bf4 h6; 15.Bxd6 hxg5; 16.Bxe7 Kxe7; 17.Ng3 Ba6; 18.c4 Rad8 and Black went on to win in Cornelison-Schiller, American Open, 1995. We'll look at the less enterprising, but fully playable move 5...e3 of Van den Bosch-Flohr in the Heroes chapter.

6.Nxf3 e6; 7.0-0 Be7. The best defense, preparing to castle.

8.Bg5. 8.Ne5 (was seen in an early game in this line. 8...Nbd7; 9.Qe2 0-0; 10.Be3 Qc7; 11.Bf4 Bd6; 12.Rad1 Nd5; 13.Bg3 N7f6; 14.Bh4 Be7; 15.Rd3 was Von Hennig-Carls, Goteborg, 1920, and Black should now play 15...Nxc3; 16.bxc3 b5; 17.Bxf6 bxc4; 18.Rg3 Bxf6; 19.Rxf6 Rb8! This game is not well known, but it is important. 8.Qe1 is an interesting plan, bringing the queen to h4) 8...0-0; 9.Bg5 Nbd7; 10.Bd3 Re8; 11.Qh4 Nf8; 12.Ne5 c5; 13.Rf4 cxd4; 14.Nxf7 Kxf7; 15.Bxf6 Bxf6; 16.Ne4 Kg8; 17.Nxf6+ gxf6; 18.Rxf6 Qe7; 19.Raf1 Qg7; 20.Rxf8+ Rxf8; 21.Bxh7+ Kh8; 22.Bg6+ Kg8; 23.Rxf8+ Kxf8; 24.Qd8#, was Welling-Pardeen, Biel, 1981.

8...0-0. 8...Nbd7; 9.Qe2 Nd5; 10.Bxd5 cxd5; 11.Bxe7 Qxe7; 12.Rae1 gave White some compensation for the pawn in Szokacs-Gal, Salgo, 1978. **9.Qd2.** 9.Qe1 is more consistent with White's general strategy. The idea is to move the queen into an attacking position at h4. 9...h6; 10.Bxf6 Bxf6; 11.Qe4. White plans to retreat the bishop to d3, creating a powerful battery on the b1–h7 diagonal. 11...g6; 12.Ne5 was played in Peilen–Joyner, Alabama, 1986. White captured on e5, which was suicidal. The bishop is needed to defend the dark squares. White has no immediate threats, so Black could bring one of the queenside pieces to the defense.

12...Nd7! Black will capture at e5 with the knight and then retreat the bishop to g7. White can exchange at d7 or try radical sacrifices. 13.Nxd7 (13.Nxg6 fxg6; 14.Qxg6+ Bg7; 15.Bxe6+ Kh8; 16.Bf5 Nf6; 17.Rad1 Bxf5; 18.Rxf5 Qe8. Every exchange increases Black's advantage. 13.Bxe6 fxe6; 14.Qxg6+ Bg7; 15.Qxe6+ Kh8; 16.Ng6+ Kh7; 17.Rxf8 Nxf8; 18.Nxf8+ Qxf8 and Black is clearly better.) 13...Bxd7; 14.Rae1 Bg7. White does not have enough compensation for the pawn, but it will take some time for Black to untangle the pieces. Moving the queen to b6 and advancing the c-pawn seems the best plan.

So, Black has no problems against 9.Qe1, and we turn to analysis of **9.Qd2**, to which Black responds **9...Nbd7.**

White has only the semi-open e- and f-files in compensation for the pawn. Black has many pieces available for defense, but the bishop at c8, and the rook in the distant corner, are very hard to activate. Therefore one must be careful not to allow White to mobilize all of the forces for an overwhelming kingside attack.

10.Rae1 c5. This is a standard method of opening the center, making it easier to develop. If Black can activate the queenside forces, the extra pawn will be decisive.

11.Kh1 a6. The immediate capture at d4 is a reasonable alternative. Black's move provokes White's response, which weakens the b4-square. 11...cxd4; 12.Nxd4 Re8 is more accurate. There is nothing to be gained by a sacrifice at e6, and Black can always defend with ...Nf8. **12.a4 cxd4; 13.Nxd4 Nb6.** 13...Re8! looks much stronger. The knight can go from d7 to f8. **14.Bd3 Nfd5.**

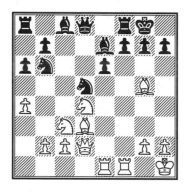

White's position is more precarious than it looks. There is tension on both flanks, and in the center, too. It is perhaps understandable that I managed to misplay the position.

15.Ne4? 15.Bxe7 Nxe7; 16.a5 Nbd5; 17.Nxd5 Nxd5 gives White more compensation for the pawn. There are some attacking chances on the kingside, and Black has a bad bishop. **15...Nxa4?!** 15...f5! would have been a killer. 16.Bxe7 Nxe7 and both knights are under attack in the middle of the board.

16.Bxe7 Nxe7; 17.Ng5 Nf5; 18.c3? What can I say? It was a terrible move! I really had to capture on f5 here, but just didn't want to part with the bishop. This faulty reasoning led to the loss of my material investment. 18.Bxf5 exf5; 19.b3 Nc5; 20.Qe3 h6; 21.Nxf5 Bxf5; 22.Qxc5 Bg6; 23.Ne4 was relatively best, though White really doesn't have very much for the pawn. 23...Rc8; 24.Qa7 Rxc2; 25.Qxb7 Qd3; 26.b4 Bxe4; 27.Qxe4 Qxe4; 28.Rxe4 Rfc8 is ugly, but not impossible to defend.

18...h6; 19.Ngf3 Nxd4; 20.cxd4.

White is simply down a pawn with no compensation. **Black went on to win.**

MILNER-BARRY GAMBIT

1.e4 c6; 2.d4 d5; 3.Nc3 dxe4; 4.f3

We have an invitation to enter the Blackmar-Diemer Gambit by transposition (1.d4 d5; 2.e4 dxe4; 3.Nc3 c6; 4.f3.) Capturing at f3 is risky, though Black should be able to survive and make use of the extra pawn. Your opponent is likely to be well prepared to play a gambit. We choose to decline the offer, and take the opportunity to strike in the center of the board. If White really wants to offer a gambit, then the Von Hennig Gambit, 4.Bc4, is a better choice.

1.e4 c6; 2.d4 d5; 3.Nc3 dxe4; 4.f3 e5

In the Milner-Barry Gambit, Black can react in the center and obtain an equal position quickly. **5.Nxe4**. White has many other tries.

5.d5 Bb4; 6.Bd2 e3; 7.Bxe3 Bxc3+; 8.bxc3 cxd5 was clearly better for Black in "Radar"-Schiller, ICC, 1997.

5.Be3 Bb4; 6.Bc4 Bf5; 7.g4 Bg6; 8.h4 h5 with an advantage for Black in Kennedy-Sawyer, Hatboro, 1989.

5.dxe5 Qxd1+; 6.Nxd1 exf3 gives White a difficult decision. Capturing with the knight means living with a weak isolated pawn, but after 7.gxf3 Be6, White has other weaknesses to deal with.

5...f5; 6.Ng3 Qxd4; 7.Bd3 Bb4+; 8.c3 Bxc3+; 9.bxc3 Qxc3+; 10.Bd2 Qxd3 was winning for Black in "Jeanlou"-Schiller, ICC 1997.

ADVANCE VARIATION

1.e4 c6; 2.d4 d5; 3.e5

Once considered harmless, except by Nimzowitsch who appreciated its potential, the Advance Variation is now the most feared weapon available to White. The maniacal variations after 3...Bf5, including the sharp Van der Wiel Variation 4.Nc3 e6; 5.g4!? and the quiet strangulation in the Short Variation with 4.Nf3, are under constant review in the chess laboratories all over the world. We will adopt the Kavalek Defense, a rare line which often leads to the sort of play found in the Gurgenidze Defense (1.e4 c6; 2.d4 d5; 3.Nc3 g6).

White already committed to the structure with the pawn at e5, but this is not necessarily the best way to deal with the Gurgenidze. Black will develop the knight from b8 not to d7, but via a6 to c7. The e6-square is not occupied by a pawn unless necessary, as the square can prove quite useful to the knight at c7, and Black will want to get the bishop developed along the c8-h3 diagonal.

VAJDA VS. TSEITLIN
Budapest, 1996
1.c4 c6; 2.d4 d5; 3.e5 Na6

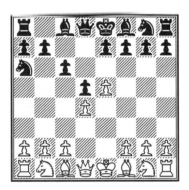

The Kavalek Defense has never been judged harshly by the theoreticians, who have mostly ignored it entirely. Black avoids all the complicated theories of the main lines of the Advance Variation but pays a price. There is not much room to maneuver behind the barrier of pawns Black must erect, often fianchettoing on the kingside. This system has not been seen in enough proper games to give a good picture of the openings, so I have included references to some of my games on-line at the Internet Chess Club. It should be understood that these are casual games. I have only replaced pseudonyms when the real name of the opponent was publicly available.

4.c3 is the most common reply, so that if the bishop captures at a6, Black will be forced to recapture with the pawn, not having ...Qa5+ available.

Another way to eliminate the check is 4.Nc3, but now the knight can receive support from a bishop at c8 after 4...b6!?

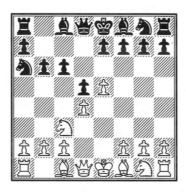

Why not? This obscure move has solid logic behind it. The knight at a6 is better defended, and Black can regroup with ...Nc7 and ...Ba6. The only potential drawback is the possibility of a capture at a6 followed by an advance of the e-pawn by White, but I don't see any concrete danger here.

5.Bxa6 Bxa6; 6.e6 fxe6; 7.Qh5+ g6; 8.Qe5 Nf6; 9.Qxe6 gets the pawn back, but after 9...Qd7; 10.Qxd7+ Nxd7; 11.Nf3 Bg7. Black has excellent pressure in the center and the advantage of the bishop pair. 5.Bg5 g6; 6.Nf3 Bg7; 7.Be2 Nc7; 8.0-0 Ne6 is solid for Black. 5.Nf3 is the most promising move. 5...Nc7; 6.Bd3 Bg4. (6...g6 looks like a better form of defense to me. 7.0-0 Bg7; 8.Re1 Nh6 and Black can follow up with ...Nf5 or ...0-0.) 7.h3 Bh5; 8.Bg5 Qd7; 9.Qd2 Bxf3; 10.gxf3 e6; 11.0-0-0 Be7; 12.h4 and White controlled greater space in Lepeshkin-Simagin, Tallinn, 1965.

Ultra-quiet players might select the wimpy 4.Be2, an open declaration that the knight at a6 is not going to be captured anytime soon.

Black has a choice of many plans against this quiet move. Let's stick with the Classical approach and get our bishop to f5. 4...Bf5; 5.Nf3 e6; 6.0-0 Bg6; 7.b3 Nc7; 8.c4 Nh6; 9.Na3 Be7; 10.Nc2 0-0; 11.Bf4 (11.Bxh6 gxh6; 12.Qd2 is better for White, now that Black has castled kingside. But Black can try to fight back with 12...f6 since 13.Rad1 fxe5; 14.Nxe5 Bg5; 15.Ne3 Bf4 and the pressure mounts at e5. 16.Nxg6 hxg6; 17.g3 Qg5; 18.Kh1.

Now Black can force a transition to the endgame. 18...Bxe3; 19.Qxe3 Qxe3; 20.fxe3 is an endgame which is not bad for Black because White cannot open lines for the bishop and the knight at c7 cannot be dislodged) 11...dxc4; 12.bxc4 b5; 13.Ne3 Nf5; 14.Rc1 Qd7; 15.Nxf5 Bxf5; 16.Bd3 bxc4; 17.Rxc4 Bxd3; 18.Qxd3 Nd5; 19.Bg5 Rab8; 20.Rfc1 Rb6; 21.Bxe7 Qxe7; 22.g3. There is no way for White to make any progress against Black's weak pawns, so a draw was agreed in Bernardo-Soppe, Buenos Aires, 1997.

4.c4 is more confrontational.

A very committal move, and Black can now safely adopt the plan with ...Bf5. 4...Bf5; 5.Nc3 Nb4; 6.Be3 Nc2+; 7.Kd2 Nxa1; 8.Qxa1 dxc4; 9.Bxc4 e6 and White does not have enough compensation for the exchange. 10.Nge2 Bb4; 11.Ng3 Ne7; 12.Ke2 0-0; 13.Nce4 Bxe4; 14.Nxe4 Nf5; 15.Qd1 Qh4; 16.Qd3 Qg4+; 17.Kf1 Rfd8; 18.h3 Qg6; 19.g4 Nxd4!

Black won easily in Buscher-Molinaroli, Germany, 1994. Non-committal in the extreme is 4.Nf3.

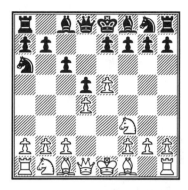

When the knight is developed quickly to f3, the option of ...Bg4 becomes available. The fianchetto plan can be combined with this, or can stand alone. 4...g6 gets us going. 5.a3 is sometimes played to keep the knight off of b4, so that the bishop can safely come to d3. This is a slow plan, however. It makes no sense if White later plays c3, so the plans with c4 are more appropriate.

5...Bg7; 6.c4 Nc7; 7.Nc3 Nh6; 8.h3 f6!? Castling is much safer. 9.exf6 exf6; 10.Be2?! (10.Bf4! Ne6; 11.Bxh6 Bxh6; 12.cxd5 cxd5; 13.Bb5+ looks marginally better for White, but the king may safely move to f7. 13...Kf7; 14.0–0) 10...0–0; 11.0–0 Be6; 12.c5 Qd7; 13.Bf4. Chances are equal, Leconte-Akl, Paris; 1994.

Of course White can continue to live a peaceful life after 5.Be2 Nc7; 6.0–0 h5; 7.Bg5 Nh6; 8.Nbd2 Bg4; 9.c4 Ne6; 10.h3 Nxg5; 11.Nxg5 Bxe2; 12.Qxe2 e6.

This position is very solid. Black has control of critical squares at g4, f5, and e4. The Black king is safe, and the bishop will come not to g7, but to e7. Black can then castle or walk the king to g7. 13.Ngf3

Nf5; 14.Rfd1 Be7; 15.Rac1 Qd7; 16.c5 g5; 17.Nf1 0-0-0; 18.b4 Rdg8.

Black's kingside attack is faster. 19.b5 g4; 20.hxg4 hxg4; 21.N3h2 g3!; 22.fxg3 Nxg3; 23.Nxg3 Rxg3; 24.Rc2 Rg7; 25.a4 Bg5; 26.Rd3 Bf4; 27.Nf1 Qd8; 28.Rf3 Qh4; 29.g3 Bxg3. White resigned. Pareja-Velasco, Spain, 1993.

Another form of straightforward development is seen on 5.Bd3 Bg7, 6.0-0 Bg4, 7.Bg5 h6, 8.Bh4 Qd7, 9.Be2 g5, 10.Bg3 e6, 11.Qd2 Ne7, 12.Nc3 Nf5. Black has a good game, Perth-Schiller, ICC, 1997.

Last, and least promising is the pointless 5.h3.

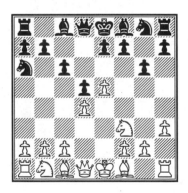

This is designed to keep a bishop off g4, but it wastes precious time. 5...Bg7; 6.Be2 Nh6!; 7.0-0 Nc7; 8.b3 0-0; 9.c4 f6! gives Black good counterplay, for example: 10.Nc3 Be6; 11.Bf4 Nf7; 12.exf6 exf6; 13.Re1 Nd6 with a comfortable position for Black in Jevtic-Vlasov, Novi Sad II, 1992. Of course we must look at the immediate capture, which perhaps deterred many players from adopting the 3...Na6 Variation. Many computer programs used to play 4.Bxa6, which is what Black is aiming for!

The queen will take care of recovering the piece, and will sit comfortably at a6, since there is no light-squared bishop to harass her. Eventually, after ...c5, she can slide over to the kingside.

4...Qa5+; 5.c3 Qxa6; 6.Qf3 e6. (6...g6; 7.h4 Bf5; 8.h5 Be4; 9.Qg3 Qd3; 10.f3 Bf5; 11.Qf2 0-0-0; 12.Ne2 gxh5; 13.Rxh5 Bg6; 14.Nf4 Qa6; 15.Rh1 Bh6; 16.Nxg6 Bxc1; 17.Nxh8 Nf6; 18.Nxf7 Rf8; 19.Nh6 Ne4; 20.Qc2 Ng3; 21.Qxc1 Qe2#. 0-1 Piper-Schiller, ICC, 1998.) 7.Ne2 Ne7, 8.0-0 Nf5; 9.Nd2 Bc7; 10.Nb3 h5; 11.Ng3 h4; 12.Nxf5 exf5; 13.h3 g5; 14.Re1 Be6; 15.Nc5 Bxc5; 16.dxc5 Rg8; 17.Qh5 g4; 18.Qxh4 gxh3; 19.Qxh3 0-0-0; 20.Bf4 Qc4. Black has sufficient compensation for the pawn, "ManoTheGreat"-Schiller, ICC, 1997.

Yet another plan for White is 4.Ne2 Bf5; 5.Ng3 Bg6; 6.h4. Here we try 6...Qa5+, a new move, based on a tactical trick.

7.Bd2 (7.c3 Bxb1!; 8.Qb3! Bxa2; 9.Rxa2 Qb6 and Black has an extra pawn) 7...Qa4! and if the c-pawn advances to protect its brother at d4, then Black can exchange queens or even try ...Bc2!? and drill into the White position. If White captures at a6, Black cannot recapture with the queen, so that line is important. 8.Bxa6 bxa6. (8...Qxa6??; 9.h5 and the bishop falls after 9...Be4; 10.f3.) 9.c3 Qxd1+; 10.Kxd1 Rb8; 11.h5 Bd3 and Black is in no immediate danger.

Suppose White decides to try to occupy all central dark squares with pawns? 4.f4 Qa5+; 5.c3 g6; 6.Bd3 Bg7 looks like a reasonable plan, followed by ...Nh6 and ...Bf5. 7.b4 Qb6; 8.a4 is too extravagant. 8...Nxb4; 9.cxb4 Qxb4+; 10.Qd2 Qxd4; 11.Bb2 Qb6; 12.a5 Qc7; 13.e6.

This is one fascinating possibility. Black can exchange bishops or play ...f6, hoping the pawn at e6 will fall. A high risk game, but I think Black is up to the task! 13...f6!?; 14.f5 (this is forced) 14...gxf5; 15.Bxf5 Nh6!; 16.Bh3 Qd6; 17.Qe2 0-0; 18.Nf3 f5; 19.Bxg7 Kxg7; 20.a6 b6 and the e-pawn falls.

4.Bd3 g6; 5.h3 (5.c3 Bg7; 6.Ne2 Nh6; 7.Ng3 Nf5; 8.Nxf5 Bxf5; 9.Bxf5 gxf5; 10.e6 fxe6; 11.Qh5+ Kd7; 12.0-0 Qe8; 13.Qe2 Qg6; 14.Re1 Nc7; 15.Bf4 Rac8; 16.Nd2 Rhg8. Black has a solid game, "AlmostDecent"-JackStraw, ICC, 1997.) 5...h5; 6.Nf3 Nh6; 7.0-0 Nc7; 8.Re1 Bf5; 9.Bf1 Qd7; 10.Nbd2 Bg7; 11.c3 Ng8 and Black was fine in Kreiman-Sidelnikov, New York, 1993.

Finally, 4.Be3 g6; 5.Nc3 Nc7; 6.Qd2 h5; 7.Nf3 Nh6; 8.0-0-0 Bg4; 9.Be2 Nf5; 10.Ng5 Bxe2; 11.Nxe2 Nxe3 brought Black equality in Greger-Hartvig, Ringsted, 1995.

After that lengthy diversion, let's return to the sensible 4.c3. We will develop our bishop on the obvious square with **4...Bf5.**

This is a challenging continuation. Black is now willing to allow the weakening of the queenside. That is not necessary, however. There are two other plans for Black which can be kept in reserve.

4...Nc7; 5.Bd3 g6; 6.Nd2 h5; 7.Nf1 Nh6; 8.Ne3 Ng4; 9.Nf3 Nxe3; 10.fxe3 Bf5; 11.Ng5 e6; 12.e4 dxe4; 13.Bxe4 Be7; 14.h4 Nd5. The position is equal, Van der Wiel-Kavalek, Wijk aan Zee, 1982.

4...Qb6; 5.f4 (5.b4 Bf5; 6.a4 e6; 7.a5 Qc7; 8.Bxa6 bxa6; 9.Nf3 Qb7; 10.Nbd2 Qb5; 11.Nb3 is "Lucky-MC"-Schiller, ICC, 1997. Here Black should play 11...Qc4 or the solid 11...Ne7) 5...Bf5; 6.Bd3 Bxd3; 7.Qxd3 e6; 8.a3 c5!; 9.Nf3 Nh6; 10.Nbd2 cxd4!; 11.cxd4 Rc8; 12.0-0 Be7; 13.Nb3 0-0; 14.Bd2 Nb8!; 15.Rac1 a6! The game is even, Schotten-Tseitlin, Crailsheim, 1996.

5.Nf3. 5.Nd2 Qb6; 6.Ngf3 e6 is approaching equality. 5.Bxa6 bxa6 needs to be checked out:

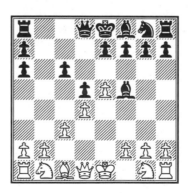

The exchange is not an effective strategy. 6.Qa4 Qb6; 7.Nf3 Qb5 8.Qxb5 axb5 is no worse for Black.; 5.Ne2 lets Black use the fianchetto plan. 5...g6 can lead to some forcing play after 6.Ng3 Bxb1; 7.Rxb1 Qa5 8.Qb3 Qb6 9.Qxb6 axb6.

10.Bd3 Nc7; 11.a3 h5 looks solid enough for Black. 5. Ne2! is an interesting new move, seen in Magen Badals-Schiller, New York Open 1998. Black should play 5...Qa5!?

So, we go back to the main game with the normal 5.Nf3, and this time we will advance the e-pawn. **5...e6; 6.Be2.**

6...Ne7. I don't like this move, which eliminates any counterplay based on ...f6. 6...Qb6 is interesting. Black defends against a capture at a6 and keeps pressure on the pawn at b2. Black may even consider queenside castling. 7.Qb3 creates a tense standoff on the b-file. I think that Black can afford to get queens off immediately. 7...Qxb3; 8.axb3 Nc7; 9.0-0 Ne7; 10.Be3 Ng6; 11.Nbd2 Be7.

This is the sort of position Black aims for in the Kavalek Variation. Black can meet an advance of White's h-pawn with ...Nh4. White's pawn structure is a little shaky. After 6...Ne7, the dangers inherent in the position become apparent as White falls for the temptation to chase the bishop with **7.Nh4?** A terrible move that gets punished in brutal fashion. 7.0-0 is stronger. 7...Nc7; 8.Re1 Qd7 is solid but very cramped.

7...Be4!; 8.Nd2 Nf5!; 9.Nxe4. 9.Nhf3 Be7; 10.0-0 0-0; 11 Nxe4 dxe4; 12.Nd2 e3; 13.Ne4 exf2+; 14.Rxf2 and here the question is whether Black must play passively with ...Nc7 or can get away with a bolder plan, for example 14...c5; 15.Bxa6 bxa6; 16.g4 Nh4; 17.Be3 cxd4 should be no better for White no matter which way White recaptures.

9...Nxh4 10.Bg5.

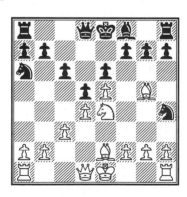

White fails to anticipate Black's shot, and it proves fatal. **10...Nxg2+!!; 11.Kf1 Qb6.** Both the knight on e4 and pawn at b2 are en prise.

12.Nc5. 12.Nd6+ Bxd6; 13.exd6 h6!; 14.Kxg2 hxg5; 15.Qd2 0-0-0! is clearly bettter for Black since the White queen must stay at d2 and guard the b-pawn. **12...h6!; 13.Bxa6.** (13.Nxe6 hxg5; 14.Nxf8 Nf4 and White loses the knight.) **13...hxg5!; 14.Bxb7.**

Now if Black moves the rook White can play Qa4. But there is a stronger move! **14...Nf4!!** 14...Bxc5?; 15.Qb3 Rb8; 16.Qxb6 Bxb6; 17.Bxc6+ Ke7; 18.Kxg2 is a very good endgame for White. **15.Bxa8.** Otherwise Black can safely move the rook. **15...Bxc5.**

Can White afford to capture the bishop? Keep in mind that White's bishop at a8 is going to fall sooner or later. **16.Qb3.** Or 16.dxc5 Qb5+.

This position is not simple. Black is down a whole rook, but has a fierce attack. White's king can move toward the center or toward the flank. 17.Ke1 Rh3. The plan is Qc4-e4+. White has two tries. The attempt to defend the light squares with 18.Qc2 is logical. Black plays 18...Nd3+; 19.Kf1 Rf3; 20.Kg1 Qxc5; 21.Rf1 Nf4 and threatens to squirm out with a draw. 22.c4!? (22.Bxc6+ Qxc6; 23.h4 d4! sets up the deadly threat of ...Rxc3 and ...Qg2#. 24.Re1 prepares to defend with Qe4, but Black cuts across that plan. 24...d3!, 25.Qd2 Rh3! and Black wins) 22...g4; 23.b4 Nh3+; 24.Kg2 Nf4+ illustrates the drawing theme.

18.Bxc6+ reduces Black's army, but there is still enough firepower to inflict damage. 18...Qxc6; 19.Qb3 f6!; 20.exf6 d4! and Black wins, according to Tseitlin. This requires further explanation.

21.Qb8+ Kf7; 22.Qxa7+ Kxf6; 23.Kd2 saves the rook at h1, and White now has the exchange and two extra pawns. If only the position could hold up for a few more moves, but it can't! 23...dxc3+; 24.bxc3 Qd5+; 25.Kc2 Qd3+; 26.Kb3 Qxc3+; 27.Ka4 Qc4+; 28.Ka5

Ra3+; 29.Kb6 Qb4+; 30.Kc6 Rxa7 and mate with ...Qa4 and ...Rd7 follows.

What about moving the king to the center? 17.Kg1 needs work. Tseitlin clams 17...Rh4 is clearly better for Black, but I don't think so! 18.h3 Qc4. (18...Ne2+; 19.Kg2) 19.Bxc6+ Kf8; 20.Qb3! and White wins. So, we must look at 17...Kd7; 18.b4 Rxa8!

I think Black is not worse here. White's pawns are pathetic and the Black knight has an excellent outpost at f4. This should be worth the exchange.

Back to the game, where we take advantage of the exposed position of White's king with **16...Qa6+!**

17.c4. 17.Kg1 0–0! gives Black a strong game, since 18.dxc5? is still not on. 18...Nh3+; 19.Kg2 Qd3!; 20.Qa4 Nf4+; 21.Qxf4 gxf4; 22.Bxc6 Qe4+!; 23.f3 (23.Kg1 f3; 24.Rd1 Qg4+; 25.Kf1 Qg2+; 26.Ke1 Qxh1+; 27.Kd2 Qxh2 and Black wins.) 23...Qe2+; 24.Kh3 Qxf3+; 25.Kh4 f6; 26.exf6 Rxf6 and mate in 5. 18.Bxc6 Qxc6; 19.dxc5? is not an improvement. 19...d4! and checkmate cannot be avoided. So

White should settle for 19.h3 Be7. 20.Re1 is relatively best, but on 20...f6!; 21.exf6 gxf6; 22.h4 e5! has the subtle point that ...Qd7-g4 is now possible!

23.hxg5 Qd7; 24.Rh2 Qg4+; 25.Kh1 and Black doesn't have to settle for a draw with 25...Qf3+, since there are avenues of attack that have not been used. White has no better than to exchange queens and go into an inferior endgame. 25...Rf7; 26.Qd1! Qxd1; 27.Rxd1 fxg5; 28.dxe5 Rf5; 29.Re1 Nd3; 30.Re2 Nxe5; 31.Rxe5 Rxe5 and Black is a piece up in the endgame.

Black continues boldly with **17...dxc4!**

A truly amazing move, offering White the rook at h8! **18.Qb7.** 18.Qb8+? is too greedy. 18...Kd7; 19.Qxh8 c3+; 20.Kg1 cxb2; 21.Rb1 Qd3; 22.Bxc6+ Kc7!

Black declines the bishop, since capturing at c6 would allow the White queen to use checks to get back into the game. 23.h3 Qxd4; 24.Rh2 Qd3! White is lost. **18...Qxb7; 19.Bxb7 Bxd4; 20.Bxc6+ Ke7.**

The game has settled down a bit. White has a slight material advantage, but the pawns at e5 and b2 cannot be defended. **21.Rd1.** 21.Rc1 Rb8! 22.Rxc4 Rxb2 and now 23.Rxd4 gets mated after 23...Rb1+.

21...Bxe5; 22.Bb5 Rb8; 23.Bxc4 Rxb2; 24.h3 Bd4! The mating theme on the back rank comes into play again. **25.Rh2.** If 25.Rxd4, then 25...Rb1+. **25...f5; 26.Bb3 e5.**

White's forces were no match for the Black army and the end came before long.

27.Rc1 Kd6; 28.Bc2 e4; 29.a4 Ke5; 30.Ke1 Bc3+; 31.Kd1 Rb4; 32.Bb1 Kd4! ; 33.f3 Nd5! ; 34.fxe4 Ne3+; 35.Ke2 Rb2+; 36.Bc2 Nxc2; 37.Kf3 Ne1+!; 38.Rxe1 Rxh2; 39.Rd1+ Rd2. White resigned.

PANOV ATTACK
1.e4 c6; 2.d4 d5; 3.exd5 cxd5; 4.c4 Nf6; 5.Nc3 Nc6

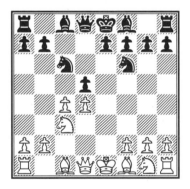

Against the once-dreaded Panov Attack, Black has three main plans. The solid 5...e6 leads to positions from the Queen's Gambit Declined or Nimzoindian, and that's fine if you happen to have those defenses in your repertoire. White usually gets an isolated d-pawn, and the position resembles a reversed Tarrasch Defense. The reversed Classical Tarrasch can be reached via 5...g6. If you play the Tarrasch repertoire presented in my *Complete Defense to Queen Pawn Openings*, then this may a good choice. In this book, however, I'd like to concentrate on the third plan, with 5...Nc6. It leads to many vary exciting positions with unbalanced pawn structures.

There are four different types of structures which arise, as we learned in the introductory chapters. White can develop with Nf3, play Bg5 with or without the gambit of the c-pawn, or advance to c5 before long.

White Plays Nf3

ANAND VS. KAROLYI
Frunze, 1987
1.c4 c6; 2.e4 d5; 3.exd5 cxd5; 4.d4 Nf6; 5.Nc3 Nc6; 6.Nf3 Bg4

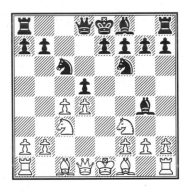

The pin is used to provide additional indirect pressure against d4. Black delays development on the kingside, but counts on having enough time to catch up later. **7.cxd5.** White releases the tension in the center. 7.Be2 dxc4; 8.d5 Bxf3; 9.Bxf3 Ne5; 10.0-0 Qd7; 11.Qe2 Qf5! is a strong improvement over the existing analysis. Theory gives only 13...0-0-0 13.b3!, Mikenas-Flohr, Folkestone 1933.

7...Nxd5; 8.Qb3. 8.Bb5 Rc8; 9.h3 Bxf3; 10.Qxf3 e6; 11.0-0 a6; 12.Bxc6+ Rxc6; 13.Nxd5 Qxd5; 14.Qxd5 exd5; 15.Re1+ Re6. Black has nothing to worry about, Joksic-Vukic, Yugoslav Championship, 1976. 8.Be2 e6; 9.0-0 Be7; 10.Nxd5 Qxd5; 11.h3 Bh5 is very comfortable for Black. 12.b3 0-0; 13.Bb2 Rfd8; 14.Rc1 Rd7; 15.Re1 Rad8; 16.Qd3 e5; 17.Qc4 Qxc4; 18.Rxc4 Bxf3; 19.Bxf3 Nxd4; 20.Bxd4 exd4 should draw. Zabiran-Postnova, Russian Girls, 1997. **8...Bxf3; 9.gxf3.**

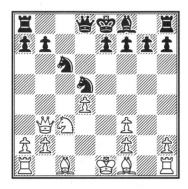

The safer path is to head for an endgame here, but moving the knight to b6 is more exciting and ambitious.

9...Nb6; 10.Be3. This is considered strongest at present. 10.d5 is met by the strong centralizing move 10...Nd4! This is examined in the next game, Greenfeld-Shirov. **10...e6.**

Castling queenside is the preferred plan. **11.0-0-0.** There are several alternatives. 11.Rg1 is discussed in Ehlvest-Kasparov in the Heroes chapter. Here are some other tries.

11.d5 Nxd5!?; 12.Qxb7 Ndb4 is complicated, but seems to work well for Black. 13.Bb5 Rc8; 14.a3 Nc2+; 15.Ke2 Qc7; 16.Qxc6+ Qxc6; 17.Bxc6+ Rxc6; 18.Rac1 Nxe3; 19.fxe3 Bd6; 20.Nb5 Kd7; 21.Nxd6 was drawn in Nordstrom-Edelsvard, Postal, 1976.

11.Rd1 Bb4; 12.a3 (12.Bb5 Nd5; 13.Ke2 Qa5; 14.Bxc6+ bxc6; 15.Nxd5 cxd5 leaves White with a rotten bishop and even more decrepit pawn structure.) 12...Ba5; 13.Bd3 Rc8. (13...Qd5!; 14.Qxd5 Nxd5; 15.Rc1 Rd8 is certainly better for Black.) 14.Rg1 0-0; 15.Kf1! was about even in Marin-Magem, Berga, 1995.

11.Bb5 Be7; 12.0–0 (12.a4 0–0; 13.a5 Nd5; 14.Nxd5 exd5; 15.a6 Na5; 16.Qa4 bxa6 was clearly better for Black in Howell-Ubach, Barcelona, 1993) 12...0–0; 13.Rad1 Qc7; 14.d5 Na5; 15.Bxb6 Qxb6; 16.Qa4 a6; 17.Bd3 Qxb2; 18.Qe4 g6 and Black used the extra pawn to win in Sikkila-Puhakka, Helsinki, 1988.

11...Be7! Black wants to get castled before the center can get blasted open.

12.d5. This aggressive move is the main line. White jettisons the weak pawns and opens lines for bishops and rooks. There are lots of alternatives to consider. 12.Rg1 0–0; 13.d5 (13.Bd3 Rc8; 14.Kb1 Na5. Black has the initiative. Murshed-Cavendish, London, 1989.) 13...exd5; 14.Nxd5 Nxd5; 15.Rxd5 Qc7; 16.Kb1 (16.Qc3!? might be worth a look) 16...Qxh2; 17.Rg2 Qh1; 18.Rd1 Rad8; 19.Rc1 Bf6; 20.Bc5 Rd2; 21.Ba3 Qh5. White resigned. Nunn-Chandler, Bristol, 1981.

12.Kb1 is a cautious alternative, getting the king off the dangerous c-file immediately. 12...0–0.

13.d5. (13.Rg1 Nd5; 14.Nxd5 Qxd5 is equal, Payen-Jones, Singapore, 1990. An immediate draw is available on 15.Bc4 Qf5+; 16.Bd3 Qd5; 17.Bc4 etc.; 13.f4 Na5; 14.Qc2 Rc8; 15.f5 Nd5; 16.fxe6 fxe6; 17.Bh3 Kh8 looks a bit better for Black, because 18.Bxe6 meets with the surprising sacrifice 18...Rxc3!; 19.bxc3 Qb6+; 20.Ka1 Qxe6.) 13...exd5; 14.Nxd5 Nxd5; 15.Qxd5 Bf6; 16.Bc4 Qc7; 17.Qf5 Ne7; 18.Qf4 Qxf4; 19.Bxf4 Rac8. The game is balanced. Abramovic-Matulovic, Yugoslavia, 1984.

Another plan, rather too optimistic, is 12.f4 0–0; 13.f5 exf5; 14.d5 Ne5; 15.Kb1 Ng4; 16.Bd4 Bf6; 17.h3 Bxd4; 18.hxg4 Bxc3; 19.Qxc3 fxg4. White did not have enough to justify two pawns in Wolff-Bauer, Newton, 1988.

12.Bd3 0–0; 13.Be4 Na5; 14.Qb5 led to an interesting encounter. 14...Nac4; 15.Qh5 g6; 16.Rhg1 Qe8; 17.Bh6 Kh8. White now sacrifces the queen. 18.Bxf8! gxh5; 19.Bg7+ Kg8. White repeated the position to draw in Pribyl-Pergericht, Prague, 1990. The result is deceptive, however. White could play on with 20.Be5+ Kf8; 21.Bxh7 when White threatens to recover the queen with Rg8+. Black must give up a bishop to avoid that. 21...Bg5+; 22.Rxg5 Ke7 with a genuinely unclear position. White has a bishop, rook and a weak pawn for the queen, but the h-pawn may fall.

Finally, 12.Re1 Bf6; 13.Ne4 Qc7; 14.Kb1 0–0–0; 15.Bb5 Kb8; 16.Rc1 is De Wit-Rohner, Netherlands, 1992. Black should now capture at d4. 16...Bxd4!; 17.Bxc6 bxc6; 18.Rc4 Bxe3; 19.fxe3 Ka8. It is not clear that White can justify the sacrifice.

Back in the main game, White has advanced immediately to d5, and Black captures. **12...exd5.**

13.Nxd5. This capture is by no means obligatory. 13.Bxb6 Qxb6, 14.Qxb6 axb6, 15.Nxd5 Rxa2, 16.Kb1 Ra5 is a common sequence.

White now has a strong move based on a potential fork at c7. 17.Bb5! Kf8!; 18.Nxe7 Kxe7; 19.Rhe1+. This position was agreed drawn in Ribli-Miles, Indonesia, 1982, but was re-examined in a later game.

19...Kf6; 20.Rd6+ Kf5; 21.Bxc6 bxc6; 22.Re7 f6?! (22...Rc5; 23.Rxf7+ Ke5; 24.Rd2 g5 would have been more active.) 23.Rxc6 Rd8; 24.Rxb6 Rd1+; 25.Kc2 Rf1; 26.Re2 Rh1. Black may be able to hold this endgame, but failed to do so in Kalinichev-Starck, Dresden, 1986. 13.Bh3 d4; 14.Nb5 0–0; 15.Nxd4 Nxd4; 16.Bxd4 Qc7+; 17.Kb1 Rad8; 18.Bf5.

White is building a strong attack, based on the potent cleric at d4. Black uses an enterprising exchange sacrifice to defuse the threat. 18...Rxd4!? (18...Qf4 deserved consideration.) 19.Rxd4 Qc5; 20.Qd3 Bf6; 21.Rg4 h5; 22.Rgg1 Qe5. Black has a serious initiative. The game played itself out as follows: 23.Qc2 Nc4; 24.Kc1 Qf4+; 25.Kb1 Na3+; 26.bxa3 Qe5; 27.Kc1 Rd8; 28.Bh7+ Kh8; 29.Rd1 Qa1+; 30.Qb1 Qc3+; 31.Qc2 Qa1+; 32.Qb1 Qc3+. Thipsay-Parr, Torquay, 1982.

White can concentrate on the queenside with 13.Bb5 0-0; 14.Bxb6 (14.Nxd5 Nxd5; 15.Qxd5 Qc7; 16.Qd7 Rfc8; 17.Kb1 Bf6; 18.Qxc7 Rxc7; 19.Bxc6 bxc6 led to an even game in Onischuk-Koutsin, Nikolayev, 1995) 14...Qxb6; 15.Nxd5 Bg5+; 16.f4 Qc5+; 17.Kb1 Nd4; 18.Qc4 Qxb5; 19.Qxd4 Bd8; 20.Rhg1 f6; 21.Rg3 Rf7; 22.Qe4 Rc8; 23.Rb3 Qa6? (23...Qc4; 24.Qe8+ Rf8; 25.Qe6+ Kh8; 26.Rc3 Qa4!; 27.b3 Rc6! was best, but is a very hard line for a human to calculate using only a naked brain. I found it only with the help of a computer.) 24.f5 Qd6; 25.Qe6.

Black resigned, Novoselski-Maehrlein, Boblingen, 1985. So, we are left with the exchange at d5 as seen in our game. **13...Nxd5.**

White can capture with either piece. **14.Rxd5.** 14.Qxd5 Qc7; 15.Bb5 a6; 16.Bxc6+ Qxc6+; 17.Qxc6+ bxc6; 18.Rhg1 0-0; 19.Rg4 Rfd8; 20.Rc4 Rxd1+; 21.Kxd1 Rc8; 22.Kc2 Kf8; 23.Ra4 was drawn in Schenning-Schuurman, Tilburg, 1991.

14...Qc7; 15.Kb1. 15.Qc4 0-0; 16.Rg1 Bf6; 17.Rf5 Qe7; 18.Bd3 Ne5; 19.Qe4 Nxd3+; 20.Qxd3 Rfd8. Black has the better pawn structure and better attacking chances, Wuts-S.Lalic, Chamberi, 1995. **15...0-0.**

Both kings have sufficient defensive resources to withstand a direct atttack, but White must avoid exchanges which will espose the weakness of the pawn structure in the endgame. 16.f4. The only move mentioned in ECO, which stops citing this game with an evaluation of better for White. There are other moves to look at before we call their judgement into question.

16.Be2 Rad8; 17.Rc1 (17.Rhd1 Rxd5; 18.Rxd5 Bd6 was fine for Black in Korneyev-Izeta, Alcobendas, 1994.) 17...Rxd5; 18.Qxd5 Rd8; 19.Qe4 Bf6; 20.f4 (20.Bxa7 Qe5; 21.Qxe5 Bxe5; 22.Be3 Bxh2; 23.f4 leaves the bishop offside, but in Pyhala-Kropsch, Jyvaskyla, 1993. Black could have solved the problem with 23...Rd6!) 20...Qa5; 21.a3 g6; 22.Bc4 Kg7; 23.Bb3 Qb5; 24.Qc4 Qxc4; 25.Bxc4 Nd4 gave Black a good endgame in Pyhala-Partanen, Jyvaskyla, 1987.

16.Qc2 Rad8; 17.Rxd8 Rxd8; 18.Bd3 g6; 19.Be4 Bf6; 20.Qc5 Kg7; 21.f4 Rd6; 22.Rc1 Qe7; 23.Bg2 b6; 24.Qc4 Nd4 gave Black the initiative in Rachels-Miles, World Open, 1987.

16.Rb5 b6; 17.Bd3 Na5; 18.Qa4 Rad8; 19.Qe4 g6; 20.Rc1 Qd7; 21.Be2 Bf6; 22.Qf4 Qd6; 23.Qxd6 Rxd6. Black had the advantage in the endgame, Sulaiti-Lim, Asian Juniors, 1989.

16.Bg2 Nb4; 17.Rd4 (17.Rb5 Qc6; 18.Rf5 Rad8; 19.Rd1 Rxd1+; 20.Qxd1 Qe6 won quickly for Black in Repkova-Radu, Mamaia, 1991.) 17...Qc6; 18.Rg4 Rfd8 was drawn in Kraut-Schlemermeyer, Germany, 1990.

16.Rg1 should be met by 16...Qxh2; 17.Rg2 Qh1; 18.Rd1 Rad8 where White is in deep trouble. 19.Rc1 (19.Re1 Qh5; 20.Bd3 Bf6; 21.Be4 Nd4; 22.Qxb7 Rb8; 23.Qd5 Ne2 . White resigned. Rozentalis-Lauritsen, Postal, 1992) 19...Bf6; 20.Bg5 Bxg5; 21.Rxg5 Nd4; 22.Qxb7 Nxf3; 23.Ka1 Qh6. Black eventually won in Jonsson-Angqvist, Vaxjo 1992.

16.Bb5 Rad8 17.Rc1 Qxh2 18.Bxc6 bxc6 19.Rxd8 Rxd8 20.Bxa7 Bg5 21.Re1 Qd6 was eventually drawn in Cossette-Filipovich, North Bay 1996.

So, White has occupied f4 with a pawn, and gets control of e5, though the bishop at e3 no longer has an active role in the kingside attack.

16...Nb4. This is logical, but not the only playable move. 16...Bf6; 17.Bg2 Rad8; 18.Rc1 Rxd5; 19.Qxd5 Rc8; 20.Qf5 Qd8 was certainly no worse for Black in Manca-Ruxton, Sas van Gent Juniors, 1988. What's wrong with 16...Rad8?; 17.Bg2 Bd6; 18.Rb5 Bxf4; 19.Rxb7 Qd6, 20.Rxc6 Qxc6; 21.Rc1 Qe4! gave Black a nice initiative in McTavish-Filipovic Toronto, 1992, which was eventually won by Black.

17.Rd4. 17.Re5 Bd6; 18.Rg5 Bxf4; 19.Rg4 Bxe3; 20.fxe3 Nc6 gave Black an extra pawn in Stein-Finegold, Dortmund, 1990.

17...Nc6; 18.Rd1. 18.Rd5 Nb4; 19.Rd4 Nc6; 20.Rd5 was agreed drawn in Reinderman-Van Mil, Gyor, 1990. **18...Bf6.** 18...Rfd8; 19.Bg2 Bf6; transposes. **19.Bg2 Rfd8; 20.Be4.** Leading authorities claim an advantage for White here, but it doesn't look like much to me.

20...Rxd1+. Black decides to eliminate the rooks, but suffers a bit as a result. 20...h6 is a solid move. Let White exchange the rooks.

21.Rxd8+ Rxd8; 22.Rd1 Rxd1+; 23.Qxd1 Qa5 is more comfortable for Black than the game. **21.Rxd1 Rd8; 22.Rxd8+ Bxd8; 23.Qd3!**

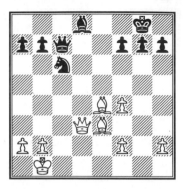

White forces a favorable position. After Black deals with the threatened capture at h7, White can take the knight at c6. Black must then recapture with the pawn, since the queen must stay on c7 to guard the bishop at d8.

23...h5; 24.Bxc6 bxc6. White wins a pawn, again based on the codependency of the Black queen and bishop. **25.Bxa7 Qxa7.** (It might have been better for Black to keep bishops on the board, for example **25...Bf6; 26.Be3 h4.) 26.Qxd8+ Kh7; 27.Qd3+ g6; 28.Qe3 Qd7; 29.b3.**

The endgame should be winning for White, who can advance the a-pawn while keeping the king sheltered. **30.Kc1 Qf6; 31.a4 c5.** 31...Qa1+; 32.Kc2 Qa2+; 33.Kc3 Qa3; 34.Kc4 and there are no more checks.

32.Kc2 Qb6; 33.f5! The decisive breakthrough. **33...Qd6; 34.fxg6+ fxg6; 35.a5 Qc6; 36.Qe2 Kh6; 37.a6 Qb6.** Now that the

Black queen is tied down, White switchers flanks and quickly wraps things up. **38.h4! g5; 39.hxg5+ Kxg5; 40.Qe7+ Kg4; 41.a7. Black resigned.**

GREENFELD VS. SHIROV
European Club Cup Final, 1996

Shirov is not generally a Caro-Kann player, but here we see how the Caro-Kann can grow from roots in the English Opening. Shirov's play illustrates a fine understanding of the Panov Attack.

1.c4 c6; 2.e4 d5; 3.exd5 cxd5; 4.d4 Nf6; 5.Nc3 Nc6; 6.Nf3 Bg4; 7.cxd5 Nxd5; 8.Qb3 Bxf3; 9.gxf3 Nb6; 10.d5 Nd4.

When White advances the d-pawn without controlling the d-file, the Black knight leaps to d4. Here it drives back the enemy queen. It is true that retreat to b5, c6, and e6 is no longer possible, but there is no danger of the knight getting trapped. **11.Qd1.**

11.Bb5+ Nd7 12.Qa4 is a very popular alternative.

12...Nxf3+ is considered bad, but is it?

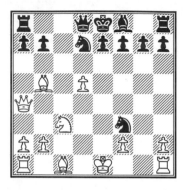

There are two king moves. First let's look at 13.Ke2 Nfe5; 14.Bf4 (14.f4 Ng4; 15.Kf3 Ngf6; 16.Re1 a6; 17.Bd2 axb5; 18.Nxb5 Ne5+. White resigned. Ginzburg-Bilalic, World Junior Championship, 1996.) 14...a6! (14...Ng6; 15.Bg3 a6; 16.Bxd7+ Qxd7; 17.Qxd7+ Kxd7; 18.Na4. Black resigned. Carlier-Boersma, Amsterdam, 1987.) 15.Bxe5 axb5; 16.Qd4 Nxe5; 17.Qxe5 Qd7 and I don't believe White has compensation for the pawn.

So, we turn to 13.Kf1 with 13...Nfe5!?; 14.Bf4 a6; 15.Bxd7+ (15.Bxe5!? axb5; 16.Qxb5 Ra5; 17.Qe2 Nxe5; 18.Qxe5 Qd6; 19.Qxd6 exd6; 20.Re1+ Kd7; 21.Rg1 g6 is not worse for Black) 15...Nxd7; 16.d6 (16.Re1 b5; 17.Qd4 Qb6; 18.Qxb6 Nxb6 is bad for White) 16...b5; 17.Qd4 Nf6; 18.Re1 Qd7; 19.Rg1 Rc8? The rook should have moved to d8. 20.Rxg7 Qh3+; 21.Rg2 Rg8; 22.Bg3. Black was in serious trouble in Bashkov-Marusenko, Police, 1992.

The general prescription is 12...Nxb5; 13.Qxb5 g6!

White has tried four plans here. We start our examination with the immediate capture at b7. 14.Qxb7 Bg7; 15.0-0 0-0; 16.Bg5 *(16.Bf4 Ne5!)* 16...h6; 17.Bh4 g5; 18.Bg3 Ne5; 19.Kg2 Rb8; 20.Qxa7 Rxb2 gives Black sufficient compensation for the pawn.

If the bishop moves to g5, we confront it immediately. 14.Bg5 h6!; 15.Bf4 Bg7; 16.0-0 0-0; 17.Rfe1 (17.Qxb7 deserves consideration. 17...Nc5; 18.Qb5 could lead to an exciting variation. 18...Bxc3; 19.Qxc5 Bxb2; 20.Bxh6 Bxa1; 21.Bxf8 Bf6; 22.Bh6 Rc8; 23.Qxa7 Qxd5 and I'd rather be Black) 17...Nb6; 18.Rad1 Rc8; 19.a4 Nc4; 20.Rd3 b6; 21.Kg2 Nd6; 22.Qa6 was seen in Peelen-Kuijf, Amsterdam, 1989. 22...Nc4 and the pressure at b2 gives Black the upper hand. Retreating in the other direction with 15.Bh4 is also possible, for example 15...Qb6; 16.0-0 Bg7.

Black has done well from this position. 17.Rfe1 (17.d6 g5; 18.Bg3 Bxc3; 19.Qxb6 axb6; 20.bxc3 e5 led to a better endgame for Black in Nijboer-Astolfi, Nimes, 1991.) 17...g5; 18.Qe2 0-0; 19.Bg3 Rfe8; 20.Nb5 e5 was similarly good for Black in Mesebitsky-Pyshkin, Postal, 1991.

Another aggressive plan is 14.d6, and Black must leave the matter of the pawn to be dealt with later. 15...e6; 15.0-0 Bg7; 16.Bg5 a6; 17.Bxd8 axb5; 18.Be7 Bxc3; 19.bxc3 was drawn in Guerra-Orr, Dubai Olympiad, 1986. Black could well play on with 19...Ra3.

Saving the best for last, 14.0-0! is the move that causes the most difficulty. 14...Bg7; 15.Bg5! (15.Re1 Considered best in ECO3, but it isn't. 15...0-0; 16.Bg5 f6!?; 17.Be3 Ne5 is far from clear, but in the long run the White pawns are weak. 15.Qxb7 0-0; 16.Rd1 Ne5 provided Black with sufficient counterplay in Werner-Kranewitter, Balatonbereny, 1996) 15...f6!? (This is an attempt to improve on. 15...h6; 16.Bxe7 Kxe7; 17.Qb4+ Ke8; 18.Rae1+ Be5; 19.f4 Qh4; 20.Qe4 Qg4+; 21.Kh1 of Von Gleich-Fette, Hamburg, 1987, where White had an indisputable advantage.)

16.Bf4 g5; 17.Bg3 f5; 18.d6 f4; 19.Rfe1 e5; 20.Nd5 0-0; 21.Nc7 lets Black offer the exchange with 21...Rf7!; 22.Nxa8 Qxa8; 23.Rad1 b6. White must return the bishop for a pawn, and then Black's minor pieces are better than the rook.

So, White usually retreats the queen to d1, and now Black hits the center with **11...e5.**

White now must capture at e6, en passant, as otherwise the pawn at d5 is too weak. **12.dxe6.** The two alternatives are not a problem if you are prepared with the right moves. 12.Be3 Bc5; 13.f4 Nxd5; 14.Qa4+ Kf8; 15.0–0–0 f6. (15...Nxf4! and Black is clearly better. Now the game ends swiftly in disaster.) 16.Qc4 and in Soylu-Trikaliotis, Budva, 1981. Black resigned because the double attack in the center forces 16...Nxc3; 17.Qxc5+. 12.f4 Bb4; 13.Bg2 Nxd5; 14.0–0 Bxc3; 15.bxc3 Nxc3; 16.Qe1 0–0 was agreed drawn in Urday-Cruz, Elgoibar 1992. 12.Bg2 Bd6; 13.f4 0–0; 14.fxe5 Bxe5; 15.0–0 Nf5; 16.Qg4 Nd6. Black has a good game, with excellent control of the dark squares. Landtman-Kuijf, Netherlands, 1992.

12...Bc5. 12...fxe6 is main line, but there are two interesting alternatives. We'll take the bishop move as our main choice, but keep 12...Qf6 in reserve as an alternative. There is no need to capture at e6, though that is a playable option, too. 12...Qf6 has not done well statistically, but I am not sure the results were the result of the opening. Consider these examples:

13.exf7+. The obvious move, but there are some others we'll look at below. 13...Kxf7 is the most obvious continuation. White will play Bg2, but now, or later? 14.Bg2 (14.Be3 can be met by 14...Nxf3+ 15.Ke2 Re8 as in the suggestion to the Valco-Shipman game below.) 14...Qe6+ (14...Rd8; 15.0–0 Bd6 deserves consideration.)

15.Be3 Nf5. (15...Rd8; 16.0–0 Bc5; 17.Ne4 Qc4; 18.Re1 Bb4; 19.Bf1 Qd5; 20.Qxd4 Qxd4; 21.Bxd4 Rxd4 is a computer-inspired fantasy which ends up in an endgame where White is a little better, though the bishops of opposite color and weak pawns work against an endgame win.) 16.Qb3 Qxb3; 17.axb3 Bb4; 18.Ke2 Bxc3; 19.bxc3 Nd5; 20.Bd2 Rhe8+. Wahls-Hermann, Delmenhorst, 1988.

White can exchange a few pieces via 13.Bb5+ Nxb5; 14.exf7+ Kxf7; 15.Qb3+ Qe6+; 16.Qxe6+ Kxe6; 17.Nxb5 Bb4+; 18.Ke2 Nd5; 19.Be3 a6; 20.Nd4! Kf6; 21.f4 Rhe8; 22.Kf3 is Makropoulos-Chevaldonnet, Pernik, 1981. Now Black played the rook to c8, a classic "wrong rook" move. 22...Rad8!, 23.Rad1 g6, 24.h4 Rd7, 25.h5 Red8, 26.hxg6 hxg6 would have left White with only a minute advantage.

13.Be3 is Valvo-Silman, New York, 1987. Black should have accepted the offer at f3. 13...Nxf3!, 14.Ke2 Rd8; 15.exf7+ Qxf7; 16.Qb1 Ne5; 17.Qe4 Qc4+; 18.Qxc4 Nbxc4 is fine for Black. (13.f4 Qxe6+; 14.Be3 Rd8; 15.Bg2 Nf5; 16.Qe2 Nxe3; 17.Qxe3 Bc5; 18.Qxe6+ fxe6; 19.0–0 0–0 wound up drawing in Ligterinkt-Christiansen, Wijk aan Zee, 1976.)

13.exf7+. White has fewer options here. 13.Bb5+ Kf8; 14.Be3 Nxe6 is better for Black. **13...Kxf7.**

White has a useless extra pawn, and is way behind in development. If left unmolested, the Black king will retreat to g8 and h8, after the rook moves to the e-file.

14.Be3 Re8; 15.Bd3 Qh4. This defends the h-pawn, and the kingside in general. **16.Ne4 Rad8; 17.Bxd4 Rxd4; 18.0–0 Bd6.**

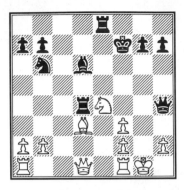

Bishops of opposite color may be useful as a drawing device in the endgame, but in the middlegame they are powerful attacking weapons!

19.Qb3+ Kf8; 20.Nxd6 Rxd6; 21.Rae1 Qg5+; 22.Kh1 Rxe1; 23.Rxe1 Qd2; 24.Rd1. Play has been quite forced, and the reduction of material would lead toward a drawn endgame were it not for the fact that both kings are vulnerable on the open board.

24...Qxf2; 25.Bxh7 Nc4! The threat of ...Qxf3+ keeps White from taking the knight. **26.Rg1 Rh6; 27.Qb4+ Nd6; 28.Qf4+ Rf6; 29.Qg4 Qxf3+; 30.Qxf3 Rxf3.**

An endgame with even material, but that is what Caro-Kann players love to see. Shirov has no intention of agreeing to a draw!

31.Kg2 Rf4; 32.Re1 Rg4+; 33.Kh3 Rb4; 34.Re2. White doesn't want to put pawns on light squares unless necessary for defense.

34...Kf7; 35.Bd3 Kf6; 36.Kg3 Rd4; 37.Bc2 g5; 38.Rf2+ Ke5; 39.Re2+ Kf6; 40.Rf2+ Ke5.

Time control is reached, and Black covers more important terri-tory. Still, it is hard to see how Black can take advantage of this. The knight on d6 is superb, but one wonders if Black would have tried so hard to win this position had it not been played in a team event.

41.Re2+ Kd5; 42.Re3 a5; 43.Bd3 b5; 44.Kf2 Rh4; 45.h3. A small concession. The pawn is easier to defend on the light square, but there is even less room to maneuver. **45...Kd4; 46.Rg3 b4.** The g-pawn is safe while the rook at g3 is tied to defensive duties.

47.Ke2 Nf7; 48.Bf5 Rh6; 49.Kd1 Rf6; 50.Bh7. 50.Bg4 Rf2; 51.Be2 a4; 52.Rf3 Rxf3; 53.Bxf3 Ne5; 54.Be2 should draw. **50...Rf2; 51.Kc1 Rh2; 52.a3 Ne5; 53.axb4 axb4; 54.Bf5 Rf2.**

White must have been overjoyed at the good fortune of being allowed to feast on the g-pawn. The dish proves to be poison, how-ever. **55.Rxg5?** 55.Bc2 Rf1+; 56.Kd2 Rf2+; 57.Kc1 would have been a more fitting conclusion to the game.

55...b3! White sees the mating net coming after the knight moves to f3, but how can the threat be dealt with?

56.Rg3. I think the best line is 56.Bg6! Nf3 (56...Nxg6 57.Rxg6 Rc2+; 58.Kb1 Rh2; 59.Rg4+ Kc5; 60.Kc1 Rxh3; 61.Kd2 is a draw.) 57.Rg4+ holds, but the defense is not simple. 57...Kc5. (57...Ke5; 58.Bd3 Rh2; 59.Bf1 Rc2+; 60.Kd1 Rxb2; 61.Bc4! Rd2+; 62.Kc1 b2+; 63.Kb1 Kf5; 64.Rg8 and White survives.) 58.Bd3 Rh2; 59.Bf1 Rc2+; 60.Kd1 (60.Kb1 Nd2+; 61.Ka1 Rc1#) 60...Rxb2; 61.Rc4+ Kd5; 62.Rb4 Ke5; 63.Bc4 and White can sacrifice a piece if necessary to draw. 63...Nd4; 64.Bxb3 Nxb3; 65.Ke1 Kf5; 66.h4 and the king cannot cross the meridien.

56...Nf3; 57.Rg4+ Kc5; 58.Kd1 Rd2+; 59.Kc1 Rh2; 60.Kd1 Rh1+ and the bishop falls. **61.Ke2 Nd4+; 62.Kd3 Nxf5; 63.Rg5 Rxh3+. White resigned.** 64.Ke4 Rh2; 65.Rxf5+ Kc4; 66.Rf8 Rxb2; 67.Rc8+ Kb4; 68.Kd3 (68.Rb8+ Kc3; 69.Ke3 Rc2 wins.) 68...Rh2; 69.Rb8+ Ka3; 70.Ra8+ Kb2; 71.Rb8 Rh3+; 72.Kd2 Kb1; 73.Ra8 b2; 74.Ra7 Rh2+; 75.Kd1 Rc2; 76.Re7 Rc8. Black wins by chasing the king from the d-file, moving the king to c1, and promoting the pawn.

White Gambits the D-Pawn

VRONA VS. VAN WELY
Holland, 1993
1.e4 c6; 2.d4 d5; 3.exd5 cxd5; 4.c4 Nf6; 5.Nc3 Nc6; 6.Bg5 dxc4; 7.Bxc4

In this line, White recovers one pawn immediately, but gives up the d-pawn. **7...Qxd4**. This is the correct capture. 7...Nxd4?; 8.Nf3 Nxf3+; 9.Qxf3 gives White enough compensation for the pawn. 7...e6!?, of Yudasin-Seirawan, Biel, 1993, is a fully acceptable alternative. But why not grab the pawn, if we are convinced it is safe to do so?

8.Qxd4 Nxd4; 9.0-0-0 e5. Please avoid 9...Nc6 as it proves embarassing after 10.Nb5 and Black resigned in Janko-Lumsdon, Disentis 1991. **10.f4.**

Here theory proclaimed the position better for White, citing 10...Ng4. Black has a much better use for that square! Before we explore that line, we need to step aside and consider another complicated line.

10.Nf3!? Nxf3; 11.gxf3. White's pawn structure is shattered.

Black can offer to return the favor with ...Bd6, but it is better to make a little breathing room for the king, to reduce the effect of a check at b5. 11...Be7; 12.Rhe1 (12.Bb5+ Kf8; 13.Rhe1 a6; 14.Bd3 Be6; 15.Rxe5 Rc8 returns the pawn for a queenside attack. Black will have the advantage if the rook at h8 can get into the game) 12...0-0; 13.Rxe5 Bd8; 14.Ne4! Black cannot afford to capture at e4, as development is lagging. 14...Nd7!; 15.Rf5 Bc7!!

This fine move guarantees equality. 16.Nd6?! was seen in Poluljahov-Maiorov, Krasnodar 1995. Black untangles the position with (16.Be7 Ne5; 17.Rh5! Re8; 18.Bd6 Nxc4; 19.Bxc7 is even) 16...Nb6!!; 17.Rc5 Bxd6; 18.Rxd6 Nxc4; 19.Rxc4 Be6; 20.Rc7 with a likely draw in the end. 10.Bb5+ Nd7; 11.Nge2 Bc5 is better for Black.

Let's get back to the main line now, and the supposedly powerful 10.f4.

The correct move here is **10...Bg4!; 11.Nf3.** On 11.Re1, Black can afford to simplify the position with 11...Rc8; 12.Rxe5+ Be7; 13.Bb5+ Nxb5; 14.Rxb5 b6; 15.Re5 Rc5; 16.Nf3 Bxf3; 17.gxf3 Rxe5; 18.fxe5 Nd7; 19.Bf4 0-0; 20.Nd5 Rc8+; 21.Kd2 Kf8; 22.Nxe7 Kxe7 was good for Black in Eberth-Szecsenyi, Heves, 1992, because the advanced White pawns are exposed.

11...Bxf3!; 12.gxf3 Rc8. 12...0-0-0 is acceptable if all you want is a draw. 13.fxe5 Nxf3; 14.Rxd8+ Kxd8; 15.Rd1+ Kc8; 16.exf6 Nxg5; 17.Nb5 a6; 18.fxg7 Bxg7; 19.Nd6+ Kc7; 20.Nxf7 Nxf7; 21.Bxf7 was drawn in Stein-Speckner, Dortmund, 1993.

13.fxe5 Rxc4; 14.exf6 g6; 15.Rhe1+ Ne6.

We are not out of theory yet! **16.Rxe6+.** 16.Kb1 Rc6. Black has a solid position. 17.Nd5 Bd6; 18.Bh6 Kd7; 19.Re2 Rd8; 20.Be3 Bc5; 21.Bxc5 Rxc5; 22.Rxe6 fxe6; 23.Nf4+ Rd5; 24.Nxd5 exd5; 25.Rxd5+ ended here with a draw, as the pawn at f6 cannot be saved. Hansen-Nielsen, Denmark, 1996. **16...fxe6; 17.f7+ Kxf7; 18.Rd7+ Kg8.**

Black has an extra exchange and a pawn, but the rook at h8 is pathetic. Control of the seventh rank keeps the balance, after White regains the exchange.

19.Bf6 b5; 20.Kd1 Rf4; 21.Ne4 Rxf3; 22.Bxh8 Kxh8; 23.Ng5 Rf1+; 24.Kc2 Rf2+; 25.Kb3.

Black picks off the h-pawn and simultaneously defends h7. But the White knight finds new employment.

25...Rxh2; 26.Nxe6 Kg8; 27.Rxa7 Bh6; 28.Kc3 Bc1!

A powerful move which turns the tables.

29.b3 Bb2+; 30.Kb4 Re2; 31.Ra8+ Kf7; 32.Ng5+ Kg7; 33.Ra7+ Kh6; 34.Nxh7 Rf2; 35.Kxb5 Bg7; 36.a4 Kxh7; 37.b4 g5; 38.Kc4 g4; 39.Rd7 g3; 40.Rd3 Rf4+. White resigned.

Panov Gambit

1.e4 c6; 2.d4 d5; 3.exd5 cxd5; 4.c4 Nf6 5.Nc3 Nc6; 6.Bg5 7.d5 Na5!?

This gambit idea was worked out by Panov himself in the 1930s, and has become one of the main lines in the 1990s. It resembles a reversed form of a gambit in the Tarrasch Defense (1.d4 d5; 2.c4 e6; 3.Nc3 c5; 4.cxd5 exd5; 5 Nf3 Nc6; 6 dxc5 d4; 7 Na4), but White here has an extra tempo which has been expended on Bg5.

SVESHNIKOV VS. ROEPERT
Budapest, 1988

This is a well-known and much studied game, cited widely in the literature.

1.e4 c6; 2.d4 d5; 3.exd5 cxd5; 4.c4 Nf6 5.Nc3 Nc6; 6.Bg5 7.d5 Na5!?; 8.b4. This is the only respectable continuation for White. 8.Bxc4 Nxc4; 9.Qa4+ Bd7; 10.Qxc4 g6; 11.Bxf6 exf6; 12.Nf3 Bg7; 13.0–0 0–0; 14.Rfe1 Qb6; 15.Re7 Qd6 and the bishops were worth more than the passed pawns in Rother-Schulze, Bundesliga, 1988. 8.Nf3 a6; 9.b4 cxb3; 10.axb3 e6; 11.Be2 Bb4; 12.Rc1 Qxd5 was much better for Black in Ravinsky-Tolush, Soviet Championship, 1944. **8...cxb3; 9.axb3 Bd7!**

It is important to control the light squares on the queenside, and although Black has not developed the kingside, White has yet to begin the task. **10.b4.** The alternatives are not at all promising.

10.Bxf6 gxf6; 11.b4 Rc8; 12.Ne4 Nc4; 13.Qb3 Qc7; 14.Nf3 is Sveshnikov-Vuruna, Belgrade, 1988. 14...Nd6; 15.Nxd6+ Qxd6 would have been clearly better for Black, with an extra pawn and the bishop par. 10.Bd2 b6; 11.b4 Nb7; 12.Ba6 Nd6; 13.Bf4 of Sher-Schulze, Mainz ,1995, should have been met by 13...e6 with a better game for Black. 10.Bd3 e6; 11.dxe6 Bxe6; 12.Bb5+ Nc6; 13.Qxd8+ Rxd8; 14.Rxa7 Bb4 was equal in Hector-Nielsen, Denmark, 1996.

10...Rc8; 11.Nb5. Against 11.Na4, Tischbierek's 11...Ne4 is good enough. **11...Nc4.** 11...Ne4 may be even stronger! 12.bxa5. 12...Nxg5; 13.Qe2 e6; 14.d6 a6; 15.Nc7+ Rxc7; 16.dxc7 Bb4+; 17.Kd1 Qxc7; 18.Qc4 Qe5; 19.Ra2 Qe1+; 20.Kc2 0-0. White resigned, Knoek-Bloklnd, Postal, 1983 The other capture is not much better. 12.Rxa5 Nxg5; 13.Rxa7 Qb6; 14.Qd4 Qxd4; 15.Nxd4 e5! and Black has the initiative. If 16.dxe6 then 16...Bxb4+; 17.Kd1 Nxe6; 18.Nxe6 Bxe6; 19.Bb5+ Ke7; 20.Rxb7+ Kf6 and the White king is more exposed than Black's monarch.

12.Nxa7. 12.Bxf6 Bxb5; 13.Bc3 Nd6; 14.Qb3 Bxf1; 15.Kxf1 Ne4 gave Black a strong game in Feher-Roepert, Budapest 1988. **12...e6!**

Black frees the position with this move. **13.Qb3.** 13.Nxc8? Bxb4+; 14.Ke2 Bb5!; 15.Kf3 Ne5+ is an easy win for Black.; 13.Rb1!? Na3; 14.Nxc8 Nxb1; 15.Qxb1 Qxc8 equalizes. **13...Qb6!** The Black queen takes up an active position.

14.Nxc8. 14.Bxc4? Qxb4+; 15.Qxb4 Bxb4+; 16.Ke2 Rxc4 gives Black the advantage. 14.Bxf6 gxf6; 15.Rb1 Qxa7; 16.Bxc4 Qd4; 17.dxe6 fxe6; 18.Be2 Bxb4+; 19.Kf1 Bc5 gave Black a strong initiative in Nurmi-Mertanen, Postal, 1991. **14...Bxb4+.** This is an awkward move to meet, since White is forced to move the king.

15.Ke2. 15.Kd1 Qd4+; 16.Kc2 Nd2! According to the literature, Black wins here but further investigation is surely warranted. (16...exd5 is, I think, far superior.) 17.Bxf6 gxf6; 18.Qb2 Qc5+; 19.Kd1 and I don't see any convincing continuation for Black. **15...Qc5.**

Black has an attack and Sveshnikov does not come up with the best plan, which is to capture at f6. **16.Rb1?!** Much stronger is 16.Bxf6! gxf6.

Here, there is only one way to stay in the game. 17.Ra8! 0–0; 18.Ne7+ Qxe7. White's king is just too exposed. The following analysis by Roepert is convincing.

19.Qg3+ (19.Rxf8+ Kxf8; 20.d6 Qxd6; 21.Qxc4 Qe5+; 22.Kf3 Bc6+; 23.Kg4 h5+; 24.Kh3 Qf5+; 25.Kg3 Qg5+; 26.Kh3 Be1!; 27.Nf3 Qf5+; 28.Kg3 Qg6+; 29.Kh3 Be4 and **Black wins**) 19...Kh8; 20.Rxf8+ Qxf8; 21.Qh4 exd5. Black can also try 21...Qc5!?; 22.Qxf6+ Qg7.

White has nothing better than exchanging queens, since the king is so vulnerable at e2. 23.Qxg7+ Kxg7; 24.Nf3 is unclear, but Black still has enough for the exchange.

16...Nxd5.

17.Kf3. 17.Be7 Nf4+; 18.Kf3 Nd2+; 19.Kg3 Nh5+; 20.Kh3 e5+; 21.g4 Qxf2; 22.Qxb4 Nf4+ and White must give up the queen.
17...Ne5+; 18.Kg3 Qxc8.

Black's position is superior because there is more than enough material compensation for the exchange and the White king is in a ridiculous position.

19.f4? 19.Nf3 Nc6!; 20.h4 h6; 21.Bd2 Qc7+; 22.Kh3 g5; 23.g4 h5! White has no prospects for survival against the opening of lines on the kingside. **19...Nc6.** The knight heads to f5.

20.Nf3 h6; 21.Bh4 Qb8; 22.Qc4 g5! The end is near. **23.Bxg5 hxg5; 24.Nxg5 Nxf4; 25.Kf2 Qa7+; 26.Kg3 Qe3+; 27.Nf3. White resigned**.

Advance Panov

EINARSSON VS. SCHILLER
Reykjavik, 1986
1.e4 c6; 2.d4 d5; 3.exd5 cxd5; 4.c4 Nf6; 5.Nc3 Nc6; 6.Bg5 Be6

From this basic formation White has a number of plans which involve the advance of the c-pawn and we will look at them in this game. Transpositional possibilities abound, particularly when Black exchanges at f6. **7.c5,** is the most direct method of implementing the plan.

White can aim for a quiet life by simply continuing with development. 7.Nf3 g6. (7...Ne4 is a good alternative, for example 8.Bd3 Nxc3; 9.bxc3 dxc4; 10.Be4 Bd5; 11.Qb1 h6; 12.Bf4 b6; 13.Ne5 Nxe5; 14.Qb5+ Qd7; 15.Qxd7+ Kxd7; 16.Bxd5 Nd3+; 17.Kd2 Rc8. Black had a tremendous knight and a better game in Arthur-Speelman, Aegon Machine vs. Human, 1997.)

8.Bxf6 (8.Be2 Bg7; 9.0–0 0–0; 10.cxd5 Nxd5 is a reversed Tarrasch Defense. White's extra tempo is not especially useful, though in Badvarevic-Ciric, Yugoslavia, 1966, 11.Qd2 was played to infiltrate at h6. Black should have replied 11...Re8 so that 12.Bh6 could be met by 12...Bh8) 8...exf6; 9.c5 Bg7; 10.h3 0–0; 11.Bb5 Rc8; 12.0–0 f5; 13.Qd2 h6; 14.Bxc6 bxc6.

The chances are about even. Black has the bishop pair, though the bishop at e6 looks more like a pawn at the moment. White has a potential passed pawn on the queenside. Black can use kingside pawn advances to threaten the knight at f3, which is needed to help protect the weak pawn at d4. I. Zaitsev-Shamkovich, Moscow, 1967.

7.Bxf6 is often seen. Black must now weaken the kingside pawn structure, but should he allow White a queenside pawn majority after ...exf6 or risk congestion in the center after ...gxf6? The long term damage inflicted by the capture is in any case serious. So we want to have as much counterplay as possible. This leads us to the capture with the e-pawn, because our pieces can be developed more quickly that way. In addition, from a practical standpoint, we need to keep in mind that the capture at f6 can be delayed until we eventually play ...g6, and then only the e-pawn capture will be possible. 7...exf6.

Now the advance of the White c-pawn is the correct strategy, as the pawn at d4, though weak, is not vulnerable to attack by ...e5, and the fianchetto of a bishop at g7 will take too much time. 8.c5 g6; 9.Bb5 h5.

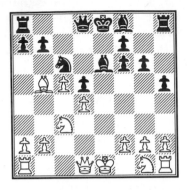

This position has been seen a few times, with very pleasant results for Black. It doesn't seem to matter much where White develops the knight from g1. Let's see what happens if it comes to e2. 10.Nge2 Bh6; 11.0-0 0-0; 12.a3.

Black should consider placing the knight at e7 at this turn or the next to defend the kingside and to eliminate the possiblility of a White capture at c6. 12...f5; 13.f4 Kh7; 14.Bxc6! bxc6; 15.b4 a5! The *Encyclopedia of Chess Openings* evaluates this positions as "unclear." 16.b5.

There is no other logical plan. 16...cxb5; 17.Nxb5 a4! Black's last move prevents White from consolidating his advantage with an advance of his own pawn to this square. White is in any case a little better, but there is plenty of defense available. 18.Rb1 Qa5; 19.Rb4 Rfb8; 20.Nec3 Bd7; 21.Nd6.

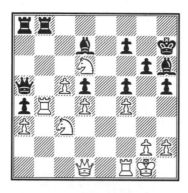

21...Bc6! (Black wisely avoids 21...Rxb4?; 22.axb4 Qxb4; 23.Nxd5+-.) 22.Qb1 (Taking the pawn would be too dangerous. 22.Nxf7 Rxb4; 23.axb4 Qxb4; 24.Qd2 Bg7; 25.Ne5 Bxe5; 26.fxe5 a3 gives Black sufficient counterplay) 22...Rf8; 23.Qa2 Rad8!; 24.Qb2 (24.Nxd5? Rxd6!; 24.Rb6? Rxd6!) 24...Bg7; 25.Rd1 Qc7; 26.Nxa4 Qe7! Black begins a regrouping maneuver that will lead to an advantage on the queenside. 27.Qd2 Ra8; 28.Re1 Qd8; 29.Nc3 Rxa3; 30.Rb6 Qa8; 31.Ndb5 Bxb5; 32.Nxb5 Ra2; 33.Qc3 Re8!

White's only defender on the back rank is challenged. Black's pieces will soon swarm in the direction of the enemy king. 34.Rxe8 Qxe8; 35.h3 Qe4; 36.Qf3 Ra1+; 37.Kh2 Qe1; 38.Nc3 h4; 39.Rb1 Rxb1; 40.Nxb1 Bxd4. White resigned, faced with mate in two, Hennigan-Tseitlin, Hastings, 1991.

10.Qa4 can be inserted before bringing the knight out. 10...Qd7; 11.Nge2 Bh6; 12.b4 0–0; 13.Bd3 a5.

Black gets the pawn to a5, in support of a future invasion of b4, before White can advance the b-pawn and attack the knight. Black's logical reasoning has a tactical flaw, however. (13...Rfe8 is correct, for example: 14.b5 Ne7; 15.0-0 Bf5; 16.Bxf5 Nxf5 with equal chances.) 14.b5 Nb4; 15.Bb1 Bg4. Here 16.a3! Bxe2; 17.Nxe2 Na6; was correct. White may have overlooked 18.c6! Qg4 (18...bxc6; 19.bxa6 Rxa6; 20.Bd3 is hopeless for Black.)

19.bxa6 Rfe8; 20.0-0! bxc6; 21.Nc3 Bd2; 22.Na2 Rxa6; 23.Bd3. White is clearly better. Instead, 16.f3 is an invitation to disaster. 16...Bf5; 17.Qd1 Rae8. Black has serious attacking chances. 18.a3 Re3; 19.Bxf5 Qxf5; 20.axb4 axb4; 21.Na4 Rd3; 22.Qb1 Re8; 23.Kf2.

White is trying to get the king to safety, but between the black rooks and the bishop at h6, there is no escape. A pretty combination now ends the game. 23...Rxe2+; 24.Kxe2 Rd2+; 25.Kf1 Qg5. White resigned, Estrin-Groszpeter, Kecskemet, 1979.

7.Qd2 g6; 8.g3 Na5; 9.Bxf6 exf6; 10.c5 h5; 11.Bg2 Bh6; 12.Qc2 0-0; 13.Nge2 Re8; 14.0-0 Bf5 gave Black equality in Sveshnikov-Tseitlin, Sochi, 1985.

7.a3!? Qd7! White has to look hard for a good plan. 8.c5 Ne4! yields instant equality. 8.Bxf6 gxf6; 9.c5 Bg4!; 10.f3 Bf5; 11.Bb5 was played in Lanka-Leko, Budapset, 1996. Here Black should play 11...h5, followed by ...Rg8 and ...Bh6, which leads to an unclear position with counterplay for Black, according to Lanka. The best line is 8.b4! dxc4!; 9.Bxf6 gxf6.

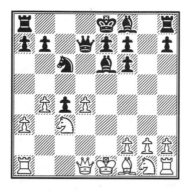

Taking with the e-pawn may be possible, but so far the g-pawn has been the universal choice. 10.d5 0-0-0; 11.Bxc4!? (11.dxe6? Qxe6+; 12.Qe2 Ne5; 13.Qe3 can be countered by 13...Bh6!; 14.Qc5+ Kb8 and White should probably resign here, as the king is a sitting duck. 11.dxc6 Qxc6; 12.Qa4 Qb6; 13.Rd1 Bh6; 14.Nf3 Rhg8 gives Black a strong attack which makes up for the material deficit) 11...Ne5; 12.Bb5 Qc7; 13.Nge2 is Lanka-Adianto, Adelaide, 1990. Black can equalize here with 13...Bf5, according to Lanka.

7.Be2 should be answered by 7...Qa5!; 8.Nf3 and now the c-pawn can be captured.

8...dxc4. If Black tries to increase the pressure with 8...Ne4, White can castle, offering a powerful gambit. Although it seems that White can force the advance of the d-pawn, this is not dangerous for us as long as we play carefully. 9.0-0 Rd8; 10.Qc1 (10.Re1!? b5; 11.Bxf6 gxf6; 12.d5 Nb4 is very good for Black) 10...h6; 11.Bd2 Nxd4!; 12.Nxd4 Rxd4 and again we find a resource for White in 13.b4!

   This is the only move that has any chance of getting some compensation for the pawns. Black will soon be able to develop the bishop and castle unless White takes the initiative immediately. 13...Qd8; 14.Be3 Rd7. Now 15.Bd1 a6 worked well for Black in Rogers-Dreyev, Biel Interzonal, 1993. White really has to grab the a-pawn instead. 15.Bxa7! g5; 16.Nb5. Rogers evaluates this as unclear.

   After 16...Bg7; 17.Bxc4 Bxc4; 18.Qxc4 Ne4; 19.Rac1 Nd2! (19...Bb2; 20.Nc7+ Kf8. White can complicate things with 21.Bb6, which threatens Ne6+.) 20.Qc8 0-0. (20...Nxf1; 21.Bb6! 0-0; 22.Bxd8 Rfxd8; 23.Qc4 Nd2; 24.Qe2 Black does not have enough for the queen.) 21.Qxd8 Rfxd8; 22.Rfe1 Rd5, the chances are about even.

   So, we return to the immediate advance of the c-pawn at move 7. It is appropriate for Black to leap into the center with **7...Ne4.**

   7...Ne4; 8.Be3. 8.Nxe4 dxe4; 9.Be3 Bd5 is fine for Black, who has blockaded the enemy d-pawn and can eventually attack it with ...e5. For example: 10.Ne2 e5; 11.Qa4 leads to some exciting complications, but is nothing for White in the end. 11...exd4; 12.Nxd4 Bxc5;

13.Nxc6 Bxc6; 14.Bb5 Bxe3; 15.Bxc6+ bxc6; 16.Qxe4+ Kf8; 17.Qxe3 Qa5+; 18.Qc3 Qxc3+; 19.bxc3 Ke7 is a dead even endgame.

8...g6; 9.Bd3 Nf6. 9...Nxc3; 10.bxc3 is a reversed Tarrasch structure that is quite promising for White, because it will be difficult for Black to achieve the critical ...e5 break.

10.Nf3 Bg7; 11.h3 0–0 (12.0–0).

Black can be satisfied with the results of the opening. The castled position is well-defended, the center is strong, and eventually the central break ...e5 can be organized. Black should also try to exchange light squared bishops when possible. White will try to take advantage of extra space on the queenside.

12...Qc8. The queen moves to support ...Bf5. **13.a3 Bf5; 14.b4 a6; 15.Re1 Rd8; 16.Na4 Bxd3; 17.Qxd3 Qc7.**

Black's position is very solid, except for the hole at b6. **18.Qb3 Re8; 19.Nb6 Rad8; 20.Bg5 e6.** Unfortunately, the liberating advance of this pawn to e5 was not possible. 20...e5; 21.Bxf6! Bxf6; 22.Nxd5 Rxd5; 23.Qxd5 Rd8; 24.Qb3 exd4; 25.Qd3 does not give Black enough for the exchange.

21.Rad1 Ne7; 22.Ne5 Nh5. The knight moves to expose the power of the bishop. Although White's center seems strong, it has a weakness—the weakness of the pawn at d4. **23.Bc1 Nc6; 24.g4.**

If the knight retreats to f6, as expected, then the bishop at g7 is shut in the cupboard again. Black has a fine sacrifice that quickly turns the tables.

24...Nxd4!; 25.Rxd4 Bxe5; 26.Rxe5 Qxe5; 27.Qd1. My opponent perhaps anticipated this position, calculating that when the knight retreats, then White plays Bf4. The queen must move, and the bishop gets to c7, at least winning back the exchange. I had a surprise ready, however!

27...Ng3! 27...Ng7; 28.Bf4 Qf6; 29.Bc7 Qh4; 30.Qd3 is not quite so awful for White. **28.fxg3.** The capture is forced, as on 28.Bf4 Ne2+ wins. **28...Qxg3+; 29.Kf1 Qxh3+; 30.Kf2 Qh2+; 31.Kf1.** Black still has a big material advantage, with a rook and three pawns for two minor pieces. But rooks need open lines, and there aren't any. So I made one.

31...e5!; 32.Rxd5 Qh1+; 33.Ke2 Qg2+; 34.Ke1 Qg1+; 35.Ke2 Qxg4+; 36.Ke1 Qg1+; 37.Ke2 Qxd1+; 38.Rxd1 Rxd1; 39.Kxd1 f5; 40.a4 Kf7.

Time control was reached. Black has the same material advantage, but in an endgame where the win is relatively straightforward.

41.b5 axb5; 42.axb5 Re6; 43.Nd5 f4; 44.Nc7 Re7; 45.b6 Rd7+; 46.Ke2 Rd8. This was the sealed move, and the game was adjourned. The second session did not take long, as the Black pawns are just too powerful. 46...g5; 47.c6 Rd6 also wins.

47.Bb2 e4; 48.Be5 f3+; 49.Ke3 Rd3+; 50.Kxe4 f2; 51.Kxd3 f1Q+; 52.Kd4 h5; 53.Nd5 Qd1+; 54.Ke4 h4; 55.Ne3 Qa4+; 56.Kd5 h3; 57.Nf1 Qd1+. White resigned.

ACCELERATED PANOV ATTACK

1.e4 c6; 2.c4

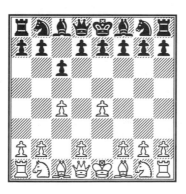

The Accelerated Panov Attack is a blunt attempt to prevent Black from playing 2...d5, but it does not succeed. All that White gains from the exchanges at d5 is the dubious privilege of an isolated d-pawn. The position can lead to a reversed Tarrasch Defense, where the extra move is not so important, though it does make it somewhat easier to play.

Readers of *Complete Defense to Queen Pawn Openings* will be well familiar with the Tarrasch Defense and the handling of isolated pawns. In our repertoire, we will include a sharp line which is, in fact, the reversed Tarrasch, if White chooses to adopt that strategy. There are other ideas, but the isolated pawn features prominently in all of them.

2...d5. Naturally we take up the challenge! **3.exd5 cxd5; 4.cxd5 Qxd5.** An alternative, and more common strategy, is 4...Nf6. We will develop the knight to that square, but will use our queen to recapture the pawn.

5.Nc3. White sensibly develops a knight with tempo. **5...Qd6.** There is no need to retreat all the way to d8, which would leave us behind in development. **6.d4.** Sooner or later White must play this, in order to complete development. **6...Nf6.**

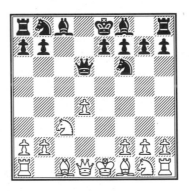

This exits the best known theoretical manuals, which discuss only the advance of the e-pawn to e6. White now has many different plans. Developing the other knight is most consistent with the reversed Tarrasch Defense, but we must pause to consider alternatives.

7.Nf3. 7.Bg5 Nc6; 8.Nf3 Bg4 should provide instant equality.

7.Bc4!? is a reasonable move. White plans Nge2, and then Bf4. The position is similar to that of the Schiller Defense, which can be reached from the Caro-Kann via 1.e4 c6; 2.d4 d5; 3.exd5 Qxd5; 4.Nc3 Qd6; 5.Bc4 Nf6, except that here the c-pawns are gone. This gives White access to b5 in some variations. It also gives Black the ability to control the c-file, and the pawn at d4 remains weak. 7...g6; 8.Qb3 e6. The slight structural weakness is offset by the vulnerable pawn at d4. 9.Nge2 Nc6; 10.Bg5 Bg7. (10...Nxd4; 11.Nxd4 Qxd4; 12.Bxf6 Qxf6; 13.Bb5+ would make me uncomfortable as Black.) 11.Bxf6 Bxf6; 12.Ne4 Qd8; 13.d5 exd5; 14.Nxf6+ Qxf6; 15.Bxd5 0-0; 16.0-0 Re8; 17.Rfe1 Be6 is dead even.

7.Bb5+ Bd7; 8.Nge2 e6; 9.Bf4 Qb6; 10.a4 Bb4; 11.0-0 0-0 gave Black equality in Hamilton-Sarwer, Saint John, 1988.

7.g3 Bg4; 8.Qb3 Qb6; 9.Bb5+ Bd7; 10.Be3 Bxb5; 11.d5 Qa5; 12.Qxb5+ Qxb5; 13.Nxb5 Nxd5; 14.0-0-0 e6!? (14...a6; 15.Rxd5 axb5; 16.Kb1 b4 17.Rb5 e6; 18.Rxb7 Nc6 is nothing special for White.) 15.Rxd5 exd5; 16.Nc7+ Kd7; 17.Nxa8 Nc6; 18.Nf3 Be7; 19.Rd1 Rxa8; 20.Rxd5+ Ke6 led to an even endgame in Rohde-Christiansen, New York Open 1987. 7.Nge2!? is a strange-looking move but it has a point.

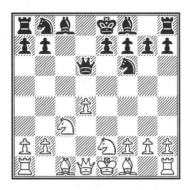

The plan here is to annoy the enemy queen with Bf4. 7...e6; 8.g3 (8.Bf4 deprives b2 of its defender, and Black can equalize with 8...Qb6.) 8...Be7! This resource is neglected in many books. It is consistent with our general theme of kingside castling.

White is committed to castling in the same direction because of the fianchetto plan. 9.Bg2 0-0; 10.0-0 (10.Bf4 Qa6; 11.0-0 Bd7; 12.d5 exd5; 13.Nxd5 Nxd5; 14.Bxd5 Bg4; 15.Qb3 Nc6; 16.Nc3 Rad8; 17.Bc4 is Bhandari-Kourkounakis, Gausdal, 1992. Black should confront the enemy queen right away. 17...Qb6; 18.Qxb6 axb6; 19.Nd5 Bc5; 20.Bc7 Rd7! Black stands well, because White cannot capture the pawn at b6. 21.Bxb6?! Rxd5!; 22.Bxd5 Bxb6 and the minor pieces are better than the rook.) 10...Rd8.

Black will now aim for the liberating advance ...e5, supported by a knight at c6. 11.Qc2 (11.Be3 Nc6; 12.Rc1 Ng4; 13.Bf4 Qb4 looks safe enough for Black. I doubt that 14.a3 Qxb2; 15.Rb1 Qxa3; 16.Nb5 Qa2; 17.Nc7 e5!; 18.Nxa8 exf4; 19.Ra1 Qc4; 20.Rc1 Qb4; 21.gxf4 Bf6 is going to appeal top players of the White pieces) 11...Qa6; 12.Be3 Nc6; 13.a3 Bf8; 14.Rfd1 Ne7; 15.Bg5 Nfd5; 16.Nxd5 exd5 was drawn in Nunn-Miles, Biel, 1986. The position is level after 17.Bxe7 Bxe7; 18.Nf4 Be6.

7...g6. Usually White plays 7...e6, but that limits the scope of the bishop at c8 and fails to put pressure on the isolated pawn.

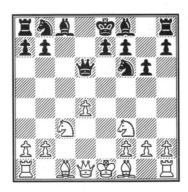

This is an interesting alternative strategy for Black. The position resembles a reversed Tarrasch Defense, though Black is not helped by the lack of development and the position of the queen at d6.

8.Bc4. 8.Bg5 Bg7; 9.Rc1 0-0; 10.Nb5 Qe6+; 11.Be2 Na6; 12.a3 Bd7; 13.0-0 Qb6; 14.Nc3 Rac8; 15.b4 was about even in Hebden-Schiller, London, 1986. I should have played 15...Nc5. 8.Be2 Bg7; 9.0-0 0-0; 10.Re1 Nc6; 11.Bg5 is a reversed Tarrasch where White has an extra tempo and the Black queen at d6 is artificial. Still, there does not seem to be any tangible advantage for White. Black can play the quiet 11...Bf5; 12.Rc1 Rac8. There is no constructive plan for White here, that I can see. The position is level, but still very interesting.

8...Bg7; 9.Nb5

White threatens to check at c7 if the Black queen moves away, so there are very few options for Black.

9...Qb4+. Black must try this active move. 9...Qd8; 10.Bf4 Na6. (10...Qa5+ comes into consideration.) 11.0-0 0-0; 12.Qb3 Bd7; 13.Nc3 Qb6; 14.Qxb6 axb6; 15.Ne5. White has a serious advantage in the center, and much more active pieces, Todorovic-Kostic, Cetinje, 1993.

10.Nd2 Na6; 11.Qe2 0-0; 12.a3 Qa5; 13.Qxe7 Be6

This is a very complicated, but extremely important position. If Black is not in trouble here, then the superior development is worth a pawn. Let's consider the logical follow-up, 14.Bxe6. Of course Black will not simply capture the bishop here, since that leaves the deficit at two pawns. Given that the White king is still in the center, the choice comes down to capturing the knight at b5 or trying a direct attack. We'll choose the latter course.

14...Rae8; 15.Qxb7 Rxe6+

Now whichever way the White king runs, Black will play ...Rb8 with a clear advantage.

EXCHANGE VARIATION
1.e4 c6; 2.d4 d5; 3.exd5 cxd5

With the exchange at d5, the pawn structure becomes unbalanced. White obtains an open e-file while Black has the slightly less useful c-file to work with. Both sides will be castling on the kingside, and with the advance of the c-pawn to c3 White will be able to blunt any queenside attack by Black.

Our goals are to create as much pressure as we can on the c-file. We can exploit a potential outpost at c4. Often, we are able to launch a minority attack on the queenside.

White will be trying to create as much pressure as possible on the c-file. They have an opportunity to exploit a potential outpost at e5. We must watch for attempts to undermine Black's kingside and center by advancing the f-pawn

If Black can weather the kingside storm, then there are sunny skies on the queenside and in the endgame. Often Black will exchange the dark-squared bishops and the light-squared bishop for an enemy knight. The contour of the middlegame may depend on positions like this:

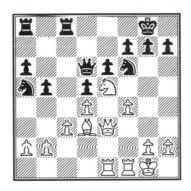

This position was proposed by Müller back in 1931 as the ideal position for both sides. Notice that Black is ready to plant the knight at c4 and then further advance the queenside pawns. As for White, the eyes are firmly fixed on the kingside.

The Exchange Variation is often recommended to beginners because if Black is not careful, White can blow up the kingside fairly easily. It is not seen much at top levels of competition, however, because when Black survives, a victory is usually the reward, unless massive liquidation reduces the game to a trivial draw.

The main line has been established for a long time and was even discussed in Müller's book. It runs 1.e4 c6; 2.d4 d5; 3.exd5 cxd5; 4.Bd3! Nc6; 5.c3 Nf6; 6.Bf4 Bg4; 7.Qb3 Qc8.

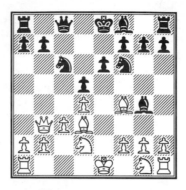

Don't be fooled by the position of the White queen. It moved to b3 only to draw the Black queen to c8. The idea of a kingside attack has not been abandoned. It is easy enough for the queen to retreat to c2 to form a battery with the bishop, aiming at h7.

TIMMAN VS. HÜBNER
Bugojno, 1982
1.e4 c6; 2.d4 d5; 3.exd5 cxd5; 4.Bd3

This is the normal move for White because it prevents Black from playing ...Bf5. Black will need to develop the bishop from c8 somewhat artificially if White refrains from an early Nf3, which would allow the pin at g4.

4...Nc6; 5.c3. The Exchange Variation is rather slow. White is content to fortify the strong pawn in the center. Plans with c4, attacking the pawn at d5, fall into the territory of the Panov Attack.

5...Nf6; 6.Bf4. If White develops the knight to f3 instead, then

Black equalizes easily with 6...Bg4, as in the game Barua-Georgiev, Biel Interzonal, 1993. White can try to double Black's pawns at the cost of the minor exchange, but over a century ago it was pointed out that 6.Bg5 is not effective, though Black must be prepared to meet it. 6...Bg4; 7.f3 Bh5; 8.Bxf6 gxf6.

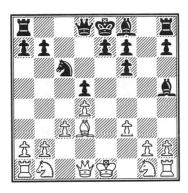

The weakness of Black's pawn structure is compensated by the open g-file and possibility of countering the strong White bishop with ....Bg6. 9.Ne2 Qb6 has the interesting forcing variation 10.Nf1 Qxb2; 11.Qb3.

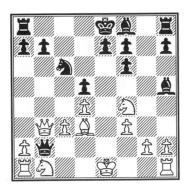

Black must not be tempted to capture either of White's rooks. Only by steering the game into a favorable, or at least equal, endgame can Black survive this position. Exchanging queens is correct. 11...Qxb3!; 12.axb3 Bg6; 13.Bxg6 hxg6; 14.Nxd5 Rd8; 15.Ne3 Bh6; 16.Ke2 Bxe3; 17.Kxe3 e5 is certainly no worse for Black!

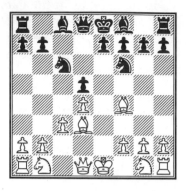

We return to the position after 6.Bf4. Black now takes advantage of the opportunity to attack the White queen. **6...Bg4; 7.Qb3!** Whenever Black develops his light-squared bishop, the b7-pawn becomes weak. 7.f3 Bh5 just helps the Black bishop on its path to g6.

7...Qc8; 8.Nd2. 8.Ne2 Bh5; 9.Be5 e6; 10.Nf4 Bg6; 11.Nd2 Be7; 12.Nxg6 hxg6; 13.Nf3 0-0; 14.0-0 a6; 15.Qc2 b5; 16.Rac1 Qb7; 17.Rfe1 Rac8; 18.Bxg6 fxg6; 19.Qxg6 Qd7. Black was able to defend with the resource Qe8, Lematschko-Danielian, Yerevan Olympiad, 1996.

8...e6.

This preliminary move makes it possible to develop the other knight at f3 without allowing Black to fracture the kingside pawn structure. Black is able to develop comfortably, but the bishop at g4 lacks room to maneuver, and will have to waste some time getting back to g6 via h5. **9.Ngf3.**

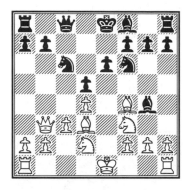

Both sides will complete their development before undertaking active operations. 9.h3 is an important alternative.

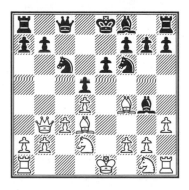

Does White gain anything by pushing the Black bishop in the direction it wanted to go anyway? Not really, but it does make possible aggressive action with g4 later.

9...Bh5; 10.Ngf3 Be7; 11.Ne5 0-0; 12.g4 Bg6; 13.Nxg6 fxg6; 14.Be3 Bd6; 15.0-0-0 Rb8; 16.f4 b5; 17.Qc2 b4; 18.Kb1 bxc3; 19.Qxc3 Qb7 with plenty of counterplay in Timman-Seirawan, Mar del Plata, 1982. No better is 11.0-0 Bg6; 12.Bb5. (Exchanging bishops transposes below to the discussion of 9.Ngf3 Be7; 10.0-0 0-0; 11.h3 Bh5.) 12...0-0; 13.Qa4 Rd8; 14.Bxc6 bxc6; 15.Ne5 c5; 16.Nc6 Qd7; 17.Nxe7+ Qxe7 presented Black with no problems in Mai-Jovanic, European Boys U-18 Championship, 1996.

Finally, 11.Qc2 Bg6; 12.a3 0-0; 13.g4 b5! gave Black good counterplay in one of the earliest examples of the 7...Qc8 defense. 14.Ne5 Nxe5; 15.Bxe5 Nd7; 16.h4 Nxe5; 17.dxe5 a5; 18.Nf3 b4; 19.h5 Bxd3; 20.Qxd3 bxa3; 21.bxa3 Rb8; 22.Nd4 f6 and Black went on to win in Loman-Reti, 1923.

9...Be7. 9...Nh5? is a poor idea, because Black has not completed his development yet. 10.Be3 Bd6; 11.Ne5! is a powerful pawn sacrifice, as the following variations show: 11...Bxe5. (11...Nxe5; 12.dxe5 Bxe5; 13.Qa4+ is hopeless for Black.) 12.dxe5 Nxe5. (12...0-0; 13.h3 Nxe5; 14.Bxh7+! Kxh7; 15.hxg4 also wins for White.) 13.Bb5+ Kf8; 14.f3 Bf5; 15.g4 and White has a sizable advantage. **10.0-0.** 10.Ne5 Nxe5 is acceptable for Black whichever way White recaptures.

We'll start with the pawn capture. 11.dxe5 Nd7 puts pressure on the center.

White has a lot of space on the kingside, but the Black minor pieces stand ready to defend their king. 12.Qc2 Bh5; 13.g4 Bxg4. (Black can also safely retreat with 13...Bg6; 14.Bxg6 hxg6; 15.Bg3 Bh4; 16.0-0-0 Qc7; 17.f4 Bxg3; 18.hxg3 0-0-0 as in Walczak-Huchla, 1993.) 14.Rg1 Bh5; 15.Rxg7 Bg6 and Black was ready to win the exchange. In Logie-Vandermeulen, Postal, 1991, White tried to break through with a sacrifice.

16.0-0-0 Bf8; 17.Rxg6 hxg6; 18.Bxg6 but Black was ready with

18...Bh6!; 19.Bg3 Qc7 and went on to win after 20.Kb1 Bxd2; 21.Rxd2 Rh6; 22.Bd3 0-0-0; 23.f4 f6. On the other hand, 12.0-0 Nc5; 13.Bb5+ Kf8 leaves White fighting for equality, despite the awkward position of the Black king. Black will gain time with ...a6 and the light squares can prove to be a problem for White, Hübner-Smyslov, Hastings, 1969.

Regarding the capture with the bishop, 11.Bxe5 0-0 12.Qc2 (12.0-0 a6; 13.a4 Qd7; 14.Rfe1 Rac8; 15.Re3 Bf5. Retreating to g6 via h5 seems wiser. 16.Bxf5 exf5; 17.Bxf6 Bxf6 was very slightly better for White in Ehlert-Kock, Germany, 1993, because of the superior pawn structure) 12...Bf5; 13.Bxf5 exf5; 14.Qb3 Qc6; 15.0-0 b5; 16.a4 a6; 17.Rfe1 Ne4; 18.Nf1 Bg5; 19.f4 f6; 20.Ne3 fxe5; 21.Nxd5 Kh8 led to uneasy complications for boths sides in Nezhmetdinov-Shamkovich, Soviet Union, 1970.

There are two other minor variants. 10.a4 0-0; 11.0-0 a6; 12.Ne5 of Regez-Umbach, 1993, should be met by 12...Nxe5; 13.dxe5 Nd7; 14.Qc2 f5 and the bishop at g4 can get back to e8 and then on to a more useful diagonal, if necessary. 10.h3 Bh5 transposes to the discussion of 9.h3, or below to 11.h3.

10...0-0. White has completed his development and is ready to take the initiative. 10...Bh5! is, perhaps, more precise but because of the many transpositional paths Black may as well castle. Here are some independent lines.

11.Ne5 Nxe5; 12.Bxe5 0-0; 13.Rac1 Bg6; 14.c4 Bxd3; 15.Qxd3 dxc4; 16.Rxc4 Qd8; 17.Ne4 Nd5; 18.Nc5 b6; 19.Qg3 g6; 20.Nd3 Rc8. Black is at least equal, Upton-Hracek, European Team Championship, 1997.

11.Rfe1 0-0; 12.Bg5 (12.h3 Bg6; 13.Bf1 Ne4; 14.Nxe4 Bxe4 was roughly level in Semeniuk-Guliev, Vladivostok, 1995) 12...Rb8; 13.Ne5

Qc7; 14.Qc2 Bg6; 15.Bxg6 hxg6; 16.Qd3 Bd6; 17.f4.

This type of position can be very dangerous for Black, if an incorrect decision is made regarding the knight at f6. Retreating to e8 can be fatal, as the following brutal example shows. 17...Ne7? (17...Nd7 maintains the balance.) 18.Qh3 b5; 19.a3 a5; 20.g4 and White had the initiative in Kristiansen-Berg, Ringsted, 1995.

After Black castles, there are again several options for White.

There are many different strategies for White, but Black usually concentrates on a single plan, advancing the queenside pawns to create a minority attack. We'll look at the move played in the game, advancing the knight to e5, in our main game. Here are some others.

11.Rae1 is a popular alternative. 11...Bh5 and now: 12.Ne5 (12.Qc2 Bg6; 13.Bxg6 hxg6; 14.Qd3 a6; 15.Ne5 Nxe5; 16.Bxe5 Qc6; 17.Nf3 b5 and Black was able to successfully carry out a minority attack in Bednar-Turov, Mlada Boleslav, 1995) 12...Nd7; 13.Ndf3 Ndxe5; 14.Nxe5 Nxe5; 15.Bxe5 Bg6; 16.Qc2 b5; 17.Bxg6 hxg6; 18.Qe2

Qc4. Black had at least equality in Caruso-Martinovsky, Geneva, 1995. 11.h3 Bh5.

This is another important deviation, which can also arise if h3 and ...Bh5 are played earlier.

12.Rfe1 Bg6; 13.Bxg6 hxg6; 14.Ne5 (14.Re2 a6; 15.a4 Na5; 16.Qc2 b5; 17.axb5 axb5; 18.b3 Nc6; 19.Qb2 Qb7; 20.Ree1 Rxa1 was drawn in Carvalho-O'Siochru, Yerevan Olympiad, 1996) 14...Nxe5; 15.Bxe5 Qc6; 16.a4 Rfc8. (16...Nd7; 17.Nf3 Nb6 provides a bit more counterplay.) 17.Nf3 Ne4; 18.Bf4 Bd6; 19.Bxd6 Qxd6; 20.Ne5. White has a slightly better position. Black must worry about the queenside. Bonaveri-Toth, Open, 1996.

12.Ne5 Nxe5; 13.Bxe5 Nd7; 14.Rae1 Re8; 15.Bg3 Nf8; 16.Re3 Bg6; 17.f4 Bxd3; 18.Rxd3 Qd7; 19.Nf3 Bd6; 20.Ne5 Qc7. Black has achieved equality. There are no weaknesses on the kingside so an attack on that flank is unlikely to succeed. Black can play on the queenside. Gaprindashvili-Kallio, European Boys U16 Championship, 1996.

12.Rae1 Bg6; 13.Bxg6 hxg6.

Black has sufficient counterplay here. 14.Re3 Na5; 15.Qb5 Nc4; 16.Nxc4 a6; 17.Nb6 (17.Qa5 dxc4; 18.Bg5 Bd8 is fine for Black) 17...axb5; 18.Nxc8 Rfxc8. Black threatens to advance the b-pawn and shred White's queenside structure, and the a-pawn is under attack. At first it seems that both threats can be parried by 19.a3, but Black marches ahead anyway: 19...b4!; 20.axb4 Ra2; 21.Re2 Rxc3; 22.bxc3 Rxe2; 23.Ra1 Ne4; 24.Ra7 Rxf2; 25.Rxb7 Bf8; 26.Rb8 Ra2.

11.Ng5 h6; 12.Ngf3 Nh5 gives Black the initiative.

11.Rfe1 can be handled by 11...Re8. Other moves such as 11...Bh5 and 11...Nh5 have been played with success, too. 12.Qc2 Bf5; 13.Bxf5 exf5; 14.Bg5 Ne4; 15.Bxe7 Rxe7 is already a strong position for Black. Watch how quickly White's position falls apart! 16.Nf1. White should have doubled rooks on the crucial e-file. 16...Qd7; 17.Rad1 Rae8; 18.c4 f4; 19.Ne5 Nxe5; 20.dxe5 Rxe5; 21.cxd5 f3; 22.gxf3 Ng5; 23.Rxe5 Nxf3+; 24.Kh1 Nxe5; 25.Ne3 g6; 26.Qe4 f5; 27.Qf4 Nf7; 28.d6 Qc6+; 29.Kg1 Re4; 30.Qg3 f4; 31.Nf5 fxg3; 32.Ne7+ Rxe7; 33.dxe7 gxf2+. White resigned, Oberst-Meduna, Germany, 1993.

So, back to the game with **11.Ne5 Bh5.**

11...Nxe5; 12.dxe5 Nd7; 13.Qc2 g6; 14.h3 Bf5; 15.Bxf5 gxf5; 16.Bh6 and White has very good prospects for an effective kingside attack, since Black's forces are uncoordinated and cannot quickly come to the defense of their monarch. **12.Qc2.**

12.Rfe1 Nxe5.

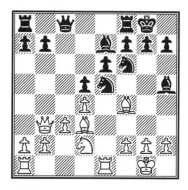

White has three ways of capturing the enemy knight. Using the rook loses to 13...Bd6, but both of the others have been tried.

13.dxe5 Nd7; 14.Qc2! Bg6; 15.Bxg6 (15.Bg3 Nc5; 16.Bxg6 hxg6; 17.Re2 was seen in Zelic-Mufic, Croatia, 1995, and here Black should just have played 17...Rd8) 15...fxg6!?; 16.Bg3 Bc5; 17.Qd3 Nb6. Black is getting ready to stick the knight at c4, with instant equality. 18.b3.

18...Qe8?! (18...Ba3 is correct, with an equal game.) 19.a4! White had a strong attack in Yudasin-Lempert, Moscow, 1991.

Capturing with the bishop changes the nature of the game. 13.Bxe5 Qc6; 14.a4 Bg6; 15.Bb5 Qc8; 16.a5 a6; 17.Bf1 (17.Ba4) 17...Qd7; 18.Bg3 Ne4; 19.Nxe4 Bxe4; 20.c4 dxc4; 21.Bxc4 Bd5; 22.Bxd5 exd5 with an eventual draw in Sznapik-Seirawan, Malta, 1980.

Playing on the dark squares also proves ineffective. 12.Bg5 Nd7; 13.Bxe7 Nxe7; 14.f4 f6; 15.Nef3 Bf7; 16.Rae1 Qc7; 17.Nh4 Rfe8; 18.Re3 Nf8; 19.Qd1 Neg6; 20.Qg4 Nxh4; 21.Qxh4 Bg6; 22.Bxg6 Nxg6; 23.Qg4 Qd6 solved all of Black's problems in Morozevich-Ekstroem, Cappelle la Grande, 1997.

A queen and double rook endgame can arise on 12.a4 Nd7; 13.Ndf3 Bf6; 14.Rfe1 Ndxe5; 15.Nxe5 Nxe5; 16.Bxe5 Bxe5; 17.Rxe5 Bg6; 18.Bxg6 hxg6; 19.Qd1 Qc4.

This is decidedly worse for Black, who was in no position to stop White on the kingside. Black should not eliminate all the minor pieces prematurely. Note in the Morozevich-Ekstroem game cited above, Black was able to play ...f6 and White was committed to f4 before the exchanges took place. Lang-Howard, London, 1996.

12.Ndf3 uses a strategy from the Colle System. There, a pawn usually is at f4 and White has a bad bishop, at least until the pawn advances to f5.

12...a6. (12...Bxf3; 13.Nxf3 Na5; 14.Qc2 Nc4 comes into consideration) and White has three notable plans. 13.Rfe1 b5!; 14.Nxc6 Qxc6; 15.Ne5 Qb7; 16.a4 b4; 17.cxb4 Qxb4; 18.Qxb4 Bxb4.

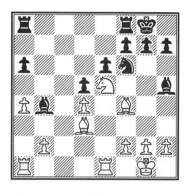

The position is objectively level, but I'd rather play Black, with convenient targets on the queenside and at d4, Orsag-Hajek, 1993. The players were under 10 years old, playing in the World Junior Championships! 13.a4 Bxf3; 14.Nxf3 Nh5; 15.Bg5 Bd6! followed by ...Nf4 gives Black a good game.

13.Nxc6 is the most consistent move. 13...Qxc6; 14.Ne5 Qc8; 15.a4 Nd7; 16.Rfc1 Nxe5; 17.Bxe5 Qd7; 18.Qa2 Rfc8; 19.b3 Bd6; 20.Bxd6 Qxd6; 21.Qd2 Bg6; 22.Bxg6 hxg6 brought Black equality in Karatekin-Tare, Balkaniad, 1993.

Since White gets nowhere with these other plans, let's return to the position after Qc2.

An important position, which Black must handle with great care.
12...Bd6!

White has a large army aimed at the kingside, and Black must prepare to eliminate some of the pieces. The threat at h7 can be parried by retreating the bishop to g6. Though Black's position seems passive, the reduction in fighting forces will make it easier to obtain counterplay. One example is: 13.Rfe1 Qc7; 14.h3 Rfc8; 15.Rac1 a6; 16.g4 Bg6; 17.Bxg6 hxg6; 18.Qd3 Nxe5. Clever, but simpler is the consistent 18...b5; 19.dxe5 Bc5; 20.b4 Bf8; 21.Qe3 Nd7; 22.c4 Qb6!; 23.Qxb6 Nxb6; 24.c5 Nd7 and Black had the advantage in the endgame, because White has a bad bishop and no useful plans for the knight. Sands-Stevens, CompuServe, 1993.

More challenging is **13.Nxc6.** White eliminates the knight that can become a source of counterplay on the queenside.

13...Qxc6; 14.Be5. 14.Bxd6 Qxd6; 15.f4 Bg6; 16.Bxg6 (16.Rf3 b5; 17.f5 Bxf5; 18.Bxf5 exf5; 19.Qxf5 b4 gave Black sufficient counterplay in Weber-Kreutzkamp, Postal, 1986.) 16...hxg6. (16...fxg6?; 17.g3 b5; 18.Rfe1 Rac8; 19.a3 Rfe8; 20.Qd3 gave White a persistent advantage in Boyd-Grainger, 1993.) 17.Rae1 b5 followed by ...b4 gives Black a reasonable game.

14...Bg6.

Now that White can no longer capture this piece with his knight, Black has a playable game.

15.Rae1 Bxd3; 16.Qxd3 Bxe5; 17.dxe5 Nd7. White has no realistic expectations of a kingside attack, so in this game the queenside became the battleground.

18.Re3 Rfc8; 19.Nf3 Nc5; 20.Qc2 Qa4; 21.b3 Qg4; 22.Rd1 Rc7; 23.Rd4 Qg6; 24.Qd1 Nd7; 25.c4 Rac8!

The game was eventually drawn, though not until there was a little excitement on both flanks!

26.Re1 Nb6; 27.Qd2 h6; 28.Qa5 dxc4; 29.Qxa7 Nd5; 30.Rxc4 Rxc4; 31.bxc4 Rxc4; 32.Qxb7 Nf4; 33.g3 Nh3+; 34.Kg2 Nf4+; 35.Kg1 Nh3+ and the peace treaty was signed.

FANTASY VARIATION

FLÜCKIGER VS. TISDAL
Bern, 1994

1.e4 c6; 2.d4 d5; 3.f3

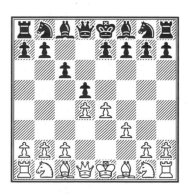

This is the Maroczy, or Fantasy Variation. White hopes that this move will lead to some fantastic flashy win, but it really is a modest and unambitious strategy, except when played as a gambit, when it takes on more unorthodox characteristics. Capturing at e4 is normal, though there is no shortage of alternatives.

Some strong players have been found on the White side, not just fans of the weird, such as Savielly Tartakower, but even such quiet positional strategists as Vasily Smyslov, not known for using unorthodox openings.

3...dxe4.

3...e6; 4.fxe4. 4.Nc3 Transposes to the Blackmar-Diemer Gambit, above. **4...e5; 5.Nf3.** 5.dxe5? is a terrible blunder because Black has 5...Qh4+!; **5...Be6.**

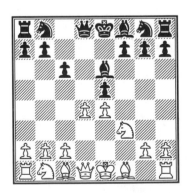

The e-pawn is safe, because if White captures with the pawn, then the queens are exchanged at d1, while if the knight blunders onto e5, ...Qh4+ is embarrassing.

6.c3. 6.Be3 exd4; 7.Qxd4 Qxd4; 8.Nxd4 Nf6; 9.Nxe6 fxe6 gave White only a marginal advantage in Klaman-Kholmov, Tbilisi, 1949. **6...Nd7; 7.Bd3.**

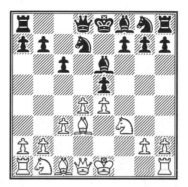

There is some tension in the center, but both sides have a long way to go before development is complete. Theory holds that the chances are about even here.

7...f6. 7...Bd6; 8.0–0 f6; 9.Be3 shows a slightly different plan for White. 9...Ne7; 10.Nbd2 Bc7; 11.Bc4 Bxc4; 12.Nxc4 exd4; 13.Nxd4 Nf8? Black should move the knight to b6 instead, when the game would be about equal. 14.Qh5+ g6; 15.Qf3. White is clearly better, Jimenez-Hort, Moscow, 1963.

8.Qe2 Bd6; 9.0–0 Qe7; 10.Nbd2.

Taking stock of the position, we can conclude that White's pieces, though well coordinated, are not in effective positions. The semi-open f-file is relatively useless, the bishop at c1 has no immediate future, and the bishop at d3 sits and stares at the pawn at e4, wishing it were somehow out of the way. Black will bring the knight to h6, taking advantage of the blocked c1–h6 diagonal.

10...Nh6. 10...0-0-0 signals more aggressive intentions, but is also worth considering. **11.Nc4 Nf7.** There is no need for Black to try to preserve the bishop pair. The White knight at c4 has scope over many important squares and is not likely to give its life for the bishop in any case.

12.Ne3 Nb6; 13.Nf5. White momentarily occupies the only hole in Black's position. **13...Bxf5; 14.exf5 0-0-0!** Black logically places his king on the queenside, as White does have some prospects of a kingside attack.

15.dxe5 Nxe5; 16.Nxe5 Qxe5; 17.Qxe5 Bxe5.

This sterile position led to an eventual draw in Flueckiger-Tisdall, Bern, 1994. For the sake of completeness, here are the remaining moves.

18.Bc2 Nc4; 19.Bb3 Nd2; 20.Be6+ Kc7; 21.Re1 Rd3; 22.Re2 Rhd8; 23.g3 a5; 24.Bxd2 Rxd2; 25.Rae1 a4; 26.a3 b5; 27.Kf2 R2d6; 28.Rc1 Rd2; 29.Rce1 h5; 30.Rxd2 Rxd2+; 31.Re2 Rxe2+; 32.Kxe2 c5; 33.Kd3 Kb6; 34.Bf7 h4; 35.gxh4 Bxh2; 36.b3 axb3; 37.c4 b2; 38.Kc2 Be5; 39.h5 b4; 40.axb4 cxb4; 41.Be6 Kc5; 42.Bg8 Bd4; 43.Bf7 Kd6; 44.Be8 Ke5; 45.Bd7 Kf4; 46.Kb1 Kg5; 47.c5 Bxc5; 48.Kxb2 Kxh5; 49.Be8+ Kg5; 50.Bg6. Draw agreed.

TWO KNIGHTS VARIATION
1.e4 c6; 2.Nc3 d5; 3.Nf3

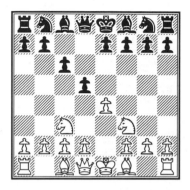

White has only modest goals in the opening. Simple development will suffice. Black responds by pinning the knight at f3. When provoked, Black's bishop captures the knight and continues to develop. White has the bishop pair, but it has no effect in such a closed position. In our selected game, British Grandmaster William Watson, known for his aggressive play on the Black side of the Sicilian Dragon, shows that even the quietest variations of the Caro-Kann can be explosive.

GHINDA VS. W.WATSON
Thessaloniki Olympiad, 1988
1.e4 c6; 2.Nc3 d5; 3.Nf3 Bg4

The pin cannot be exploited immediately, but White almost always challenges the bishop right away.

4.h3. 4.d4 dxe4; 5.Nxe4 e6; 6.Bd3 Nf6; 7.h3 Bh5; 8.0–0 Nxe4; 9.Bxe4 brought equality in Spassky-Petrosian, Soviet Union, 1955.

4...Bxf3; 5.Qxf3 Nf6.

This is an ambitious plan for Black. The solid 5...e6 leads to a quieter, but less interesting life. **6.d4.** 6.e5 is an obvious alternative. 6...Nfd7.

This is a very committal plan. White can at best get to a position similar to the French Defense, but where Black does not suffer from a bad bishop. There is also the aggressive advance of the e-pawn to be considered.

7.e6 fxe6; 8.d4 e5! Black gets rid of the problematic pawn right away. 9.dxe5 Nxe5; 10.Qg3 Nf7; 11.Be3 e5; 12.0–0–0 Nd7; 13.f4 e4; 14.Be2 Nf6. Black has a clearly superior position, Godes-Gorshkov, Soviet Union. 1974.

7.d4 can be met by the simple advance of the e-pawn, but there is a more interesting line. 7...Qb6!; 8.Qd1 e6; 9.f4 c5; 10.Na4 Qa5+; 11.c3 cxd4; 12.b4 Qc7; 13.Qxd4 Nc6; 14.Qf2.

Black can liven the game up by advancing the d-pawn. 14...d4!; 15.b5 (15.a3!? dxc3; 16.Nxc3 a6 is solid for Black) 15...Ne7 was played in Kupreichik-Kaunas, Cuxhaven, 1993. Kaunas gives the following analysis. 16.Qxd4 Nf5; 17.Qc4 Qxc4; 18.Bxc4 Rc8; 19.Bb3 Ng3; 20.Rg1 g5! and in his opinion, Black stands better. That evaluation is not unreasonable, since White's extra pawn is more than offset by the horrendous coordination of his pieces.

7.Qg3 e6; 8.d4 Qb6 gives Black an easy game. The only line that requires specific attention is the offer of the d-pawn. 9.Bd3 Qxd4; 10.0-0 was played in Ozsvath-Eperjesi, Hungary, 1967. Black should have had the courage to munch another pawn. 10...Qxe5; 11.Bf4 Qd4; 12.Rad1 Qb4 and I really don't see any satisfactory compensation for White.

6.g3 is a minor line, used just to get out of the books. 6...dxe4; 7.Qe2 Nbd7; 8.Bg2 g6; 9.Nxe4 Nxe4; 10.Qxe4 Bg7; 11.0-0 0-0 gave Black a solid position in Kudrin-Christiansen, USA Championship 1983.

6.d3 e6 is a very common continuation.

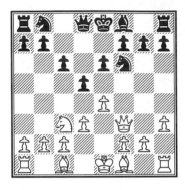

White's unambitious play is not likely to cause any trouble, but many plans have been tried. We'll look at five distinct strategies, saving the best, the prophylactic advance of the a-pawn, for last.

7.Bd2 Bb4; 8.a3 Bd6; 9.g4?! is a rather eccentric line. 9...d4; 10.Ne2 Qb6; 11.0–0–0 Nfd7; 12.Qg2 e5; 13.f4 Nc5.

White already has some worries on the queenside, and the game quickly exploded in Black's favor. 14.fxe5 Na4; 15.b3 Bxa3+; 16.Kb1 Nb2; 17.Bc1 Nxd1; 18.Bxa3 Qa5; 19.Bc1 c5; 20.c4 Nc6; 21.Kc2 Ne3+. White resigned, Zuckerman-Marovic, Malaga, 1968.

7.Be2 Nbd7; 8.Qg3 g6; 9.0–0 Bg7; 10.Bf4 Qb6; 11.Rab1 0–0; 12.Bf3 e5; 13.Bd2 dxe4; 14.dxe4 a5. White has nothing special here, and the Chigorinish position of the rook at b1 is not very aggressive, Karpov-Portisch, Montreal, 1979.

7.g3 Bb4; 8.Bd2 d4; 9.Nb1 Qb6; 10.b3 a5; 11.a3 Bxd2+; 12.Nxd2 0–0 give Black good counterplay, for example: 13.Bg2 a4!?; 14.0–0 axb3; 15.cxb3 Nbd7; 16.Qe2 Ra6 with chances for both sides in Stripunsky-Guliev, Beloreshchensk, 1993.

7.Bg5 Be7 is harmless. So, White usually plays 7.a3 and Black responds 7...Bc5.

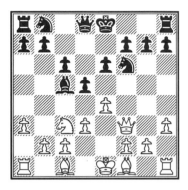

This plan is best known from an old game Fischer-Larsen game. The bishop stands well here. 8.e5 Nfd7; 9.Qg3 Bd4; 10.f4 0–0; 11.Ne2 Bb6; 12.Be3 Bxe3; 13.Qxe3 is Hickl-Schlosser, Altensteig, 1990. Here 13...Qb6 proved a bit risky, so I recommend 13...c5.

8.Be2 0–0; 9.0–0 Nbd7; 10.Qg3 Bd4; 11.Bh6 looks aggressive, but Black has no problems after 11...Ne8; 12.Bg5 Ndf6; 13.Bf3 Qd6, for example: 14.Bf4 Qc5; 15.Rab1 dxe4; 16.dxe4 e5. (16...Nh5 is more logical, getting rid of one of the White bishops.) 17.Bg5 Bxc3; 18.bxc3 b5; 19.c4! a6; 20.Bd2 Qe7; 21.Bb4 Nd6; 22.Rfd1 Rfd8; 23.cxb5 cxb5 was eventually drawn in Fischer-Larsen,Zurich, 1959.

8.g4 is another radical attempt to launch an early kingside attack. It is premature. 8...0–0.

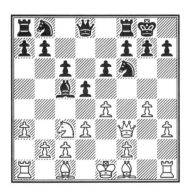

Black has a comfortable position. 9.h4 Nbd7; 10.g5 Ne8; 11.Bh3 f5; 12.exf5 exf5; 13.Bf4 Qe7+ was eventually drawn in Tal-Portisch, Candidates Match, 1965.

6...dxe4. Capturing the pawn is correct. White cannot recapture at e4, because then the pawn at d4 will fall without compensation. **7.Qe3.**

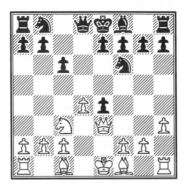

Black has many plans here, but we will adopt the standard approach with the advance of the e-pawn. **7...e6.** 7...g6!?; 8.Nxe4 Bg7 is a reasonable alternative.

8.Nxe4 Nxe4; 9.Qxe4 Nd7. The knight heads to f6, or b6, and then to d5. **10.c3 Nf6.**

Black is not even behind in development, and has an excellent pawn structure. **11.Qf3 Be7.** 11...Qd5 is a good move too, since White's bishop pair cannot be very effective in a closed position. 12.Qxd5 exd5; 13.Bd3 Bd6 is unlikely to lead to a decisive result.

12.Bd3. 12.Bc4 Nd5!?; 13.0-0 0-0; 14.Re1 Bd6 is not going to cause Black any worries.

12...0-0. 12...Qd5 is still a good alternative. **13.0-0 Qb6; 14.Bg5 Rfd8; 15.Rfe1 Rd5!; 16.Bh4 Rad8; 17.Bc4 R5d7.**

Black's pieces are in good positions and the pawn structure is solid. **18.Re2!?** 18.b4 a5; 19.a3 Nd5 is considered equal, but after 20.Bxe7 Rxe7; 21.Bb3. White has a slight advantage. So I think that Black should play 18...e5.

18...c5! This typical freeing maneuver focuses the battle on the d-file. **19.dxc5?!** It is probably better for White to allow the exchange of pawns to take place at d4. 19.Rae1! is preferred by Watson.

In view of what might follow, I'd give serious thought to 19...Kf8 instead, since the e-file seems to need support. After 19...cxd4. White should not capture in the center. 20.Bxf6?! Bxf6; 21.Rxe6 fxe6!; 22.Rxe6 Qc7. (22...Qc5!? is given by Watson in his notes to the game, but he overlooked the immediate 23.Re8#!)

23.Rc6+ Kh8; 24.Rxc7 Rxc7 is evaluated by Watson as equal, but I think it more accurate to say that Black has all the chances, though the bishops of opposite color make a draw, the likely result. 20.Rxe6! is best, when Watson likes 20...Qc5, but I feel that the position after 21.Bxf6 gxf6. (21...Bxf6??; 22.Re8+.) 22.cxd4 Qxc4; 23.Rxe7 Qxd4;

24.Qg3+ Kf8; 25.Qa3 is clearly in White's favor.
   19...Qxc5.

Now the pawn structure favors Black, who controls the d-file. **20.Bb3?** White fails to appreciate the danger which will become evident after Black's next move. 20.Bxf6 Qxc4; 21.Re4! Qc5 should lead to a draw.

20...g5!! A brilliant stroke. Although the move would seem to weaken the Black kingside, it actually releases all the pressure and allows Black to consider taking the initiative on that flank. **21.Bg3.** 21.Qg3 is just too risky. 21...Nh5; 22.Qg4 Nf4; 23.Re3 is not as bad for White as the literature suggests. 23...h5; 24.Qf3 gxh4; 25.Qxf4 Bg5 does not win for Black, as Watson suggests, because White has the saving plan 26.Re5! Bxf4; 27.Rxc5 and a draw is likely, because of the bishops of opposite color. I think Black does better to play 24...Nd5, with the better chances.

   21...Rd3; 22.Re3.

White wants to alleviate the pressure by exchanging a pair of rooks, but there is a structural price to be paid. **22...Rxe3; 23.fxe3.** 23.Qxe3 Qxe3; 24.fxe3 Rd2 is clearly bad for White. **23...Rd2;**

24.Qxb7!? White gives up the e-pawn in return for Black's b-pawn. Each side will now have a passed pawn, but White's king is still airy.

24...Qxe3+; 25.Kh2 Ne4; 26.Qb8+ Kg7.

The threat is ...Nxg3, then ...Bd6. **27.Be5+.** 27.Re1?? fails to 27...Qxe1; 28.Bxe1 Bd6+; 29.Qxd6 Rxd6 and the bishop pair is insufficient compensation for the exchange.

27...Bf6; 28.Rd1!? Rxb2; 29.Rd8 Kh6!

The king is remarkably safe here, and White is the one who needs to worry about survival. **30.Bd4.** 30.Rd1 loses to 30...Bxe5+; 31.Qxe5 Rxg2+; 32.Kxg2 Qf2+; 33.Kh1 Ng3+; 30.Bxf6 Qf2!; 31.Bxg5+ Nxg5; 32.Qg3 Nf3+ forces White to give up the queen.

30...Bxd4. A slight inaccuracy, though the position is still winning. Watson pointed out that 30...Qd2 is more efficient.

31.Rxd4 Rxg2+. 31...Qf2?? is a blunder that Watson managed to avoid. White would slip out of the noose after 32.Qf8+ Kh5; 33.Bd1+! Kg6; 34.Qg8+ and the king cannot escape the checks.

32.Kxg2 Qf2+; 33.Kh1 Qf1+; 34.Kh2 Qf2+; 35.Kh1 Ng3+. White resigned, Ghinda–W.Watson, Thessaloniki Olympiad, 1988.

GOLDMAN VARIATION
1.e4 c6; 2.Nc3 d5; 3.Qf3

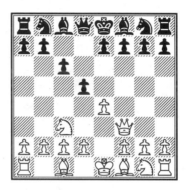

The Goldman Variation is an example of premature queen development, but it is only bad if White makes errors later. Normally, it leads to a dull equality. It is almost never seen in professional circles, but is used by amateurs as a surprise weapon.

LUTIKOV VS. PETROSIAN
Soviet Championship, 1960
1.e4 c6; 2.Nc3 d5; 3.Qf3 dxe4; 4.Nxe4 Nd7

This is played to allow ...Nf6 without the disruption of the kingside pawn structure.

5.d4. This is the usual move. 5.b4 is an original approach. 5...Qb6; 6.a3 Ngf6; 7.Bb2 a5; 8.Bc4 e6 was seen in Czebe-Molinaroli, Dresden, 1994 and here White could have captured at f6 with advantage: 9.Nxf6+ Nxf6; 10.Bxf6 gxf6; 11.b5!? cxb5 12.Rb1 Bd7 13.Bxb5 Bxb5 14.c4 and White can capture at b5 with the rook.

5.b3 Ngf6; 6.Nxf6+ (6.Ng3 was played in Lombardy-Brinck Claussen, Krakow, 1964. Now, according to ECO, Black should play 6...e6; 7.Bb2 Qa5 with an equal position. I'd prefer to be Black here) 6...Nxf6; 7.Bb2 Bg4; 8.Qg3 e6 is dead equal and was eventually drawn in Csom-Navarovszky, Kecskemet, 1968.

5...Ndf6.

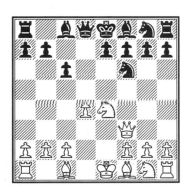

5...Ngf6; 6.Bc4 Nb6 is also playable for Black. **6.c3.** 6.Bd3 is a normal position unless Black grabs the pawn at d4. But is it safe to do so? 6...Qxd4; 7.Ne2 Qd8; 8.N2c3 g6; 9.Bg5 Bg7; 10.0–0 Nxe4; 11.Nxe4 Nf6; 12.Nxf6+ exf6; 13.Rfe1+ Be6 and Black is just a pawn up, Ozanne-Menghi, Arnhem, 1989. 6.Bc4 Bg4; 7.Qd3 Nxe4; 8.Qxe4 Nf6; 9.Qd3 e6; 10.Bg5 Be7 is fine for Black.

6...Nxe4; 7.Qxe4 Nf6; 8.Qc2 Bg4.

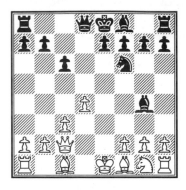

9.Ne2. Developing the bishop is no better. 9.Be2 Bxe2; 10.Qxe2 10...e6 is equal. 10.Nxe2 e6; 11.Bf4 Be7; 12.0–0 0–0; 13.h3 Qb6; 14.Qb3 Qxb3; 15.axb3 is also even, with White's pressure on the a-file compensating for the doubled pawns, Oldach-Niebling, World Seniors, 1997. 9.Bd3 Bh5; 10.Ne2 Bg6; 11.0–0 Bxd3; 12.Qxd3 is also about even.

9...e6; 10.Ng3 Qd5; 11.f3 Bh5; 12.Nxh5 Qxh5; 13.Bf4 Nd5; 14.Bg3 Qg5; 15.Qd2 Be7.

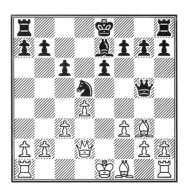

This position was agreed drawn in Lutikov-Petrosian, Soviet Championship 1960. There is plenty of play left, and the strong knight at d5 guarantees that Black's chances are at least equal, despite White's control of the bishop pair.

ULYSSES GAMBIT

1.e4 c6; 2.d4 d5; 3.Nf3 dxe4; 4.Ng5.

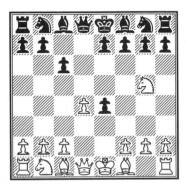

The Ulysses Gambit is not without some justification. White's knight move is not unusual in many of the Caro-Kann lines. It is now a very common reply to 1.e4 c6; 2.d4 d5; 3.Nc3 dxe4; 4.Nxe4 Nd7; 5.Ng5. The gambit is not even mentioned in ECO, but it is becoming more popular in gambit circles.

NAKAMURA VS. SCHILLER
Hawaii International, 1995

The true test must be in accepting the gambit, but I was in no mood to test the home preparation of my opponent and returned the pawn before too long.

1.e4 c6; 2.d4 d5; 3.Nf3 dxe4; 4.Ng5 Nf6; 5.Bc4 e6; 6.Nc3 Nbd7.

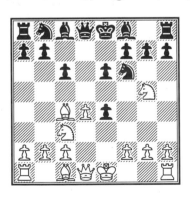

An improvised defense. I didn't want to determine the fate of my dark-squared bishop just yet. 6...Be7; 7.0-0 0-0; 8.Ncxe4 Nxe4; 9.Nxe4 was better for White in Nakamura-Perry, Hawaii, 1986 because Black has a bad bishop which is not likely to enter the game anytime soon. White obtains a similar advantage in this game.

6...b5 is perhaps playable. The plan is reminiscent of the Semi-Slav, but the queenside formation is quite different here, with the pawn back at c2 and the e-pawn gone from the board. Of course this involves a positional concession in that the pawn structure is weak and the bishop at c8 remains very bad.

Perhaps Black can take the initiative, for example: 7.Be2 Bb4!; 8.0-0 Bxc3; 9.bxc3 h6; 10.Nh3 0-0 where Black holds on to the pawn, though White has some compensation in the bishop pair and Black suffers from a miserable bishop at c8, which might be activated by an early ...e5.

The next sequence of moves in the game is predictable.

7.0-0 h6; 8.Ngxe4 Nxe4; 9.Nxe4 Nf6; 10.Qd3 Be7; 11.Be3 Qc7; 12.Rad1.

White certainly stands better here, with equal material, better development, and considerable pleasure from the awful bishop at c8. I decided to get the bishop into the game by fianchettoing it at b7 and playing an early ...c5.

12...b6; 13.f3 Bb7; 14.Rfe1 Rd8. There is no rush to play ...c5 right away, since Black has not finished developing.

15.Bf2 0-0; 16.Bg3 Qd7; 17.h3 c5.

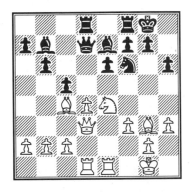

White now chose to support the pawn at d4 with **18.c3**. 18.dxc5 Qxd3; 19.Bxd3 (19.Rxd3 Nxe4; 20.fxe4 Rxd3; 21.Bxd3 Bxc5+ gives Black the better endgame) 19...Nxe4; 20.Bxe4 Rxd1; 21.Rxd1 Bxe4; 22.fxe4 Bxc5+; 23.Bf2 Bxf2+; 24.Kxf2 Rc8; 25.c3 Rc7 should be drawn, eventually.

18...cxd4; 19.cxd4 Bd5. White now prepares for an exchange at c4. **20.b3! Bc6.** 20...Bxc4; 21.bxc4 gives White control of the center.

21.a4 Nd5; 22.Nf2? Black overlooks the threats on the dark squares.

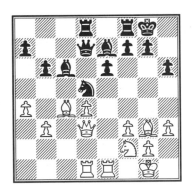

22...Bb4! White had nothing better than to give up the exchange with **23.Ng4 Bxe1; 24.Bxe1,** but after **24...Nf4!; 25.Qe3 Ng6.** Black consolidated and eventually exploited the extra material to win.

MIESES GAMBIT

MIESES VS. DAVIDSON
Scheveningen, 1923
1.e4 c6; 2.d4 d5; 3.Be3 dxe4.

Another variation on the Blackmar-Diemer theme. It is nowhere to be found in some opening referecnces, but may appear from time to time in amateur games.

4.Nd2. 4.Nc3 Nf6; 5.f3 Bf5 is good for Black, because against such a defense the White bishop usually performs more effectively from g5. **4...Nf6; 5.c3.** 5.f3 is a more Diemerish move. 5...Nd5 is so simple and strong, one wonders why Black even considers capturing on f3 or defending the pawn at e4, though those plans are often seen. **5...Bf5.** Black's extra pawn is not so important in and of itself, but it does play an important role in limiting the mobility of White's forces and hindering natural development.

6.Qc2 e6; 7.h3 Nbd7; 8.g4 Bg6; 9.Bg2. White is now ready to recover the pawn, but the kingside has been weakened irreparably. **9...Nd5 10.h4.** The threat of trapping the bishop is sidestepped in an aggressive fashion.

10...f5!; 11.Ne2 Qc7; 12.h5 Bf7; 13.gxf5 exf5. The position has been transformed, and Black's extra pawn is in the bank. The central pawnroller is picking up speed. **14.Bg5 h6; 15.Bh4 Bd6; 16.Bh3.**

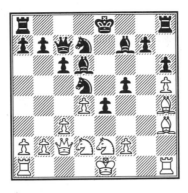

Although Black has not castled, the e-file is ready for action! **16...e3! 17.Nc4.** 17.fxe3 Nxe3 is clearly better for Black.

17...exf2+ 18.Bxf2 0–0–0; 19.Nxd6+ Qxd6; 20.Bxf5.

White has regained the pawn, but is still at a disadvantage, as the king is exposed in the center.

20...N5b6. This indirectly prevents castling queenside, as the pawn at a2 would be left undefended. 20...Rde8; 21.0–0–0 Ne3! was a better plan. **21.Bg3.** 21.0–0–0 Bxa2; 22.Rhg1 Rhf8 gives Black a strong game.

21...Qd5; 22.Be4 Qe6; 23.Bf5 Qd5; 24.Be4 Qe6? Black has the advantage, so there is no reason to settle for a draw. **25.Bf5 Qd5.** The game should have ended in a draw by repetition, but White decides to play on.

26.Rh4 Be6; 27.Be4 Qg5; 28.Bg6 Rhf8; 29.Rh2 Nf6; 30.Bh4 Qa5; 31.Rf2 Ng4; 32.Rxf8 Rxf8; 33.Qe4 Qd5.

White is eager to get the queens off the board, given the vulnerability of the king, but the exchange should have taken place at e4, rather than d5.

34.Qxd5?! Nxd5. Now the Black knights have excellent posts. **35.Kd2 Kd7; 36.b3 Nde3; 37.Be4 Nf1+; 38.Kd3 Nf2+; 39.Bxf2 Rxf2; 40.Re1.**

We have often mentioned the weakness of a pawn at h5. Here it is the most important factor in the endgame.

40...Bf7!; 41.Bg6 Rf3+; 42.Kc2 Bxg6+; 43.hxg6 Ng3; 44.Nxg3 Rxg3. The brutal liquidation of minor pieces gives Black a winning endgame.

45.Rf1 Rxg6; 46.Rf7+ Kc8. Black resigned.

INDIAN ATTACK
1.e4 c6; 2.d3

When White refrains from exercising the privilege of occupying the center, Black has an easy game. The most principled response is to take over the center right away, by playing ...e5 and ...d5. We can then develop a bishop at d6 and bring a knight to either f6 or e7, followed by kingside castling. There are no significant weaknesses on the kingside, though we will want to keep an eye on the f5-square. Black's theater of operations is the queenside, unless White chooses that territory, in which case we can launch a kingside attack.

LJUBOJEVIC VS. KARPOV
Linares, 1992
1.e4 c6; 2.d3 d5; 3.Nd2 e5; 4.Ngf3 Bd6

White has to fianchetto the bishop at g2, since the f1–a6 diagonal is blocked by the pawn at d3. Often, the queen is developed to e2, sometimes right away, as in this game. White hopes to create enough pressure on the e-file to bring results. Our options as Black include rapid kingside castling, sometimes even temporarily sacrificing the pawn at e5.

5.Qe2. 5.g3 is the immediate implementation of the fianchetto. Play can transpose into our main game if White later plays Qe2, but more often one sees a rook at e1 providing the firepower on the e-file. 5...Nf6; 6.Bg2 0–0; 7.0–0 Re8.

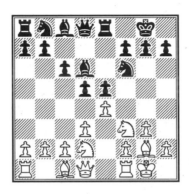

The preceding moves need no explanation. At this point, White must do something other than simple development, as there is nothing to be done with the dark squared bishop for the moment. The h-pawn can advance to h3, but this weakens the kingside slightly. Black will just retreat the bishop, as there is no need to concede the bishop pair by capturing at f3. Normally White swings the rook to e1. 8.Re1.

8.h3 Nbd7; 9.a3 a5; 10.Re1 Qc7 looks very comfortable for Black. 8.b3 weakens the dark squares so Black should play 8...d4 with a superior game.

8...Nbd7; 9.a4. (9.c3 is another try by the Yugoslav theoretician. 9...dxe4; 10.dxe4 Qc7; 11.Qc2 a5; 12.Nc4 Bf8; 13.a4 b5; 14.Na3 Ba6; 15.Bf1 Reb8; 16.b3 h6 was about equal in Ljubojevic-Karpov, Buenos Aires, 1980) 9...a5; 10.b3 was played in Planinc-Razuvayev, Polanica Zdroj, 1979. Advancing the d-pawn would now have been thematic. 10...d4; 11.Nh4 Bb4; 12.Nf5 Bc3; 13.Rb1 Nc5. Black has more chances on the queenside than White does on the kingside.

5.Be2 is wimpy. White is playing a sort of reversed Philidor Defense. 5...Ne7; 6.0–0 0–0; 7.Re1 f5; 8.c3 Nd7; 9.Bf1 Kh8; 10.g3 fxe4; 11.dxe4 Ng6; 12.Bg2 Nf6. Black has a thoroughly acceptable position, with good prospects on the kingside, Ljubojevic-Lobron, Indonesia, 1983.

Getting back to 5.Qc2, we see it is a preliminary to either the fianchetto line or an enterprising gambit. **5...Nf6.**

We will look at the fianchetto plan in our main game. 6.exd5 cxd5; 7.Nxe5 0–0 is an interesting sacrifice. Karpov's opinion is that Black has sufficient compensation, and I agree.

8.d4 Re8; 9.Ndf3 Nc6; 10.c3 Ng4 gets the pawn back with interest. 11.Be3 Ngxe5; 12.Nxe5 Nxe5; 13.dxe5 Rxe5; 14.Qd2 Bf5; 15.Be2 Qh4; 16.Qd4 Qxd4; 17.Bxd4 Re6 is likely to lead to a draw.

6.d4 is perhaps a surprising move, since the pawn has already moved once. Yet it is taken as the main line in the 1997 edition of the *Encyclopedia of Chess Openings*, where it is argued that it leads to an advantage for White. The game in which it was introduced, Timman-Seirawan, Linares, 1992, was a battle of two top theoreticians in the Caro-Kann, and it deserves careful study.

6...dxe4; 7.Nxe5 Bf5; 8.h3 h5; 9.Ndc4! (9.Rg1 h4; 10.g4 hxg3; 11.Rxg3 led to unclear complications in another contest between the same players, the very same year, in Ljubojevic-Karpov, Roquebrune, 1992.)

9...Be7; 10.Bd2! Nbd7; 11.0–0–0 Nb6; 12.Ne3!? (12.Ba5 is interesting. Seirawan indicates that this move would have given White the advantage, but I am by no means convinced. 12...Nfd5 prepares to kick out the enemy knight with ...f6) 12...Be6; 13.Ba5? (13.c4! would have been stronger. 13...Nfd7; 14.Ba5 Nxe5; 15.dxe5 Qc7; 16.Qc2 Qxe5; 17.Bc3 Qg5; 18.Qxe4 Na4; 19.Bd4 Nc5 can lead to an endgame after 20.Qe5 Qxe5; 21.Bxe5 Ne4 with a good game for Black) 13...Bxa2! Seirawan safely consumed the pawn at a2 and held the advantage.

Returning to the fianchetto plan, we must consider the position after **6.g3 0–0; 7.Bg2 Re8; 8.0–0.**

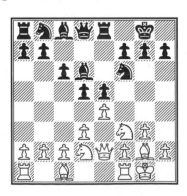

8...a5! It is time to play on the queenside. White must advance the a-pawn. **9.a3.** 9.a4 is met by 9...Na6. **9...a4.**

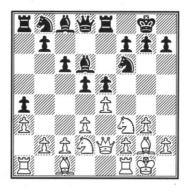

Black can be satisfied with the opening so far. There are no hindrances to the completion of the development process. White, however, has problems activating the dark-squared bishop. The normal King's Indian Attack with h4, Nf1–h2 and kingside aggression is far too slow here. Ljubojevic opts to play on the queenside instead.

10.b4 axb3; 11.cxb3 Bg4; 12.Bb2 Nbd7; 13.h3 Bh5.

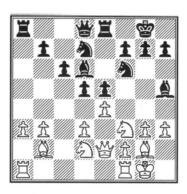

Black's position is a joy to play. All the pieces are on useful squares except the queen, whose future has not yet been determined. The Black pawn structure is far superior to White's, and the center is well controlled.

14.Qe3. 14.g4 Bg6; 15.Nh4 Nc5!? is better for Black, according to Karpov. Indeed, the White queenside pawns look very weak and may be ripe for the plucking in the endgame. **14...d4.** 14...Qe7! is stronger, according to Karpov. 15.b4 d4; 16.Qe1 Bxf3!; 17.Bxf3 b5. Black will soon break open the game with ...c5.

15.Qe1 b5; 16.Qc1 Ra6; 17.Qc2 Bxf3; 18.Bxf3 Qb6; 19.Rfc1 Rea8; 20.Nb1! White reorganizes and tries to defend all the weak squares. **20...Qd8.** 20...h5!? might have been stronger. 21.h4 g6; 22.Bd1 Bf8. Black threatens ...Bh6.

21.Bd1 Nf8; 22.Qe2 Qe7; 23.Kg2 Ne6; 24.Rc2 Nc5; 25.Nd2 Ne6; 26.Nb1 h5; 27.h4 g6; 28.Bc1 Qd7; 29.Rca2 Ng4; 30.Qc2 Be7; 31.Bf3 Kg7; 32.a4 Nf6; 33.Bd2 Nc5; 34.Be1. 34.Bb4?? would lose instantly to 34...Nxd3.

34...Qe6; 35.Nd2 R6a7; 36.Be2 Na6; 37.Nf3 Nb4; 38.Bxb4 Bxb4; 39.Ng5 Qd7; 40.axb5 Rxa2; 41.Rxa2 Rxa2; 42.Qxa2 cxb5.

The flurry of exchanges at time control has left Black with a better bishop. Karpov shows his superior endgame technique and builds his tiny advantage into a decisive one, with quite a bit of help from his opponent.

43.Qa6 Ne8; 44.Nf3 f6; 45.Ng1 Nd6; 46.Qb6?! Too adventurous. **46...Qb7!; 47.Qd8?** The queen does not have enough room to maneuver. White should have exchanged queens, though the endgame would be difficult. 47.Qxb7+ Nxb7; 48.Bd1 Nc5; 49.Bc2 would not be easy for Black to win, though the king might eventually infiltrate via b4.

47...Nf7; 48.Qe8? 48.Qd5 was better. Keeping the queens on was not the best strategy. **48...Be7!** Suddenly the White queen is out of escape squares! 49...Nd6 is a real threat.

49.Bxh5 gxh5. White's piece sacrifice does not stave off defeat for long. **50.Nh3 f5; 51.f3 fxe4; 52.fxe4 b4; 53.Nf2 Qc7; 54.Kf1 Qd6; 55.Kg2 Bd8; 56.Nh3 Qg6; 57.Kh2 Qg4; 58.Qb5 Qe2+; 59.Kg1 Qd1+; 60.Kg2 Qxb3. White resigned.**

HEROES OF THE CARO-KANN DEFENSE

THE FOUNDING FATHERS
Horation Caro

Horatio Caro was an Englishman, living in Berlin. He lived from 1862 to 1920, and is generally considered to have been an International Master in strength. He both played and wrote about his favorite defense, which quickly established him as an authority on the line. His preference after the normal 1.e4 c6; 2.d4 d5; 3.Nc3 dxe4; 4.Nxe4 was to play 4...Nf6, and after 5.Nxf6+, recapture with the e-pawn. This system is not seen very often as the pawn structure permanently favors White. We take a look at it in the following game, played at one of the grandest events of 100 years ago.

PILLSBURY VS. CARO
Vienna, 1898
1.e4 c6; 2.d4 d5; 3.Nc3 dxe4; 4.Nxe4 Nf6; 5.Nxf6+ exf6.

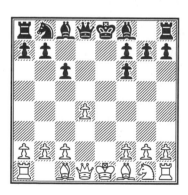

The Caro Defense, or "Original Caro-Kann" has been discarded, for the most part. White has a permanent queenside pawn majority. Black will suffer in this line, though sometimes the open diagonals and files give some counterplay for Black's rooks and bishops.

6.Nf3. 6.Bc4 is the usual move today. Queens will be exchanged on the e-file, and an early endgame is normal, with White having an advantage. **6...Bd6; 7.Bd3 Bg4?!** 7...0-0; 8.0-0 Bg4 is stronger, as in Kuijpers-Flohr, Amsterdam, 1963. White does not dare to weaken the kingside pawn structure with the advance of the kingside pawns because he has already castled on that side.

8.h3 Bh5? 8...Qe7+ is not quite so bad. **9.g4 Bg6; 10.Nh4 Nd7; 11.Nf5 Bxf5; 12.Bxf5.** White has the bishop pair as well as the better pawn structure. **12...g6; 13.Qe2+ Qe7; 14.Bxd7+!** Returning the minor exchange, White forces the Black king to move.

14...Kxd7; 15.Be3. White wants to keep queens on the board. **15...Rae8; 16.d5.**

White is clearly better, according to modern human authorities. Computers don't see much, if any, advantage in the White position but there are several long-term factors, including the weakness of f6, h6, and a7, the queenside pawn majority, and the safer White king, that add up to a problematic situation for Black.

16...c5; 17.Qb5+ Kc8; 18.0-0-0 Qc7; 19.Rd3. White is attacking at a furious pace. **19...Re4; 20.Rc3 a6; 21.Qd3.** This wins the c-pawn. **21...Rhe8; 22.Bxc5 Kd7.** 22...Bxc5; 23.d6 Qc6; 24.d7+ wins material for White.

23.Be3 Qa5; 24.a3 b5; 25.Rc6 Bf4; 26.Kb1 Bxe3; 27.fxe3 Rxe3; 28.Qd4!

The holes at g6 and a7 are exploited and Black could resign, but showed the spectators why even winning a rook here is fatal. **28...Re1+; 29.Ka2 Rxh1; 30.Qa7+** with mate in two. We acknowledge Horatio Caro for his inspiration, but his efforts have little to do with the modern handling of the Caro-Kann Defense.

Marcus Kann

Marcus Kann was a minor figure in 19th century chess. He was born in Vienna in 1820 and lived there until his death in 1886. He participated in the great German Chess Congress of 1885, at which the following game took place.

MIESES - KANN
Hamburg, 1885

1.e4 c6; 2.d4 d5; 3.e5 The Advance Variation was not well regarded at the time, and White's third move was criticized in the tournament book.

3...Bf5; 4.Bd3 Bxd3; 5.Qxd3 e6; 6.f4.

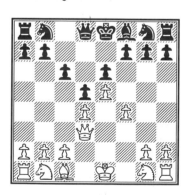

This structure invites counterplay at c5, and the game resembles a French Defense, with the important difference that the light-squared bishops are gone from the board. **6...c5.** Without a "bad bishop" at c8, Black has a very comfortable position.

7.c3 Nc6; 8.Nf3 Qb6; 9.0–0 Nh6. Another important factor is the excellent blockading post at f5. **10.b3 cxd4; 11.cxd4 Nf5; 12.Bb2 Rc8.** White is tied down to the defense of the d-pawn.

13.a3? 13.Rc1 was best, but Black has a much better bishop. Just how strong the bishop is can be seen in the game.

13...Ncxd4!; 14.Nxd4. 14.Bxd4 Nxd4; 15.Nxd4 Bc5; 16.Rd1 loses as in the game. **14...Bc5; 15.Rd1.** 15.Kh1 Bxd4; 16.Bxd4 Qxd4; 17.Qxd4 Nxd4; 18.Nd2 Ke7 gives Black an extra pawn in the endgame.

15...Nxd4; 16.Bxd4 Bxd4+; 17.Qxd4 Rc1!

This is a classic position, exploiting two pins at once, on the back rank and the a7-g1 diagonal.

18.Kf2 Rxd1; 19.Qxb6 axb6; 20.Ke2. A modern player would no doubt resign here. **20...Rc1; 21.Kd2 Rg1; 22.g3 Kd7; 23.a4 Rc8; 24.b4 Rcc1. White resigned.**

HYPERMODERN SUPPORT
Aron Nimzowitsch

Although Nimzowitsch preferred non-Classical lines, rather fitting for one of the leaders of the Hypermodern Revolution, he did play the Caro-Kann Defense and heaped enthusiastic praise on it. Here is an excerpt from his foreword to Hans Müller's classic book on the opening: "When 1...e5 has seen its final act, when 1...Nf6 or 1...c5 or even 1...e6 have taken their place in the display case of rarities, 1...c6 will always live and bloom. This openings is inspired by the genuine modern spirit. Not faster and faster development, but rather solidity, combined with a lasting initiative is the story."

LEVENFISH-NIMZOWITSCH
Vilnius, 1912

Nimzowitsch understood that a symmetrical pawn structure does not always lead to drawish positions. He was an expert in handling various Exchange Variations, and gave instructions on how to break the symmetry in his classic book *Chess Praxis*.

1.e4 c6; 2.c4 e6 This is a very slow plan, but it is not bad if you are willing to defend the ...e6 lines in the Panov Attack. It is played by modern Grandmasters such as Shabalov. **3.Nf3.** 3.d4 d5; 4.exd5 cxd5; 5.Nc3 Nf6 reaches the normal Panov Attack lines with 5...e6, if White is so inclined.

3...d5; 4.exd5 exd5; 5.cxd5 cxd5; 6.Bb5+ Nc6.

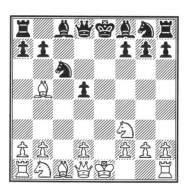

The obvious move is to castle here, as in the game, but an interesting alternative was seen in Gulko-Shabalov, Bern, 1992. **7.0–0.** 7.Qe2+ Qe7; 8.Ne5 Bd7; 9.Bxc6 was played in the cited game, and Gulko evaluates 9...Bxc6; 10.0–0 0–0–0 as slightly better for White.

7...Bd6; 8.d4 Nge7; 9.Bg5 f6. Black does not mind the slight weakening of the kight squares to get rid of the annoying pin.

10.Bh4 0–0; 11.Nbd2 Bg4.

12.Bxc6? I like Keene's description of this move: "A very strange move which is based on the pursuit of a tactical chimera." White expects Black to take with the pawn, because it seems that there is a danger on the a2-g8 diagonal.

12...Nxc6; 13.Qb3 Bb4; 14.Ne5.

This is the position White was aiming for, with pins all over the place. Black responds by giving up the dark squared bishop, after which the knight becomes a pesky invader.

14...Nxe5; 15.Qxb4 Nd3; 16.Qxb7 Be2. White should probably just give up the exchange here. **17.Rfb1? Rc8!** Nimzowitsch suggested that there was some humor in the infiltration of the rook, which is powerfully centralized on the open file.

18.Nf1 g5; 19.Bg3 f5. The wall is closing in on the dark-squared bishop, which must take refuge in the center of the board. **20.Be5 Rf7; 21.Qa6 f4.**

White senses the danger and now offers a little material to try to reduce the pressure.

22.Re1 Nxe1; 23.Qxe2. White perhaps forgot that there is a tactical trick at g2, based on a potential fork by an advancing Black f-pawn. **23...Nxg2!; 24.Nd2 Nh4; 25.Nf3 Ng6; 26.Kh1.** The White king tries to hide in the corner, but there is no defense.

26...g4!; 27.Nd2 Qd7; 28.Rg1 Rc2; 29.h3 g3. White resigned.

THE STANDARD BEARERS
Salo Flohr

Flohr had a quiet style. He would lie in wait for his opponent, like a coiled snake, ready to strike out if provoked but otherwise willing to sit still for as long as it takes. In the following game, he shows his ability to demolish opponents who overplay the position. White had several chances to escape his gloomy fate, but cracked under the relentless pressure of Flohr's deep moves. He was best known for playing the 4...Nd7 line which used to bear his name, but has now been transferred to Anatoly Karpov.

VAN DEN BOSCH-FLOHR
Hague (Match), 1932

1.e4 c6; 2.d4 d5; 3.Nc3 dxe4; 4.Bc4 Nf6; 5.f3 e3. Giving back the pawn is not necessary, but it is a reasonable defense because

White has already weakened the kingside and the a7-g1 diagonal. Indeed, the dark squares prove to be White's undoing in this game. **6.Bxe3 Bf5; 7.Nge2 e6.**

Black wants to play solidly. White wants to mix it up. Typical Caro-Kann situation! **8.g4?!** A very weakening move. **8...Bg6; 9.h4 h6; 10.Nf4 Bh7.**

11.Qd2. 11.g5 hxg5; 12.hxg5 meets with a nasty surprise. 12...Bxc2!; 13.Rxh8 Bxd1; 14.gxf6 Qxf6; 15.Rxd1 g5 and White loses more material. **11...Nd5!** Against all of White's aggression, this solid move serves notice that the Black position has no weaknesses.

12.Ncxd5 cxd5; 13.Bb5+ Nd7; 14.g5 a6. White's position is looking more and more disjointed. **15.Be2.** 15.g6 axb5; 16.gxh7 Nf6 leaves White with a horrible position.

15...Qb6; 16.g6. Aggressive, and perhaps not necessary. 16.0–0–0 Bb4; 17.c3 Rc8; 18.Nd3 Bxd3; 19.Qxd3 Qa5; 20.Kb1 would have been stronger. **16...Bxg6; 17.Nxg6 fxg6; 18.0–0–0 Be7; 19.Rdg1.**

There is no saving the pawn at g6, but Black wants to extract a price. White has a beautiful light-squared bishop, but it will have to leave the board if the g-pawn is to be recovered.

19...Nf8!; 20.Bd3 0-0-0. Now White can have the pawn. **21.Bxg6 Nxg6; 22.Rxg6 Bf6.** It is instructive to observe how Flohr takes advantage of possibilities along the third rank. **23.c3 Rhf8!** Black sets up threats against the pawn at f3. **24.f4.** gets the pawn to a stronger square, but turns the bishop at e3 into a joker.

24...Rd6!; 25.f5. White fears a coming minority attack on the queenside, so tries to reactivate the bishop. **25...exf5; 26.Qd3 Bd8; 27.Rxg7 Rg6!; 28.Rxg6 Qxg6.**

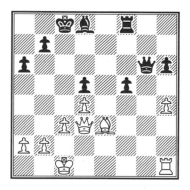

White should still be able to hold the position, with a sensible move like 29.Bf4. Instead, White moves the queen to the c1–h6 diagonal, but freely gives up the pin on the f-pawn.

29.Qd2?! f4! A wonderful little sac that allows Black to activate all of the pieces. **30.Bf2.** 30.Bxf4 Qe4; 31.Rf1 Bc7 and the pin wins. **30...f3; 31.Qe3?** 31.Rg1 Qh5; 32.Qe3 Bc7 would let White escape with 33.Qe6+ Kb8; 34.Rg8 Bf4+; 35.Kc2 Rxg8; 36.Qxg8+ Ka7; 37.Qe6! Black cannot easily make progress. **31...Bc7!; 32.Qe1 Bf4+; 33.Be3 Re8. White resigned**.

HARRY GOLOMBEK

Golombek was one of the best British players of his day, and his writings were familiar to many lovers of the game both in book form and in his reports as chess correspondent of the *Times* of London. He held the titles of Grandmaster and International Arbiter. A life-long fan of the Caro-Kann, he set forth three goals for White in the opening, with which Black should be familiar: rapid development, control of e5 and the b8-h2 diagonal in general, and the avoidance of a weakness at d4. He felt that the Caro-Kann was so strong that White should not even play 2.d4, though few authorities ever agreed with him on that point.

BROADBENT VS GOLOMBEK
British Championship Playoff, 1947

Golombek shows how effective a fianchetto defense can be against the Exchange Variation, and it is a fully respectable alternative to the defense we presented in our repertoire. This game is also a veritable lesson in the art of tactics and combinative play. Who says the Caro-Kann is dull?

1.e4 c6; 2.d4 d5; 3.exd5 cxd5; 4.Bd3 Nc6; 5.c3 Nf6; 6.Bf4 g6.

This is one of Black's reliable plans. The fianchetto formation is not easy to attack, but Black must beware of playing too passively. In particular, it is not a good idea to play for ...e5 unless there is support from a pawn at f6. Golombek demonstrates the proper strategy.

7.Nf3 Bg7; 8.Nbd2 0-0; 9.0-0 Nh5; 10.Bg3. 10.Be3 is better. **10...Nxg3; 11.hxg3 Bg4.** All of this is eminently sensible. Both sides develop and Black eliminates the powerful enemy bishop. **12.Qb3 Rb8.**

An odd move, but safe when White has no dark-squared bishop. Chigorin was fond of placing a rook behind the b-pawn when appropriate. **13.Rfe1 Qd6; 14.Rad1 b5!** The minority attack is launched, and the presence of the rook at b8 gives it added power.

15.a3 Rfe8; 16.Be2 Na5; 17.Qb4 Nc4! White can never capture this knight because after ...bxc4 there is destruction on the b-file. **18.Qb3.** Trading queens leads to an uncomfortable position for White after 18.Qxd6 exd6; 19.Bxc4 bxc4; 20.Rxe8+ Rxe8; 21.Re1 Rxe1+; 22.Nxe1 Bh6. Black threatens ...Bc1, and the doubled d-pawns effectively keep the enemy knights at bay. **18...f6!**

This is necessary preparation for the advance of the e-pawn. Although the Caro-Kann has an unjustified reputation for leading to cramped positions for Black, here it is White who is suffocating.

19.Nh2 Bf5; 20.Bf3 Kh8; 21.Nhf1 Bh6! This is a much better home for the bishop. **22.Be2 a5; 23.f4?!** I don't like this obvious move, because the center gets blasted open. 23.Bf3 would have been safer. **23...Qc7; 24.Bf3 Red8; 25.Ne3 Nxe3; 26.Rxe3 e5!**

White is now struggling to survive. Black has plenty of support in the center, and the pin on the f-pawn is an immediate concern. White tries to take the seventh rank, but Black doesn't fall for it.

27.Rde1. 27.dxe5 is answered by a new pin with 27...Qb6!; 28.Rde1 fxe5 and the f-pawn falls. I haven't seen this many pins since the film *Hellraiser*.

27...Qb6!; 28.dxe5 fxe5; 29.Kh1 exf4; 30.Re7 fxg3. White's situation is hopeless. All Black has to do is get to the h-file, and the funeral of the White monarch can't be far off. The desperate sacrifice at e4 only prolongs the suffering.

31.Ne4 Bxe4; 32.Bxe4 Bf8! The rook is trapped. **33.Bxd5 Bxe7; 34.Rxe7 Qd6!** Another double attack brings the game to a close. **35.Rf7 Qxd5!** A terminal exploitation of the back rank. **36.Rf8+ Rxf8!** White resigned.

MIKHAIL BOTVINNIK

Botvinnik used solid, classical openings throughout his career. The French Defense and Caro-Kann were infused with new life through Botvinnik's deep exploration of critical variations. In his World Championship matches with Mikhail Tal, the Caro-Kann played a pivotal role. In the 9th game of the 1960 match, Botvinnik demonstrated his famous endgame technique to bring home the point.

TAL VS. BOTVINNIK
World Championship, 1960

1.e4 c6; 2.d4 d5; 3.Nc3 dxe4; 4.Nxe4 Bf5; 5.Ng3 Bg6; 6.N1e2.
6.Bc4 e6; 7.N1e2 is an alternative move order. It was played in three
other games between Tal and Botvinnik. 7...Nf6. (7...Bd6;; 8.h4 h6;
9.Nf4 Bxf4; 10.Bxf4 Nf6; 11.Qd2 Nbd7; 12.0-0 Nd5; 13.Rde1
N7b6; 14.Bb3 Nxf4; 15.Qxf4 was played in the 15th game of the
match. White failed to achieve anything significant in the opening.)
8.Nf4 Bd6; 9.Nxg6 (9.0-0 Nd5; 10.Ngh5 0-0; 11.Bb3 Nd7; 12.Nxg6
hxg6; 13.Ng3 Qh4 equalized in the 2nd game of the 1961 match)
9...hxg6; 10.Bg5 Nbd7; 11.0-0 Qa5 also brought equality, in the 17th
game of this match. **6...Nf6.**

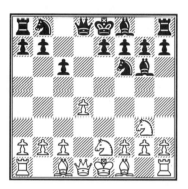

Tal tried both 7.Nf4 and 7.h4 here. **7.h4** (7.Nf4 e5; 8.Nxg6 hxg6;
9.dxe5 Qa5+; 10.Bd2 Qxe5+; 11.Qe2 Qxe2+; 12.Bxe2 Nbd7 held no
dangers for Black in a game between the same players at Moscow,
1964.) **7...h6; 8.Nf4 Bh7; 9.Bc4 e6.**

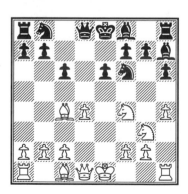

There are many move orders that can be used to reach this basic position of the Tal Attack. **10.0–0.** Two other Botvinnik games diverged here. They are included in the notes to the Tal-Vukic game in the Illustrative Games section. **10...Bd6.**

One would expect Tal to sacrifice here, and he did not disappoint. Objectively, it seems more than a little optimistic, but the Black king does come under direct attack. **11.Nxe6 fxe6; 12.Bxe6 Qc7; 13.Re1 Nbd7.** After many years, this remains the main line of the Tal Attack! **14.Bg8+.** 14.Kh1 Bxg3; 15.fxg3 Qxg3 and it is White's king that needs to be worried!

14...Kf8; 15.Bxh7 Rxh7 ;16.Nf5. Here Black wisely refrains from adventures at h2, choosing instead to get the king to safety, even at the cost of a pawn. **16...g6!** 16...Bh2+; 17.Kh1 g6; 18.Bxh6+ Rxh6; 19.Nxh6 Qf4; 20.Re3 Qxh6; 21.Kxh2 Qxh4+; 22.Kg1 Ng4; 23.Qf3+ would have given White a strong attack. **17.Bxh6+ Kg8.**

The Black king is safe. White cannot keep both bishop and knight. **18.Nxd6 Qxd6.** 18...Rxh6; 19.Re6 Rxh4; 20.Qd3 Rh6 would be less comfortable for Black. **19.Bg5 Re7; 20.Qd3.** White need not exchange rooks, as sooner or later Black is likely to do so, bringing the other rook to the e-file. 20.Rxe7 Qxe7; 21.h5 gxh5; 22.Qxh5 Nxh5; 23.Bxe7 Nf4 was possible. **20...Kg7.**

Botvinnik considers this position equal. **21.Qg3?** Tal misevaluates the endgame. White should have exchanged rooks at e7, or adopted Tal's suggestion of 21.f4. Tal wasn't guilty of carelessness, modern computers think the endgame is fine for White too! **21...Rxe1+; 22.Rxe1 Qxg3; 23.fxg3.**

White has three pawns for the piece, but there are doubled pawns, and Black's knights are well coordinated. Still, there is not all that much chance of White losing, as the Black pawns can be exchanged for White ones until there are none left. **23...Rf8!** This keeps the White king from getting into the game. Such a long-term plan is easy to overlook.

24.c4 Ng4; 25.d5 cxd5; 26.cxd5 Ndf6; 27.d6 Rf7. Sooner or later the d-pawn will fall, but White will be able to slide the king into the game. **28.Rc1 Rd7; 29.Rc7 Kf7; 30.Bxf6 Nxf6; 31.Kf2 Ke6; 32.Rxd7 Kxd7; 33.Kf3 Kxd6.**

If White could exchange all the Black pawns, then a draw would be the result. That is very difficult, however.

34.Kf4 Ke6; 35.g4 Nd5+; 36.Ke4 Nf6+; 37.Kf4 Nd5+; 38.Ke4 Nb4; 39.a3 Nc6; 40.h5.

With time control reached, Tal cleverly made his 41st move quickly, so that Botvinnik had to seal the move before adjournment. Botvinnik had to chew up a lot of clock time, but managed to find the right move. He had only twenty minutes, however, to get to the next time control at move 56.

40...g5; 41.h6 Kf6; 42.Kd5 Kg6; 43.Ke6. 43.Kd6 Na5; 44.Kc7 b5; 45.Kb8 Nc4; 46.Kxa7 Nxb2; 47.Ka6 Nc4; 48.Kxb5 Nxa3+ was analysed by Botvinnik. **43...Na5; 44.a4 Nb3; 45.Kd6 a5; 46.Kd5 Kxh6!** Although the king is far from the queenside, this move wins. **47.Kc4 Nc1; 48.Kb5 Nd3!; 49.b3 Nc1; 50.Kxa5 Nxb3+; 51.Kb4.** 1.Kb6 Kg6; 52.Kxb7 Nc5+ wins.

51...Nc1; 52.Kc3 Kg6; 53.Kc2 Ne2; 54.Kd3 Nc1+. With his flag hanging, Botvinnik buys time to reach move 56. **55.Kc2 Ne2; 56.Kd3 Nf4+; 57.Kc4 Kf6; 58.g3 Ne2. White resigned.** Magnificent endgame play by Botvinnik, much of which had to be worked out before adjournment.

Tigran Petrosian

BRONSTEIN - PETROSIAN
Leningrad, 1960

1.e4 c6; 2.Ne2.

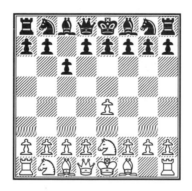

We haven't discussed this odd move yet. Petrosian brushes it off without difficulty, defeating one of the finest players of the day in under 24 moves, as Black yet!

2...d5; 3.e5 c5. Petrosian's biographer Vasiliev describes Black's move thus: "A correct rejoinder to the slightly pretentions opening system chosen by White." Black heads for a French Defense, reckoning that White's eccentric play will require the knight to lose a tempo and still not reach its natural post at f3.

4.d4 Nc6; 5.c3 e6; 6.Nd2 Nge7; 7.Nf3 cxd4.

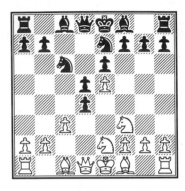

White must capture with the pawn here, of course. But Bronstein was evidently in creative mode. **8.Nexd4?** 8.cxd4 Nf5; 9.Nc3 gets the knights to their normal square, but the initiative is taken by Black, who has a permanent target at d4. 9...Qb6 creates a very awkward situation for White.

8...Ng6; 9.Nxc6 bxc6; 10.Bd3 Qc7; 11.Qe2 f6! This technique is often used in the French to undermine a pawn chain. Here it allows White to get rid of the weak pawn, but Black's center is strong. In addition, the Black king can use f7. Petrosian was fond of such plans. This is truly a contest between two great players with rather unique styles! **12.exf6 gxf6; 13.Nd4 Kf7.**

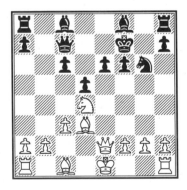

The Black king has all the defense it needs, and the Black pawn center will soon become a juggernaut. **14.f4 c5; 15.Qh5.**

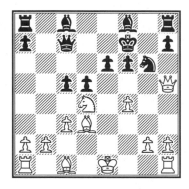

White threatens to capture at g6, since the h-pawn is pinned. Petrosian is not impressed! **15...cxd4!; 16.Bxg6+ hxg6; 17.Qxh8 dxc3; 18.Qh7+ Bg7.** White is clearly in trouble, with an exposed king, no development except the queen, and the nagging problem of ...Ba6 followed by ...Rh8, trapping the queen.

19.Be3. 19.f5 Qe5+; 20.Kd1 cxb2; 21.Qxg6+ Kf8; 22.Rb1 bxc1Q+; 23.Rxc1 Qd4+; 24.Ke2 Rb8 and the hunt is on! **19...cxb2; 20.Rd1 Ba6.** Resignation would be appropriate here. **21.f5 exf5; 22.Qh3 Qc2; 23.Qf3 Bc4. White resigned.**

MODERN HEROES
Vlastimil Hort

Hort was one of the great players of the 1960s and 1970s, and enjoyed the Caro-Kann from both sides of the board, experimenting with a variety of systems. Here we find him showing the true value of a semi-open h-file for Black.

MARIOTTI - HORT
Biel, 1982

Hort numbers this among his ten best games. The rook maneuver ...Rh4-f4 followed by the sacrifice at f3 is very instructive. I have borrowed analysis from Hort's notes in his *Begegnungen am Schachbrett*, published by Walter Rau Verlag.

1.e4 c6; 2.Nc3 d5; 3.Nf3 dxe4. Hort was fond of the Two Knights as White, and Hort had pleasant memories of a game in this line against Karpov. **4.Nxe4 Nf6; 5.Qe2.** 5.Nxf6+ exf6; 6.Be2 Bd6; 7.0-0 0-0; 8.d4 Re8; 9.Re1 Bf5; 10.Be3 Nd7; 11.h3 Be4! gave Black a good game in Karpov-Hort, Tilburg, 1979. **5...Bg4.** 5...Nxe4; 6.Qxe4 Nd7; 7.Bc4 Nf6; 8.Ne5! This is what White had in mind, forcing 8...e6 and

Black is stuck with a bad bishop.

6.h3. 6.Nxf6+ gxf6; 7.Qe4 f5 would have been followed by ...Rg8 and ...Bg7, according to Hort. **6...Bh5; 7.Ng3 Bg6; 8.Ne5 Nbd7; 9.Nxg6 hxg6.**

The hunt for the bishop has taken too much time, and White's Bf1 has difficulty getting into the game.. **10.b3.** 10.d4 would have been more logical. **10...e6; 11.Bb2 Qa5.** Black pins the d-pawn and covers the rank. The rook will come to h4, and Black dominates the open ranks. **12.a3 Rh4!; 13.Qf3.** White wants to swing the queen to c3.

13...Bd6; 14.Be2 Rf4! 14...Ne5; 15.Qe3 Nd5; 16.Qg5 Nf4 looks good, since the rook cannot be captured because of the fork at g2, but White plays 17.Kf1! Black is left without a useful move. **15.Qd3 Qc7; 16.Bf3 Be5; 17.c3.** 17.0-0-0 Bxb2+; 18.Kxb2 Ne5; 19.Qe2 Nxf3; 20.gxf3 is no fun for White. **17...Bd6; 18.Qc2?**

Hort now demolishes the enemy kingside. 18.Qe2 Qb6; 19.0-0

Qxb3 gives up a pawn, but Hort indicates that the position is not so clear. A plausible continuation is 20.d4 Nb6; 21.Rfb1 Qc4 and even after 22.Qxc4 Nxc4; 23.Bc1 the exchange sacrifice is possible. 23...Rxf3; 24.gxf3 b6; 25.Ne4 Bc7 and White's rooks look rather pathetic. Chances should be about equal.

18...Rxf3!; 19.gxf3 Bxg3; 20.fxg3 Qxg3+; 21.Kf1. 21.Ke2 Qg2+; 22.Ke3 Nd5+; 23.Kd4 e5+; 24.Kc4 b5+; 25.Kd3 Qxf3#. **21...Qxf3+; 22.Kg1 Qg3+.** Hort was probably concerned about time pressure and threw in a few repetitions to edge closer to move 40.

23.Kf1 Qf3+; 24.Kg1 Ne4. Black could resign here. The end is inevitable. **25.d4.** 25.Rh2 Ng5; 26.Rg2 Nxh3+; 27.Kh2 Nf4 and **Black wins**. **25...Qe3+; 26.Kg2 Qg3+; 27.Kf1 Qf3+; 28.Kg1 Qe3+; 29.Kg2 Qg5+; 30.Kf1 Ng3+; 31.Kg2 Nf5+; 32.Kh2 Qg3#.**

Bent Larsen

The fighting nature of Bent Larsen led him to the Bronstein-Larsen Variation (1.e4 c6; 2.d4 d5; 3.Nc3 dxe4; 4.Nxe4 Nf6; 5.Nxf6+ gxf6) so in our collection we find his games primarily in the non-Classical lines. It would be remiss of me not to give an example of Larsen in his pet variation, so here is one of his most interesting games, played in what was perhaps the most successful tournament of Larsen's career, the great Clarin tournament of 1979, where he demolished a superstar field.

SPASSKY VS. LARSEN
Buenos Aires, 1979
1.e4 c6; 2.d4 d5; 3.Nc3 dxe4; 4.Nxe4 Nf6; 5.Nxf6+ gxf6.

Larsen is closely identified with this dynamic approach to the Caro-Kann. Indeed, Ray Keene calls it the Dynamic Caro-Kann, while others call it the Bronstein-Larsen Variation. Of course the opening had a long tradition before David Bronstein and Bent Larsen took it up. It dates back to Nimzowitsch, the first player to really understand the structure. Larsen is perhaps most responsible for popularizing the opening, defeating top players with it. **6.Be2** White can choose among a variety of formations.

In ECO, where the variation has the code B16, only 6.c3 is indicated as leading to an advantage for White, and a small one at that. Still, only former World Championship candidate Kevin Spraggett of Canada uses it regularly. It does feature in the repertoire of some rising stars, such as Jennie Frenklakh. **6...Bf5.** White's move order prevents Black from placing the bishop at g4, which is the usual reply to an early Nf3. **7.Nf3 Qc7; 8.0–0 e6; 9.c4 Nd7; 10.d5.**

White's play is strong, and formed the model for an important game a few years later. During some of this fruitful period for the variation I was based in England, writing quite a bit on openings. One of my first assignments, for the journal *New Chess Player*, was to do a survey of the theory of this opening.

10...0–0–0; 11.Be3. 11.Nd4 Bg6; 12.Be3 e5; 13.Nb3 Kb8; 14.Qe1 Rg8; 15.dxc6 gave White the advantage in Ciric-Dlugy, Manchester, 1981. Future Grandmaster Maxim Dlugy was too young at the time to enjoy the gifts from the sponsor—Benedictine Liquer! Dlugy relied on the opening for some time, early in his career.

11...c5; 12.b4 Rg8.

White gives into temptation and captures on c5, but that turns out to be a strategic mistake.

13.bxc5? 13.Kh1 Be4; 14.bxc5 Nxc5; activates the pin on the d-file. 13...Bxc5; 14.Nd4?! Bh3! This wins the exchange. 15.g3. 15.Bf3 Rxg2+; 16.Bxg2 Rg8; 17.Qf3 Bxg2; 18.Qxg2 Rxg2+; 19.Kxg2 Qe5 should win for Black. 15...Bxf1; 16.Bxf1 (16.Kxf1 Ne5; 17.f4 Ng6 is also good for Black) 16...Ne5; 17.Rb1 Ng4; 18.Bc1? (18.Bg2 was the lesser evil) 18...Nxe3; 19.fxe3 Qe5; 20.Qb3 b6; 21.Qa4 would have led to a favorable endgame for Black on 21...Bxd4; 22.Qc6+ Qc7; 23.Qxc7+ Kxc7; 24.exd4 Rg4. **18...h5!** The kingside attack begins. **19.Rb3 h4; 20.Ba3 hxg3; 21.hxg3 f5!**

Black has tremendous pressure on the a7-g1 diagonal and on the g-file. The pawn at g3 is weaker than it looks. White must exchange bishops. **22.Bxc5 Qxc5; 23.Rb5 Qd6; 24.Qb3 f4**. Larsen has no fear. He carries out the attack, not showing any concern for the arrival of the White rook at b7. The Black queen provides all the defense needed, and the h-file is open for infiltration.

25.Rxb7 fxg3!; 26.Rxa7. 26.f3 does not defend. Larsen gives 26...g2; 27.fxg4 Rxg4; 28.Bxg2 Rdg8 and Black will win. **26...gxf2+; 27.Kg2 Qh2+.**

A picture tells the story. There are still landmines, however, and Larsen manages to step on one. **28.Kf3 Qh1+; 29.Kg3 Nf6+??** 29...Nh2+; 30.Kf4 Rg4+; 31.Ke3 Qe4+; 32.Kd2 Qxd4+; 33.Bd3 Qxa7 is an example of the correct approach to the hunt. **30.Kxf2 Qh4+; 31.Ke2 Qe4+; 32.Qe3.**

White survives to an endgame with one pawn for the exchange and a safer king. This is the move Larsen missed at move 29. **32...Qxe3+.** Larsen recovers his balance, not trying to avoid the endgame, but welcoming it, because the tactics are not finished yet!

33.Kxe3 Rg3+; 34.Kd2. The trap is 34.Kf4 Nh5+; 35.Ke4 f5+; 36.Ke5 Re3#. **34...exd5; 35.Nf5.** White would like to exchange all the remaining pawns, but capturing at d5 would have walked into a nasty pin on the d-file. **35...Kb8; 36.Rxf7 dxc4+; 37.Kc2 Rf3!**

What a sight the f-file is! One would think this was a composed problem, not an actual game.

38.Ng3. 38.Rxf6 Rxf1; 39.Rb6+ Ka7; 40.Rb5 Rd3 will push the king to the edge of the board. 41.Re5 Rf2+; 42.Kc1 Rc3+; 43.Kd1 Rcc2; 44.Ng3 Rfd2+; 45.Ke1 Rxa2; 46.Ra5+ is a last desperate try but 46...Kb6!; 47.Rxa2 Rxa2; 48.Ne4 Rg2 is a win. 49.Nc3 Kc5; 50.Ne4+ Kd4; 51.Nd2 c3; 52.Nb3+ Kd3; 53.Nc1+ Ke3; 54.Kf1 Rb2 and mate is inevitable. **38...Rf2+; 39.Be2 Rg8. White resigned.**

Tony Miles

One of Britain's most creative Grandmasters, endowed with a tremendous power in the endgame, Miles has used the Caro-Kann from time to time in his wide and varied repertoire. He has had a great deal of experience on the Black side of the Panov Attack, using the system we include in our repertoire.

TAL VS. MILES
Bugonjo, 1984
1.e4 c6; 2.d4 d5; 3.Nd2 dxe4; 4.Nxe4 Bf5; 5.Ng3 Bg6; 6.h4 h6; 7.Nf3 Nd7; 8.h5 Bh7; 9.Bd3 Bxd3; 10.Qxd3 Qc7; 11.Bd2 e6; 12.0–0–0 Ngf6; 13.Ne4 0–0–0.

We have used the plan of kingside castling in our repertoire, but here is a taste of the older, more traditional plan. **14.g3 Nc5; 15.Nxc5 Bxc5; 16.c4 Bb6.**

This is now the main line of the queenside castling approach, and the present game is typical of the possibilities that are contained in that line. **17.Bc3.** 17.Bf4 Qe7; 18.Qe3 Rhe8; 19.Kb1 was agreed drawn in Miles - Hort, Bath, 1983. **17...Rhe8; 18.Kb1.** 18.Qe2 was an attempt to improve, introduced months later in Van der Wiel - Miles, Tilburg, 1984.

18...a6; 19.Qc2 Re7; 20.Ne5 Ba5! An important resource, which indirectly undermines the outpost at e5. **21.b4.** This move is not in ECO, but is is better than the line they give, in my opinion.

21.c5 can be met by 21...Nd5! (21...Bxc3; 22.bxc3 would leave Black with problems on the dark squares, especially at b6.) 22.Nc4 Bxc3; 23.bxc3 b5! as suggested by Miles, would take advantage of the attack on the knight to force White either to capture the pawn, or retreat. In either case Black would no longer have a problem at b6.

The most recent edition of ECO claims it is better for White, but why? 24.Nd6+ is dealt with by 24...Rxd6; 25.cxd6 Qxd6 and the superstrong knight and extra pawn makes up for the exchange, especially since there are many weaknesses in White's position.

21...Bb6; 22.a4 Qb8! Black has a choice of creating a queen and bishop battery on either diagonal. **23.f4 Qa7; 24.Rd2 Kb8.** Black could not capture the pawn here. 24...Bxd4?; 25.Rhd1 is clearly better for White. **25.a5 Bc7; 26.g4.** 26.d5? exd5; 27.Bd4 Qa8 looks imposing but Black can slide his pieces in puzzle-like fashion and bring the king to c8 and queen to b8, after which White has nothing for the pawn, according to analysis by Miles. **26...Ka8.**

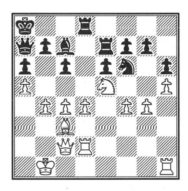

White controls a great deal of space, but Black's position is solid and his pieces have just enough breathing room. **27.g5?!** This only accentuates the weakness at f4. **27...Ne8; 28.c5?!** White seems obsessed with the dark-squares, but Black's next move shows just how weak the pawns are!

28...Qb8; 29.g6 f6; 30.Nc4 Bxf4. Black has a clear advantage now. **31.Re2 Nc7; 32.Bb2 Nb5; 33.Rhe1.** 33.Rd1 Bc7 and the rook will advance to d5, after which the h-pawn or d-pawn must fall. **33...Nxd4; 34.Bxd4 Rxd4; 35.Rxe6 Rxe6; 36.Rxe6 Qd8; 37.Re1.**

The White king is surrounded by air and Black has one extra pawn already. The game quickly resolves in Black's favor. **37...Ka7!** There will be no check at b6! **38.Ka2 Bd2!** The fork gives White no choice. **39.Rb1 Qd5.** The pin wins. **40.Kb3 Rd3+. White resigned.**

Eric Lobron

German Grandmaster Eric Lobron is almost single-handedly responsible for the development and popularization of the kingside castling approach in the Classical Caro-Kann which now bears his name.

HEIDRICH VS. LOBRON
Bundesliga, 1987

Lobron doesn't always follow the same path in the Caro-Kann, though he does usually adopt the ...Be7 formation with eventual kingside castling. Black doesn't have to castle right away. Let's consider some alternatives. In this game we will look at blasting open the c-file prepared by 13...Rc8. We'll also consider the immediate 13...c5 and 13...a5. With four playable strategies for Black in this typical position in the Classical Variation, you will be able to vary your repertoire and keep your opponents off balance.

1.e4 c6; 2.d4 d5; 3.Nd2 dxe4; 4.Nxe4 Bf5; 5.Ng3 Bg6; 6.h4 h6; 7.Nf3 Nd7; 8.h5 Bh7; 9.Bd3 Bxd3; 10.Qxd3 e6; 11.Qe2 Ngf6; 12.Bd2 Be7; 13.0–0–0.

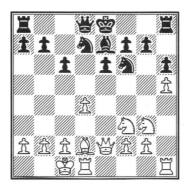

13...Rc8. It is interesting that Lobron chose this move, given his success against Grunfeld with 13...a5!? at Lugano, 1981.

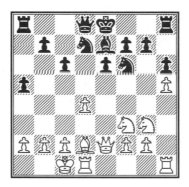

14.Ne5 a4 comes in two flavors, depending on which side will occupy the a3-square. First, let's look at 15.a3. Lobron, as White, chooses this prophylactic plan, but it hardly looks like a panacea for his queenside ills, despite the success in this game. 15...0–0; 16.Rh3.

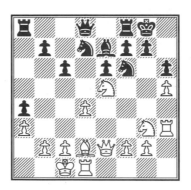

This is a critical position. I think that Black makes a mistake on his next move. 16...Qc7!? is my preference. (16...Rc8; 17.Kb1 c5; 18.Bc1 Qc7; 19.Ng6! fxg6; 20.Qxe6+ Kh8; 21.hxg6 and White is going to be able to double rooks on the h-file. Black was unable to hold the position in Lobron-Douven, Amsterdam, 1987.)

17.Ng6 fxg6; 18.Qxe6+ Kh8; 19.Qxe7 (19.hxg6 Ng8; 20.Nh5 Rae8!?; 21.Qc4 b5; 22.Qc3 Rxf2 turns out to be in Black's favor) 19...Rae8; 20.Qb4 Nd5; 21.Qxa4 Rxf2; 22.Re1 Rxe1+; 23.Bxe1 Rxg2; 24.hxg6 N7b6; 25.Qa7 c5.

What a crazy position! White seems to have all the makings of a back-rank mate, but Black targets c2 as a checkmating square. Let's try to solve the puzzle. 26.Ne4 opens up a path to the f-file for the White rook. 26...Rg1; 27.Rf3! Kg8; 28.Qa5 Qe7. Now the rook must move to deal with the threat at e4. 29.Rg3 Rf1; 30.Rg4 cxd4; 31.Qd2 seems to defend, but Black has the winning shot 31...Nc3!!

So, if White does not succeed by advancing the a-pawn, let's see what happens when Black is allowed to occupy a3. 15.f4 is met by 15...a3. Black's play is very straightforward—thrust the a-pawn at White's jugular! 16.b3 0-0; 17.f5. White correctly takes aim at the weakest square in Black's camp—e6. But the reply closes the e-file and takes the sting out of the move. 17...Nxe5!; 18.dxe5 Nd5; 19.Kb1 Qb6; 20.c4 This creates a weakness, but the knight at d5 is simply too dominating. 20...Qd4!; 21.Be1 Nc3+; 22.Bxc3 Qxc3. Black's advantage is obvious. The dark squares are under control, and the queenside lies undefended. This was played in Gruenfeld-Lobron, Biel, 1981.

So, let's get back to **13...Rc8.**

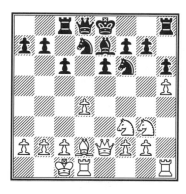

14.Ne5 0–0. 14...Nxe5; 15.dxe5 Nd5 is inconsistent with the plan of putting a rook at c8. Now ...c5 is meaningless. **15.Rhe1 b5.**

This position can be reached from 13...Rc8, as here, or from 13...0–0. **16.Nf5!?** See Sisniega - Lobron, New York, 1988 for the more conservative 16.Kb1. **16...exf5; 17.Nxd7 Qxd7; 18.Qxe7.** The little combination has created a pawn structure which would favor White were it not for the fact that his h-pawn is so weak. But the endgame is not what Black is after!

18...Qd5!; 19.Kb1. 19.Qxa7? Ra8; 20.Qc5 Qxa2; 21.Bb4 Ne4 is gruesome. **19...Rce8; 20.Qc7 Rxe1; 21.Rxe1 Qxg2; 22.Bb4 Re8!; 23.b3.** 23.Rxe8+ Nxe8; 24.Qe7 Qf1+; 25.Qe1 Qxe1+; 26.Bxe1 Nf6 is clearly better for Black. **23...Rxe1+; 24.Bxe1 Qe4; 25.Bc3 Qf3; 26.Qd8+ Kh7; 27.Kb2 Nd5.**

The old notion of good knight vs. bad bishop is exemplified here. **28.Be1 Qe4.** White resigned.

Yasser Seirawan

Unlike most of the other modern heroes, except Anatoly Karpov, Seirawan is primarily a positional player, eager to enter endgames which can exploit his creativity in that area of the game. He has relied to a large degree on the Classical Variation.

VAN DER WIEL VS. SEIRAWAN
Baden Baden, 1980

In this game Seirawan punishes a premature attack with considerable skill. The basic defensive idea was worked out by Boleslavsky.

1.e4 c6; 2.d4 d5; 3.Nd2 dxe4; 4.Nxe4 Bf5; 5.Ng3 Bg6; 6.Bc4 e6; 7.N1e2 Nf6; 8.0–0.

Castling is the primary alternative to the plans with an early Nf4. White can now try a plan with the advance of the f-pawn, rather than the h-pawn. **8...Bd6; 9.f4 Qd7!** Boleslavsky's idea. Usually this square is used by a knight, but the queen helps defend e6 and prevents sacrificial ideas. It also controls f5, by extension, and discourages the advance of White's f-pawn.

10.Bd3. This is the only move mentioned in ECO, but a number of alternatives have been explored, including the immediate sacrifice of the f-pawn. 10.f5 is a shade too ambitious. Black captures with the pawn: 10...exf5.

White now has two strategies, going after the bishop immediately or targeting the pawn at f5. 11.Nf4 0–0; 12.h4 Bxf4 (12...Re8!? is playable, since 13.h5 Bxf4; 14.Bxf4 Bxh5; 15.Nxh5 Nxh5; 16.Qxh5 allows 16...Qxd4+ and Black recovers the piece and emerges three pawns ahead.) 13.Rxf4 h6; 14.h5 Bh7; 15.Qf3 Re8 was better for Black in Hausner-Heinig, Germany, 1995, because the discomfort of the Black bishop is not worth a pawn. Black will play ...Nd5 soon.

11.Bd3 is the other plan, and now things can get interesting. 11...Ne4. (11...Bxg3; 12.Nxg3 Qxd4+; 13.Kh1 0–0 looks safe enough for Black. 14.Nxf5 Bxf5; 15.Bxf5 Qxd1; 16.Rxd1 and the bishop pair provides some compensation for the pawn.) 12.Bf4 Nxg3; 13.Nxg3 0–0; 14.Bxd6 Qxd6; 15.Bxf5 Rd8; 16.c3 Nd7; 17.Ne4 Qd5 gave Black equality in Weder-Markus, Postal, 1987.

10.Kh1 is sometimes played, so that the d-pawn might be sacrificed later without giving Black the tempo resulting from a check against the White king. 10...h5 buys some space for the bishop. 11.f5 (11.Nc3 h4; 12.Nge2 h3; 13.g3 b5; 14.Bd3 b4 gave Black a strong initiative in Walther-Khasoff, Postal, 1979.) 11...exf5; 12.Nf4 Bxf4; 13.Rxf4 h4; 14.Qe1+ Kf8.

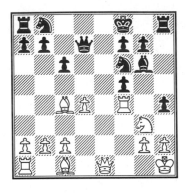

White has invested a pawn to deprive the Black king of the privilege of castling. This is not very important, however, as the h-file is useful to the rook and the king can slide to g8, and even to h7, if necessary. 15.Ne2 h3; 16.Rh4 hxg2+; 17.Kxg2 Bh5!? Kasparov would have had an advantage after exchanging rooks, but goes for more. 18.Nf4 Na6; 19.Nxh5 Nxh5; 20.Qd1 (20.Bxa6 bxa6; 21.Qb4+ would at least have given White some play on the dark squares.) 20...g6; 21.Bg5 Kg7; 22.d5 f6!; 23.Qd4 c5!; 24.Qc3 b5!

After these three strong moves, White had nothing better than sacrificing the exchange in the hopes of an attack. 25.Rxh5 Rxh5; 26.Qxf6+ Kh7; 27.Be2 Rf8. Kasparov now returns the exchange and takes over the attack. 28.Qxf8 Qxd5+; 29.Kg3 Rxg5+; 30.Kh4 Rg2; 31.Qe7+ Kg8; 32.Qe8+ Kg7; 33.Qe7+? White's best chance lay in the surprising move 33.Kh3! Qf7! The queens come off and the rest is simple. 34.Qe5+ Qf6+; 35.Qxf6+ Kxf6; 36.Bxb5 Nc7; 37.Bd3.

The future World Champion, perhaps in time trouble, misses a forced mate in four (and an alternative mate in five)! 37...Nd5?! (37...Rg4+; 38.Kh3 Ne6; 39.Bxf5 gxf5; 40.Rf1 Ng5#. Another mate is 37...Ne6; 38.Bxf5 g5+; 39.Kh5 Nf4+; 40.Kh6 Rxh2+; 41.Bh3 Rxh3#.) 38.Rf1 c4; 39.Bxc4 Ne3; 40.Kh3 g5; 41.Rc1 g4+. White resigned, Eolian-Kasparov, Soviet Junior Championship, 1977.

Against 10.Bb3 Na6; 11.c4 Nc7 is a suggestion for Black from Kasparov. With all of the alternatives exhausted, we return to the main line. White has just played 10.Bd3, and we will take up the offer to trade bishops.

10...Bxd3; 11.Qxd3 g6.

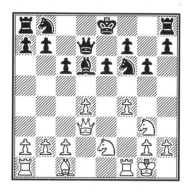

Black must accept this necessary weakening of the kingside. It turns out that the g7-square will become quite useful later, and White is in no position to exploit the c1–h6 diagonal unless the f-pawn gets out of the way. For that reason, the sacrificial advance of the f-pawn is often seen at some point in the proceedings. **12.b3.** The bishop has no future on the c1–h6 diagonal, so shifts to a potentially more useful one. There are four alternatives for White, none of which are frightening.

12.f5 can be played immediately. 12...gxf5; 13.Bg5 Be7; 14.Rae1 is best met by 14...Rg8; 15.Bh4 was played in Romero Holmes-Izeta, Albacete, 1989. Jon Speelman found a strong continuation for Black. 15...Rg4!; 16.Bxf6 Bxf6; 17.c3 Na6 and Black has the better chances, with a kingside attack coming soon.

12.Nc3 aims to transfer the knight to e4. It is a rather mechanical plan which has so far been played only by computers! 12...Na6; 13.a3 Nc7; 14.Nce4 Be7; 15.b4 0–0; 16.Bb2 Rfd8; 17.Rad1 a5 was a sensible continuation, seen in a contest between Mega IV and Turbo King in 1990.

12.Ne4 Nxe4; 13.Qxe4 0–0; 14.Be3 Na6; 15.Kh1 Nc7; 16.Rad1 Nd5 was good for Black in Reyes-Fletcher, New York Open, 1989. 12.c4 0–0; 13.Bd2 was tried in Weinitschke-Salot, Postal, 1984. Black should play 13...b5 to strike at White's pawn center.

So, White heads for the queenside fianchetto. **12...Na6**. The knight will take up a post at c7, as is normally the case when the queen occupies d7. **13.Bb2 Be7; 14.c4.** 14.Rad1 Nc7; 15.c4 0–0 transposes below to 15.Rad1. **14...Nc7.**

Black's formation is purely defensive, but it is not easy to crack, despite the weak dark squares on the kingside.

15.Qf3. 15.Rad1 has also been tried. 15...0–0; 16.Qc3 (16.Qf3 Nce8; 17.Nc1 Ng7; 18.Nd3 Qc7; 19.Nc5 Rad8; 20.Kh1 Ngh5; 21.Nxh5 Nxh5 proved solid enough in Madl-Brunner, Eurodata, 1992. Black went on to win) 16...Rfd8; 17.Rd3 Nce8; 18.Kh1 Bf8; 19.Rdf3 Bg7 is a good defense. It is hard to see what further preparation can be made for the advance of the f-pawn, but that advance fails. 20.f5?! exf5; 21.Nxf5 gxf5; 22.Rxf5 Nd6; 23.R5f4 Re8; 24.Qc2 Nde4; 25.d5 cxd5; 26.Nd4 dxc4; 27.bxc4 Nd6; 28.Nf3 Re4; 29.Rxf6 Bxf6; 30.Bxf6 was played in Hartmann-Berg, Bundesliga, 1986, where 30...Qf5; 31.Ba1 Re1!; 32.Qf2 Rxf1+; 33.Qxf1 Ne4 allowed Black to simplify the position and ward off all threats. Black went on to win.

15...0–0; 16.Nc1 Nce8! The knight transfers to g7, overprotecting the f5 square. It is a move and plan that Aron Nimzowitsch would be proud of. **17.Nd3 Ng7; 18.Ne5 Qc7.**

The position is balanced. Black's defenses are strong except for the h6 square. **19.h3 Rad8.** It would have been better to play ...h5 right away. **20.Rad1?** White could have avoided some of the coming difficulties by playing Ne2, and then a kingside attack with the advance of the g-pawn might have discomforted Black. **20...h5!** Seirawan appreciates that although White seems to be attacking on the kingside, he needs to play vigorously there, too. The idea is to advance the pawn to h4 and chase away the knight. The pawn at h4 can be defended by the bishop at e7.

21.Ne2 h4. This puts an end to White's hopes of getting a pawn to g4, so the knight may as well return. **22.Ng4 Nfh5.** The horses move into position, smelling the hole at g3. **23.Qc3 Kh7; 24.Rf3 Nf5.**

There is pressure at f4 and g3. Black's position cannot be penetrated, and White is reduced to utter passivity. 25.Ne3 Bf6; 26.Ng4 Bh8; 27.Ne5 White gets the knight to e5, counting on it to shelter the weakling at f4. Not so!

27...Nxf4!!; 28.Rxf4 Bxe5; 29.Re4 Bf6; 30.Rf1 c5; 31.Qd2 cxd4. Black resigned.

Jonathan Speelman

British Grandmaster Jon Speelman, like Salo Flohr and Anatoly Karpov, enjoys rather quiet and unambitious openings. Speelman is a noted endgame authority and is quite content to do battle in that stage of the game. He is not afraid of complicated positions, and against no less than World Champion Garry Kasparov he had a dramatic battle which deserves more analysis than can be presented here. Interested readers are referred to his excellent collection of best games, listed in the bibliography, where the game occupies ten pages of rigorous discussion.

KASPAROV-SPEELMAN
Linares, 1991

1.e4 c6; 2.d4 d5; 3.Nd2 dxe4; 4.Nxe4 Nd7. Speelman has generally adopted this approach in his games. **5.Bc4.** The immediate 5.Ng5 now shares the limelight with the bishop move. We examine that continuation in the game Kamsky-Karpov. **5...Ngf6.**

White now has two main plans, the capture at f6, and the more enterprising attack with Ng5.

6.Ng5. 6.Nxf6+ Nxf6; 7.c3 Qc7; 8.Nf3 Bf5; 9.0-0 e6; 10.Qe2 Bd6; 11.Ne5 0-0-0 is an interesting line that has brought Speelman success. 12.a4 Rhe8; 13.a5 (13.Bf4! is stronger, where Speelman evaluates the position as unclear) 13...Nd5; 14.h3 f6; 15.Nd3 g5; 16.Nc5 Bxc5; 17.dxc5 a6; 18.Rd1 Qg7; 19.Bb3 h5; 20.Bxd5 exd5; 21.Qxh5 Qd7; 22.c4 d4. Black went on to win in Tkachiev-Speelman, London,

1993. **6...e6; 7.Qe2 Nb6; 8.Bb3.** The bishop also retreats to d3 in many games. **8...a5.**

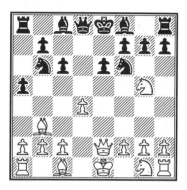

Speelman often used an early advance of the a-pawn. In most cases, Black drives back the knight on g5 first, but Speelman wanted to surprise Kasparov. Speelman writes that Kasparov "produced a magnificent look of mildly contemptuous puzzlement before replying." **9.c3!? a4; 10.Bc2 a3; 11.b3**

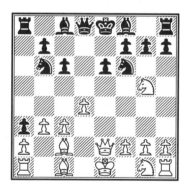

The pawn structure is set for a while. The pawn at a3 cramps the queenside, but may be weak in an endgame. **11...Nbd5; 12.Bd2 Bd6.** The tactical line 12...Nxc3; 13.Bxc3 Nd5; 14.Bd2 Nb4 is refuted by 15.Be3! Qa5; 16.Kf1 b6; 17.Qd2 as given by Speelman.

13.N1f3 Nf4; 14.Qf1 h6; 15.Ne4. 15.Nxf7? was tempting, but Kasparov saw the continuation 15...Kxf7; 16.Ne5+ Bxe5; 17.dxe5 Qa5!; 18.exf6 Qe5+; 19.Kd1 Rd8 and Black has the advantage. **15...Nxe4; 16.Bxe4 0–0; 17.g3 Nd5; 18.Qe2.**

Speelman now played the standard freeing maneuver, but it might have been premature. Perhaps retreating the knight to f6 was objectively better. **18...c5; 19.dxc5 Bxc5; 20.Ne5!** 20.0-0 Nf6; 21.Bc2 b6; 22.Rfd1 Qe7; 23.b4 Bd6; 24.Be3 Qc7 and Black plays ...Bb7 with powerful bishops. **20...Qc7; 21.0-0!**

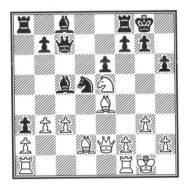

Speelman has used up three-fourths of his allotted time on half the required moves, while Kasparov was moving along at a faster clip. Speelman had no time to waste, and after contemplating his reply for less than ten minutes he decided to let it fly.

21...Be3!? An amazing move which sent Kasparov into the think tank for forty minutes. The complexities are so rich that Speelman had to substantially revise his published commentaries to the game when preparing his collection of best games. I will present only the conclusions of his analysis, and refer the reader to Speelman's book for the details. If you look at earlier commentaries to this game you will find a quite different picture, but Speelman backs up his new conclusions with detailed analysis.

22.fxe3! 22.Bxe3 was the expected reply. 22...Nxc3!; 23.Qh5 Nxe4. *(23...Ra5 comes into consideration.)* 24.Rac1 Qa5; 25.b4 Qb5; 26.Bc5 Nf6; 27.Qh4 b6!; 28.Bxf8 Qxc5; 29.Be7 Nd5 would have provided more than enough compensation for the exchange.

22...Qxe5; 23.Qd3. 23.Bc2 f5; 24.Qd3 Nf6; 25.c4 Qc7 is fairly balanced. **23...Ra6!** A useful repositioning of the rook, which can now get to d6. **24.c4 Nf6; 25.Bg2 Rd6.**

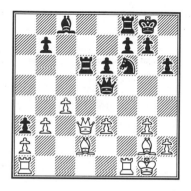

26.Qe3! Kasparov wants an endgame and he wants it now! **26...Qg5.** No way. **27.Qa5.** Another try. The players are getting very short of time, having less than ten minutes each remaining.

27...e5; 28.Bb4 Ra6; 29.Qb5 Bd7; 30.Qxb7 Qxe3+; 31.Kh1 Ra7; 32.Bd2? The correct move was 32.Qf3, but there was very little time to think. **32...Qd4; 33.Bc3 Qc5; 34.Qb4 Qc7; 35.c5.**

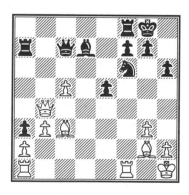

With flags hanging, Speelman missed a powerful shot. **35...Bc6?** 35...Rb8! would have picked up the c-pawn, and Kasparov would have had to fight for the draw. **36.Qb6 Bxg2+; 37.Kxg2 Nd5; 38.Qxc7 Rxc7; 39.Bxe5 Rxc5; 40.Bd6 Rc2+; 41.Rf2.**

Time control reached, Speelman is on home territory in the endgame. The control of the seventh rank is critical. Although it looks tempting to put the rook at d8, because Black has the threat of ...Ne3+ regaining the rook at c2 if White captures, Speelman analyzed it out to a win for White.

41...Rfc8. 41...Rd8; 42.Rxc2 Ne3+; 43.Kf2 Nxc2; 44.Rd1 Nb4; 45.Rd2 Nxa2; 46.Bf4! Rxd2+; 47.Bxd2. Speelman gives the following win: 47...Kf8; 48.Ke3 Ke7; 49.Kd4 Kd6; 50.b4 f5; 51.b5 g5; 52.Kc4 Kc7; 53.Be3 and with the Black king cut off from the b-pawn, White can corral the knight.

42.Bxa3 Ne3+; 43.Kg1 Ra8; 44.Bb2! 44.Bb4 is wrong because of 44...Raxa2; 45.Rxa2 Rc1+ and mate follows. (44.Bc1 Raxa2; 45.Rxc2 Rxa1; 46.Rc8+ Kh7; 47.Kf2 Ng4+ is not a problem for Black.) **44...Rxf2; 45.Kxf2 Nc2; 46.Rc1 Nb4; 47.Rb1 Rxa2; 48.Ke3 f6; 49.Kd4 Nc2+; 50.Kc3 Na3.**

This leads to a very complicated rook and pawn endgame.

51.Bxa3 Rxa3; 52.Kb2 Ra7; 53.b4 Kf7; 54.b5 Ke6; 55.Kb3 Kd7. It is hard to decide whether the king is better at d7 or d6. **56.h4?** 56.Rc1 was a better try. **56...h5; 57.Rc1 Rc7; 58.Rd1+.** 58.Rxc7+ Kxc7; 59.Kc4 leads to a draw after 59...Kb6; 60.Kd5 g5; 61.Ke6 gxh4; 62.gxh4 Kxb5; 63.Kxf6 Kc6; 64.Kg6 Kd7; 65.Kxh5 Ke8; 66.Kg6 Kf8! **58...Kc8; 59.Rd5 Re7; 60.Kc4 Re3. Draw agreed.**

Garry Kasparov

Although you won't find current PCA World Champion Kasparov defending the Caro-Kann these days, it played an important role in his development as a chessplayer. The opening suited his skills well in the late 1970s, as he was earning his Grandmaster title. Here is an exciting game from the Soviet Junior Championship. Kasparov's choice in the Caro-Kann was the Classical.

EHLVEST VS. KASPAROV
Soviet Junior Championship, 1977
1.e4 c6; 2.c4 d5; 3.cxd5 cxd5; 4.exd5 Nf6; 5.Nc3 Nxd5

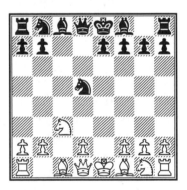

This is a more common reply to the Accelerated Panov than the one adopted in our repertoire. 6.d4 Nc6. We have now reached the Panov Attack. This position could be arrived at via 1.e4 c6; 2.d4 c5; 3.exd5 cxd5; 4.c4 Nf6; 5.Nc3 Nc6; 6.cxd5 Nxd5.

7.Nf3 Bg4; 8.Qb3 Bxf3; 9.gxf3 Nb6. 9...e6; 10.Qxb7 Nxd4; 11.Bb5+ Nxb5; 12.Qc6+ Ke7; 13.Qxb5 Qd7; 14.Qa5 Nxc3; 15.Qxc3 f6; 16.Be3 Kf7 gave Black the advantage in Tseitlin-Kasparov, Soviet Union, 1978. **10.Be3 e6; 11.Rg1.** This is sometimes played in order to tie down the bishop at f8 to the defense of the g-pawn, and station the rook on a useful open file. **11...Bb4.**

White can go after the g-pawn or address the question of development. **12.Bb5.** 12.Rxg7 Nd5; 13.0-0-0 Rc8; 14.Kb1 Bxc3; 15.bxc3 is Alexandria-Zaitseva, Tbilisi, 1979. 15...Na5 was best, I think. 16.Bb5+ Kf8; 17.Qa3+ Qe7! (17...Kxg7??; 18.Rg1+ Kf6; 19.Bg5+ and White wins.) 18.Qxe7+ Kxe7; 19.Bd2 Nxc3+; 20.Bxc3 Rxc3; 21.Bd3 is better for Black, as the White pawn structure is wretched.

The most important line is: 12.0-0-0 Bxc3; 13.bxc3 (13.Qxc3 Rc8! gives Black a strong queenside attack.) 13...g6 (13...0-0!; 14.Bh6 g6; 15.Bxf8 Qxf8 is considered a promising sacrifice by Jansa. Black's knights have more scope than White's rooks. Still, it requires practical tests. 14.d5 Nxd5; 15.c4 Rc8; 16.Qb2 and White was clearly better in Jansa-Kraut, Germany, 1988.

12...Nd5; 13.Rxg7. 13.0-0-0 Bxc3; 14.bxc3 0-0; 15.Bh6 g6; 16.Bxc6 bxc6; 17.Bxf8 Qxf8 illustrates Jansa's suggestion. 18.Kc2 c5; 19.Qa3 Rc8 20.dxc5 Rxc5 21.Rd3 a5 22.Rg4 Qc8 23.h4 was agreed drawn in Breyther-Hermann, Germany 1988, but I would have played on with 23...h5. **13...Qb6.**

14.Kf1. 14.Bxc6+ is stronger. 14...Qxc6; 15.Bd2 Bxc3; 16.bxc3 Nb6; 17.Rb1 gave White strong pressure in Breyther-Holzapfel, Germany, 1989. **14...Nxc3; 15.Bxc6+ Qxc6; 16.bxc3 Bf8; 17.Rg5 Be7.**

White has a small advantage, based on the control of the open files. There are still many weaknesses in the pawn structure, however, and that limits his options. **18.Rb5 Qxf3; 19.Rxb7 0–0.** Even 14-year old Kasparov manages to avoid the tactical disaster 19...Qh1+; 20.Ke2 Qxa1; 21.Qb5+ Kf8; 22.Bh6+ Kg8; 23.Rb8+ Rxb8; 24.Qxb8+ Bf8; 25.Qxf8#. **20.Rb1 Bf6; 21.Qd1.** White wants an endgme where the extra pawn matters.

21...Qh3+; 22.Ke2 Kh8. The g-file is vacated so that a rook can take up a position there. **23.Qh1 e5; 24.Qf3 Qe6; 25.d5 Qa6+; 26.Ke1 Bg7!** The f-pawn is sacrificed to open up more lines. **27.Rxf7 e4; 28.Rxf8+ Rxf8; 29.Qxe4 Bxc3+; 30.Kd1 Bg7; 31.a4 Rc8; 32.Rb5 Qf6.** Kasparov is still down two pawns but is hoping to find a way to infiltrate the White position. Still, Black has no immediate threats and could afford to grab the a-pawn.

33.Qg4 Rd8; 34.Ke2 Qc3; 35.Rb7. This looks decisive. Time pressure may have played a role. This game was played at a 45-move time control, with each player having 135 minutes.

35...Qc2+; 36.Kf1 Qd3+; 37.Kg1. Now Black can defend while simultaneously threatening a discovered pin. **37...Rg8!; 38.Bg5.** 38.h4 Bd4!; 39.Bg5 Rf8 exploits a different pin. **38...Qxd5; 39.Rxg7??** This looks so simple, but there is a big tactical hole. 39.Rd7 Qe5; 40.Rd8 Rxd8; 41.Bxd8 Qe1+; 42.Kg2 Qe8 would be difficult to win for White, but was relatively best. **39...Rxg7; 40.Bf6?**

This looks convincing, but the pins work both ways, and the d1 square is open. 40.h4 Qe5; 41.Kg2 h6; 42.Qh5 Qe4+; 43.Kh2 Rg6! In the end, Black would win.

40...Qd1+! White resigned.

RETURN TO THE WORLD CHAMPIONSHIP

We have seen that a number of World Champions used the Caro-Kann, but it has become most closely identified with Anatoly Karpov, the current FIDE titleholder. The Caro-Kann has played a role in several World Championship matches in the 1990s.

Anatoly Karpov

The current FIDE World Champion has been relying on the Caro-Kann for many years now. He took the quiet variation 1.e4 c6; 2.d4 d5; 3.Nc3 dxe4; 4.Nxe4 Nd7, which had been variously named for Smyslov, Flohr, Filip and several others, and established his own patent on the system, which is now generally referred to as the Karpov Variation. Although our repertoire prefers the Classical Line, here is an example of the Karpov Variation (which he modestly calls the Petrosian-Smyslov Variation!) as played by its leading exponent.

KAMSKY VS. KARPOV
Dortmund, 1993

The most interesting part of this game is the period just before time control. Both sides make errors under tremendous time pressure, and I present some new analysis of the key positions. The game also serves as an introduction to one of the most topical lines in the Caro-Kann, which Karpov has used to battle with challengers including Gata Kamsky in their 1996 title bout.

1.e4 c6; 2.d4 d5; 3.Nd2 dxe4; 4.Nxe4 Nd7; 5.Ng5 Ngf6; 6 N.f3 6.Bc4 e6; 7.Qe2 Nb6 transposes to Kasparov-Speelman. **6...e6.**

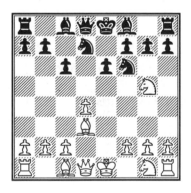

This has become one of the most hotly debated positions of the 1990s. **7.N1f3.** 7.Ne2 Bd6; 8.0–0 h6; 9.Nf3 Qc7; 10.c4 b6; 11.b3 Bb7; 12.Bb2 c5; 13.Ng3 0–0 was seen in Christiansen-Karpov, Roquebrune, 1992 but the FIDE World Champion now prefers 7...h6.

7...Bd6. 7...h6 led to a famous debacle in the final game of the 1997 DEEP BLUE vs. Kasparov match. 8.Nxe6 Qe7; 9.0–0 fxe6; 10.Bg6+ Kd8; 11.Bf4 b5; 12.a4 Bb7; 13.Re1 Nd5; 14.Bg3 Kc8; 15.axb5 cxb5; 16.Qd3 Bc6; 17.Bf5 exf5; 18.Rxe7 Bxe;7 19.c4 and an embarrassed Kasparov resigned. **8.Qe2.**

This is the most active continuation. Castling is less threatening. 8.0–0 h6; 9.Ne4 Nxe4; 10.Bxe4 0–0; 11.c3! c5. Karpov used to play 11...e5, but that is now considered better for White. 12.Bc2 Qc7; 13.Re1 Rd8; 14.h3 Nf6; 15.Qe2 cxd4; 16.Nxd4 Bh2+; 17.Kh1 Bf4; 18.Nb5 Qb8; 19.a4 Bd7; 20.Bxf4 Qxf4; 21.Nd4 Bc6 gave Black equality in Kamsky-Karpov, Tilburg, 1991. **8...h6; 9.Ne4 Nxe4; 10.Qxe4.**

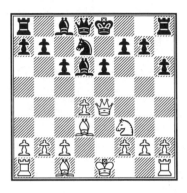

According to theory, Black should develop the knight, as in this game, but we should take note that in 1997 Karpov adopted a different move order. **10...Nf6.** 10...c5!? is Karpov's current choice. 11.0–0 Nf6. (11...Qc7; 12.Qg4 Kf8; 13.c3 b6; 14.Qh4 Bb7; 15.Be4 Bxe4; 16.Qxe4 Rd8; 17.dxc5 Nxc5; 18.Qe2 Ke7 was even in Illescas-Karpov, Dos Hermanas, 1997.) 12.Qh4. (12.Bb5+ Ke7; 13.Qe2 Qc7; 14.dxc5 Qxc5; 15.Be3 Qc7 was solid enough for Black in Topalov-Karpov, Dos Hermanas, 1997) 12...Qc7; 13.Re1 Bd7; 14.Bg5 Be7; 15.dxc5 Qxc5; 16.Ne5 Bc6 also seems satisfactory for Black, Ivanchuk-Karpov, Dortmund, 1997.

11.Qh4?! White usually retreats the queen to e2, and that is considered a superior plan. Play usually continues along the path of 11.Qe2 Qc7; 12.Bd2 b6; 13.0–0–0 Bb7.

This is a position which has had plenty of high-level tests. 14.Rhe1 should be met by kingside castling. 14...0-0. (14...0-0-0; 15.Ba6 Bxa6; 16.Qxa6+ Kb8; 17.Qe2 worked out well for White in A. Sokolov-Karpov, Belfort, 1988.) 15.g4 c5; 16.g5 hxg5; 17.Nxg5 Bf4; 18.h4 Rad8; 19.dxc5 bxc5; 20.Be3 Rd4!?; 21.Rg1 Bxe3+; 22.fxe3 led to a balanced game in Kamsky-Karpov, FIDE World Championship, 1996.

Another plan is 14.Ne5 c5; 15.Bb5+ Ke7; 16.dxc5 Qxc5; 17.a3 (17.Bc3 Rhd8; 18.Bd4 Qc7; 19.Rhe1 Kf8; 20.c3 a6; 21.Bd3 b5 with a good game for Black, Leko-Karpov, Dortmund, 1995) 17...Qc7; 18.Bf4 Nd5; 19.Bg3 Rhd8; 20.Rd4 Kf8; 21.Kb1 a6; 22.Rc4 Qe7; 23.Nc6 Bxc6; 24.Bxc6 Ra7; 25.Bxd5 exd5; 26.Bxd6 Qxd6; 27.Rd4 b5 is better for White, but Black managed to draw in Kamsky-Karpov, FIDE World Championship, 1996.

14.Kb1 Rd8; 15.c4 (15.Rhe1 0-0; 16.Ne5 c5; 17.f4 cxd4; 18.g4 is more interesting. Kasparov gained the advantage against Yepishin in a 1995 quick game, and White certainly has compensation for the pawn) 15...0-0; 16.Bc3 Rfe8; 17.Ne5 c5; 18.dxc5 Bxc5; 19.f3 a5; 20.Bc2 Ba6; 21.Ba4 Rxd1+; 22.Rxd1 Rd8; 23.Rxd8+ Qxd8 was better for Karpov, playing Black in his 1995 game against Almasi, at Groningen.

Karpov now plays a rather shocking move. **11...Ke7!!**

No, this isn't a typo. Karpov really did play the king to e7. It is an idea he discovered in 1988 during preparations for a game against Kasparov. He revealed his secret weapon in this game. Kamsky sees the target in the center and goes after it with a pawn sacrifice.

12.Ne5. 12.0-0 begs for a kingside attack with 12...g5; 13.Qh3 g4, as suggested by Blatny. **12...Bxe5; 13.dxe5 Qa5+; 14.c3.** 14.Bd2 Qxe5+ 15.Be3 would invite Black to take the b-pawn, but the offer is best declined. **14...Qxe5+; 15.Be3 b6; 16.0-0-0.**

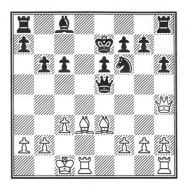

White has a nice bishop pair and open lines to use in the attack.

16...g5; 17.Qa4. 17.Qh3 c5; 18.Rhe1 is very complicated, according to Karpov. A plausible continuation is 18...Bb7; 19.Bc2 Be4; 20.Bb3 Bf5; 21.Qf3 . I think Black's position holds more potential. **17...c5; 18.Rhe1 Bd7; 19.Qa3 Rhd8.**

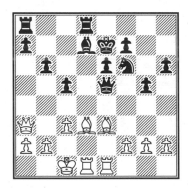

This is a critical position. All of White's pieces are in postion, and clearly the break at f4 is the goal. Karpov had correctly analyzed the position. **20.g3.**

Much attention has been paid to the alternative 20.f4!? gxf4; 21.Bd4 Qg5! Karpov provides the following analysis. 22.Re5 Qh4!; (22...Qxg2?; 23.Rxc5! lets White build a powerful attack.) 23.g3 fxg3; 24.hxg3 Qxg3, for example: 25.Rxc5? bxc5; 26.Qxc5+ Ke8; 27.Bxf6 Qf4+ and **Black wins.** 20.b4!? is suggested by Korchnoi, but 20...Ke8; 21.Bxc5 Qxh2; 22.Bd4 is clearly better for White.

20...Qc7; 21.Bd4. 21.f4 Ng4; 22.Bd4 gxf4; 23.h3 Ne3 was a line Karpov was looking forward to. **21...Be8!** The d-file is activated. **22.Kb1 Rd5.** 22...Bc6!?; 23.Be5 Qd7; 24.Bc2 Qb7 might have been even stronger, according to Karpov. **23.f4!** This powerful move keeps White in the game. **23...Rad8.** 23...gxf4; 24.gxf4 Qxf4? would lose to 25.Rf1.

24.Bc2! 24.Be5 Qc6!; 25.c4 R5d7; 26.Qc3 Ng4; 27.fxg5 hxg5; 28.Rf1 Rd4! Karpov's analysis leads to a definite advantage for White. 24.fxg5 hxg5; 25.h4 gxh4; 26.gxh4 e5 creates serious problems for White. **24...R5d6; 25.Bxf6+.** 25.Be5 Rxd1+; 26.Rxd1 Rxd1+; 27.Bxd1 Qd7; 28.Be2 Qd2. Black has a powerful initiative. **25...Kxf6; 26.fxg5+ hxg5; 27.Rxd6 Rxd6.**

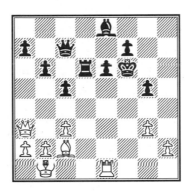

White must now do something to activate the useless queen. **28.c4 Ke7; 29.Qe3 f6; 30.h4.** Both players were in time trouble, but Karpov had no difficulty in declining Kamsky's peace offering here. Black has every reason to play on.

30...gxh4; 31.gxh4 Qd7; 32.Qh6 e5? Black should ignore the kingside and get to the seventh rank. Correct was 32...Rd2! The threat is ...Qd4, defending f6 and creating a horizontal pin against the bishop at c2. 33.Rf1 Qd4; 34.h5 Bf7; 35.Rc1 Rh2; 36.Qg7 e5; 37.Rf1 e4; 38.Rd1 Rd2; 39.Rxd2 Qxd2; 40.b3 Qg5; 41.Qxg5 fxg5; 42.h6 (42.Bxe4 Bxh5 is hopeless for White) 42...Bg6. The bishop endgame is winning for Black. There aren't any other serious alternatives, since 33.Qg7+ Bf7; 34.Bg6 gets mated. 34...Rd1+; 35.Kc2 Qd2+; 36.Kb3 Qb4+; 37.Kc2 Rd2+; 38.Kc1 Qxb2#.

33.h5 Qg4. Again Karpov misses the power of moving a rook to d2. **34.Qh7+ Kd8.**

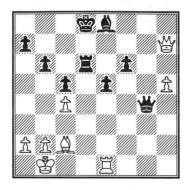

The game is far from over, and the analysis of this position in the literature gives the mistaken impression that White's loss is all but inevitable. In fact, many resources were missed in the time scramble. **35.h6.** 35.Qxa7 has been rejected because of 35...Bxh5; 36.Qb8+ Ke7 with consideration only of the immediate check at c7. There is a stronger move, however. 37.Ba4! Bg6+; 38.Ka1 Qd4; 39.Qc7+ Kf8; 40.Rh1! The final position is unclear.

35...Rd2; 36.Qf5. 36.Qxa7! would have been strong enough to equalize. 36...Qxc4; 37.Qxb6+ Ke7; 38.Bb3! Bg6+; 39.Ka1 and the Black queen must abandon the defense of the c-pawn. Karpov makes no mention of this. **36...Qxf5; 37.Bxf5 Bd7.** Karpov criticizes the move, but does not tell us what would have been better. 37...Rh2; 38.h7 Ke7; 39.Rg1 Bf7; 40.Rg8! Rxh7; 41.Bxh7 Bxg8; 42.Bxg8 f5 leaves only White with winning chances.

38.Bg6? 38.Kc1! would have drawn, at least 38...Rd4; 39.Bxd7 Rxc4+!; 40.Kb1 Rh4; 41.Rd1 Rxh6; is given by Karpov, and Konikowski extends the analysis to 42.Bf5+ Kc7; 43.Rd7+ Kc6; 44.Rxa7 where Black will be fighting for the draw. **38...Rh2.**

The h-pawn is doomed, and the Black pawnroller moves inexorably forward toward the promotion squares. **39.h7 Ke7; 40.Bd3 Be6; 41.Rg1 f5; 42.Rg7+ Kf6; 43.Rxa7 e4; 44.Be2 f4; 45.b3 f3; 46.Bd1 Bf5**. The threat of advancing the e-pawn with discovered check also picks off the h-pawn.

    47.Kc1 Bxh7; 48.Rb7 Ke5; 49.Rxb6 Rxa2. White resigned.

SELF-TEST

Here are some critical positions for you to use to evaluate your understanding of the repertoire. These are questions of positional judgment and familiarization, not tactical tests. In each case you can go to the referenced game to see the answer and analysis of the position. The diagrams are found in the game as presented below. By having to spot the diagram, instead of simply flipping to a page number, you need to have the position in your mind's eye.

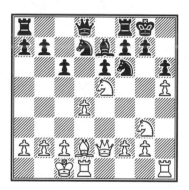

This is a position from Sisniega-Lobron. Should Black advance the c-pawn right away or prepare it with ...Rc8? (Page 53)

Kupreichik-Lobron reached this position. What standard theme does Black use to obtain equality? (Page 60)

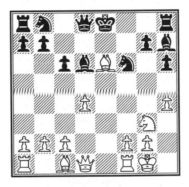

In Tal-Vukic, Black chose the correct defensive strategy. What is it? (Page 74)

In the Vajda-Tseitlin game, this is an important early position? (Page 115)

What are Black's two strategies? (Page 141)

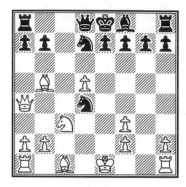

This is a popular line for White, seen in the notes to Greenfeld-Shirov. Can Black take the pawn at f3? Is it a good idea? (Page 141)

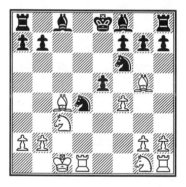

In Vrona-Van Wely, Black played the correct move here. What is it? (Page 148)

This is a crucial position from the Accelerated Panov Attack. You must know the proper move here or risk losing! (Page 167)

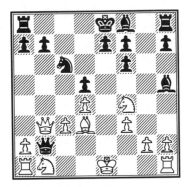

We encountered this position in Timman-Hübner. What is the correct plan for Black? (Page 174)

In the notes to Ghinda-Watson, you'll find that this position presents an excellent opportunity for Black to take action. How does the position play out? (Page 191)

When White adopts the King's Indian Attack, where does Black arrange counterplay, and how? The position is discussed in Ljubojevic-Karpov. (Page 209)

WHERE TO GO FROM HERE

After reading this book, you can go on to incorporate openings that you find interesting into your own repertoire. There are thousands of books available on specific opening strategies, and for proficiency you'll need to turn to the extensive literature on each opening. A selection of recommended opening books from many different publishers is available from Cardoza Publishing, as well as many of my new up-to-date titles on opening play, at www.cardozapub.com. My recent 1700 page trilogy, *World Champion Openings*, *Standard Chess Openings*, and *Unorthodox Chess Openings*, contains many more openings you may find of interest.

Additional information on the openings is available at http://www.chessworks.com, which is the web site of the author. Also, look for the new free online chess magazine where I am editor-in-chief, Chess City, www.chesscity.com. There will be loads of resources and information available here for free, and articles, columns, gossip, and much more from some of the best writers in the chess world.

Armed with the knowledge you gain in this book, you can also deepen your understanding of the ideas behind the Caro-Kann by examining collections of games by the strong players who use this system. You can find many books devoted to the games of the great masters. There are also plenty of sources on the Internet where you can find collections for free!

See you at the chessboard.

LITERATURE

Here are some selected works on the Caro-Kann that can help you further explore the opening. Not all are in print, but they are worth seeking out. I also include references to important works cited in the text.

Caro-Kann: Classical Variation by Garry Kasparov and Alexander Shakharov. Batsford 1983.

Caro-Kann B17 by Anatoly Karpov. Chess Informant 1994.

Caro-Kann 4...Nd7 by Leonid Shamkovich and Eric Schiller. Chess Enterprises 1988.

Encyclopaedia of Chess Openings, Volume B (3rd Edition) by Chess Informant. Chess Informant 1997.

How to Play the Caro-Kann Defense by Raymond Keene and Shaun Taulbut. Batsford 1988.

Isolated Pawn by Andrei Mikhalchischin, Yakov Srokowski and Vladimir Braslavsky. Chess Academy, 1994.

Jon Speelman's Best Games by Jon Speelman. Batsford, 1997.

Play the Caro-Kann by Egon Varnusz. Pergamon.

Panov Attack: At the Crossroads of Opening Theory by Eric Schiller. Volumes 1-3. Chess Enterprises, 1995-98.

Praktische Eröffnungstrategie: Die Eröffnung Caro-Kann by Hans Müller. Schachverlag Hand Hedwigs's, 1931.

The Caro-Kann Advance by Byron Jacobs. Chess Press, 1997.

The Caro-Kann in Black and White by Anatoly Karpov and Alexander Belyavsky, R & D Publishing 1994.

The Classical Caro-Kann Rejuvenated by Eric Schiller, Chess Enterprises 1995.

Understanding the Caro-Kann Defense by Raymond Keene, Andy Soltis, Edmar Mednis, Jack Peters and Julio Kaplan. RHM Press 1980.

CHESS PRODUCTS CATALOG

For the latest updated listings, go to our web site
www.cardozapub.com

KASPAROV TALKING COACH™

SAITEK - The World Leader in Intelligent Electronic Games

AMAZING NEW TALKING TECHNOLOGY - Wow everyone with this incredible table top computer chess unit that not only informs and encourages you throughout the game but provides tremendous flexibility for both playing and coaching. Even more amazing, this **talking chess computer** retails for under $100!

POWERFUL AND VERSATILE - SETTINGS FOR EVERYONE - Play at any level you like - **384 level/setting combinations** and a built-in library of 134 opening moves allow a full range of options. Beginners can use the levels and features to learn, intermediate players to become stronger, and higher level players to take the challenge head on.

GREAT FOR LEARNING - Improve your chess or play for fun! The user-selectable **Talking Coach** includes learning, coach and warning modes (lets you know if a piece is in take), while the smart hint key suggests moves when you need help. If you change your mind and want to see how a game plays out differently, use the take-back feature; it allows take back up to 6 moves.

READY FOR ACTION - Sensory style chess board comes with built-in handy storage compartment for the pieces. Turn off current game at any time and continue play later - computer remembers position for up to two years.

To order, send just $99.95 for the <u>Kasparov Talking Coach</u>.

KASPAROV CHESS GK2100™
SAITEK - The World Leader in Intelligent Electronic Games

THE BEST VALUE MONEY CAN BUY! - The **fabulous** Kasparov GK2100 is the **most popular** chess computer we sell. Using a super high speed **RISC** computer chip and rated at a **2334** USCF rating, you'll have consistent challenges and excitement. Coaching features and fun levels makes it suitable for novices; masters and experts will want to choose higher levels.

GREAT DESIGN - Packaged in a sleek, handsome cabinet suitable for your living room. No need to find a partner to play - **take on the Champion**!

POWERFUL PROGRAM FEATURES - **64 levels of play** include sudden death, tournament, problem solving and beginner's. Shows intended move and position evaluation, take back up to 50 moves, and user selectable **book openings library**. Also choose from **Active, Passive, Tournament, complete book, no book.** Select the high speed **Selective Search** or play against the powerful **Brute Force.** program. Thinks in opponents time for best realism. Shutoff, shut on memory - remembers game for 1 year!

GREAT FOR BEGINNERS AND MASTERS ALIKE! - This **awesome program** can beat over 99% of all regular chess players, yet it is still suitable for beginners and intermediate players: Simply set the skill level to the appropriate strength for the best challenges. Matching your skill to the correct level of play ensures a **challenging** and **exciting** game.

EVEN MORE FEATURES - Opening library of 35,000 moves, **large LCD** shows full information and keeps track of playing time. Modern ergonomic design goes well in living room.

To order, send $199.95 for the Kasparov Chess GK2100

CARDOZA PUBLISHING CHESS BOOKS

- OPENINGS -

WINNING CHESS OPENINGS by Bill Robertie - Shows concepts and best opening moves of more than 25 essential openings from Black's and White's perspectives: King's Gambit, Center Game, Scotch Game, Giucco Piano, Vienna Game, Bishop's Opening, Ruy Lopez, French, Caro-Kann, Sicilian, Alekhine, Pirc, Modern, Queen's Gambit, Nimzo-Indian, Queen's Indian, Dutch, King's Indian, Benoni, English, Bird's, Reti's, and King's Indian Attack. Examples from 25 grandmasters and champions including Fischer and Kasparov. 144 pages, $9.95

WORLD CHAMPION OPENINGS by Eric Schiller - This serious reference work covers the essential opening theory and moves of every major chess opening and variation as played by all the world champions. Reading as much like an encyclopedia of the must-know openings crucial to every chess player's knowledge as a powerful tool showing the insights, concepts and secrets as used by the greatest players of all time, World Champion Openings (WCO) covers an astounding 100 crucial openings in full conceptual detail (with 100 actual games from the champions themselves)! A must-have book for serious chess players. 384 pages, $18.95

STANDARD CHESS OPENINGS by Eric Schiller - The new definitive standard on opening chess play in the 20th century, this comprehensive guide covers every important chess opening and variation ever played and currently in vogue. In all, more than 3,000 opening strategies are presented! Differing from previous opening books which rely almost exclusively on bare notation, SCO features substantial discussion and analysis on each opening so that you learn and understand the concepts behind them. Includes more than 250 completely annotated games (including a game representative of each major opening) and more than 1,000 diagrams! For modern players at any level, this is the standard reference book necessary for competitive play. A must have for serious chess players!!! 768 pages, $24.95

UNORTHODOX CHESS OPENINGS by Eric Schiller - The exciting guide to all the major unorthodox openings used by chess players, contains more than 1,500 weird, contentious, controversial, unconventional, arrogant, and outright strange opening strategies. From their tricky tactical surprises to their bizarre names, these openings fly in the face of tradition. You'll meet such openings as the Orangutang, Raptor Variation, Halloween Gambit, Double Duck, Frankenstein-Dracula Variation, and even the Drunken King! These openings are a sexy and exotic way to spice up a game and a great weapon to spring on unsuspecting and often unprepared opponents. More than 750 diagrams show essential positions. 528 pages, $24.95

GAMBIT OPENING REPERTOIRE FOR WHITE by Eric Schiller - Chessplayers who enjoy attacking from the very first move are rewarded here with a powerful repertoire of brilliant gambits. Starting off with 1.e4 or 1.d4 and then using such sharp weapons such as the Göring Gambit (Accepted and Declined), Halasz Gambit, Alapin Gambit, Ulysses Gambit, Short Attack and many more, to put great pressure on opponents, Schiller presents a complete attacking repertoire to use against the most popular defenses, including the Sicilian, French, Scandinavian, Caro-Kann, Pirc, Alekhine, and other Open Game positions. 192 pages, $14.95.

GAMBIT OPENING REPERTOIRE FOR BLACK by Eric Schiller - For players that like exciting no-holds-barred chess, this versatile gambit repertoire shows Black how to take charge with aggressive attacking defenses against any orthodox first White opening move; 1.e4, 1.d4 and 1.c4. Learn the Scandinavian Gambit against 1.e4, the Schara Gambit and Queen's Gambit Declined variations against 1.d4, and some flank and unorthodox gambits also. Black learns the secrets of seizing the initiative from White's hands, usually by investing a pawn or two, to begin powerful attacks that can send White to early defeat. 176 pages, $14.95.

COMPLETE DEFENSE TO QUEEN PAWN OPENINGS by Eric Schiller - This aggressive counterattacking repertoire covers Black opening systems against virtually every chess opening except for 1.e4 (including most flank games), based on the exciting and powerful Tarrasch Defense, an opening that helped bring Championship titles to Kasparov and Spassky. Black learns to effectively use the Classical Tarrasch, Symmetrical Tarrasch, Asymmetrical Tarrasch, Marshall and Tarrasch Gambits, and Tarrasch without Nc3, to achieve an early equality or even an outright advantage in the first few moves. 288 pages, $16.95.

COMPLETE DEFENSE TO KING PAWN OPENINGS by *Eric Schiller* - Learn a complete defensive system against 1.e4. This powerful repertoire not only limits White's ability to obtain any significant opening advantage but allows Black to adopt the flexible Caro-Kann formation, the favorite weapon of many of the greatest chess players. All White's options are explained in detail, and a plan is given for Black to combat them all. Analysis is up-to-date and backed by examples drawn from games of top stars. Detailed index lets you follow the opening from the point of a specific player, or through its history. 288 pages, $16.95.

SECRETS OF THE SICILIAN DRAGON by *GM Eduard Gufeld and Eric Schiller* - The mighty Dragon Variation of the Sicilian Defense is one of the most exciting openings in chess. Everything from opening piece formation to the endgame, including clear explanations of all the key strategic and tactical ideas, is covered in full conceptual detail. Instead of memorizing a jungle of variations, you learn the really important ideas behind the opening, and how to adapt them at the chessboard. Special sections on the heroes of the Dragon show how the greatest players handle the opening. The most instructive book on the Dragon written! 208 pages, $14.95.

- MIDDLEGAME/TACTICS/WINNING CONCEPTS -

WORLD CHAMPION COMBINATIONS by *Keene and Schiller* - Learn the insights, concepts and moves of the greatest combinations ever by the greatest players who ever lived. From Morphy to Alekhine, to Fischer to Kasparov, the incredible combinations and brilliant sacrifices of the 13 World Champions are collected here in the most insightful combinations book written. Packed with fascinating strategems, 50 annotated games, and great practical advice for your own games, this is a great companion guide to *World Champion Openings*. 264 pages, $16.95.

WINNING CHESS TACTICS by *Bill Robertie* - 14 chapters of winning tactical concepts show the complete explanations and thinking behind every tactical concept: pins, single and double forks, double attacks, skewers, discovered and double checks, multiple threats - and other crushing tactics to gain an immediate edge over opponents. Learn the power tools of tactical play to become a stronger player. Includes guide to chess notation. 128 pages, $9.95

ENCYCLOPEDIA OF CHESS WISDOM, The Essential Concepts and Strategies of Smart Chess Play by *Eric Schiller* - The most important concepts, strategies, tactics, wisdom, and thinking that every chessplayer must know, plus the gold nuggets of knowledge behind every attack and defense, is collected together in one highly focused volume. From opening, middle and endgame strategy, to psychological warfare and tournament tactics, the *Encyclopedia of Chess Wisdom* forms the blueprint of power play and advantage at the chess board. Step-by-step, the reader is taken through the thinking behind each essential concept, and through examples, discussions, and diagrams, shown the full impact on the game's direction. You even learn how to correctly study chess to become a chess master. 400 pages, $19.95.

- BASIC CHESS BOOKS -

THE BASICS OF WINNING CHESS by *Jacob Cantrell* - A great first book of chess, in one easy reading, beginner's learn the moves of the pieces, the basic rules and principles of play, the standard openings, and both Algebraic and English chess notation. The basic ideas of the winning concepts and strategies of middle and end game play are shown as well. Includes example games of great champions. 64 pages, $4.95.

BEGINNING CHESS PLAY by *Bill Robertie* - Step-by-step approach uses 113 diagrams to teach novices the basic principles of chess. Covers opening, middle and end game strategies, principles of development, pawn structure, checkmates, openings and defenses, how to write and read chess notation, join a chess club, play in tournaments, use a chess clock, and get rated. Two annotated games illlustrate strategic thinking for easy learning. 144 pages, $9.95

- MATES & ENDGAMES -

303 TRICKY CHECKMATES by *Fred Wilson and Bruce Alberston* - Both a fascinating challenge and great training tool, this collection of two, three and bonus four move checkmates is great for advanced beginning, intermediate and expert players. Mates are in order of difficulty, from the simple to very complex positions. Learn the standard patterns and stratagems for cornering the king: corridor and support mates, attraction and deflection sacrifices, pins and annihilation, the quiet move, and the dreaded *zugzwang*. Examples, drawn from actual games, illustrate a wide range of chess tactics from old classics right up to the 1990's. 192 pages, $12.95.

MASTER CHECKMATE STRATEGY by *Bill Robertie* - Learn the basic combinations, plus advanced, surprising and unconventional mates, the most effective pieces needed to win, and how to mate opponents with just a pawn advantage. also, how to work two rooks into an unstoppable attack; how to wield a queen advantage with deadly intent; how to coordinate pieces of differing strengths into indefensible positions of their opponents; when it's best to have a knight, and when a bishop to win. 144 pages, $9.95

BASIC ENDGAME STRATEGY: Kings, Pawns and Minor Pieces by *Bill Robertie* - Learn the mating principles and combinations needed to finish off opponents. From the four basic checkmates using the King with the queen, rook, two bishops, and bishop/knight combinations, to the King/pawn, King/Knight and King/Bishop endgames, you'll learn the essentials of translating small edges into decisive checkmates. Learn the 50-move rule, and the combinations of pieces that can't force a mate against a lone King. 144 pages, $12.95.

BASIC ENDGAME STRATEGY: Rooks and Queens by Bill Robertie - The companion guide to *Basic Endgame Strategy: Kings, Pawns and Minor Pieces*, you'll learn the basic mating principles and combinations of the Queen and Rook with King, how to turn middlegame advantages into victories, by creating passed pawns, using the King as a weapon, clearing the way for rook mates, and other endgame combinations. 144 pages, $12.95.

EXCELLENT CHESS BOOKS - OTHER PUBLISHERS
- OPENINGS -

HOW TO PLAY THE TORRE by *Eric Schiller* - One of Schiller's best-selling books, the 19 chapters on this fabulous and aggressive White opening (1. d4 Nf6; 2. Nf3 e6; 3. Bg5) will make opponents shudder and get you excited about chess all over again. Insightful analysis, completely annotated games get you ready to win! 210 pages, $17.50.

A BLACK DEFENSIVE SYSTEM WITH 1...D6 by *Andrew Soltis* - This Black reply - so rarely played that it doesn't even have a name - throws many opponents off their rote attack and can lead to a decisive positional advantage. Use this surprisingly strong system to give you the edge against unprepared opponents. 166 pages, $16.50.

BLACK TO PLAY CLASSICAL DEFENSES AND WIN by *Eric Schiller* - *Shows you how to develop a complete opening repertoire as black.* Emerge from *any* opening with a playable position, fighting for the center from the very first move. Defend against the Ruy Lopez, Italian Game, King's Gambit, King's Indian, many more. 166 pages, $16.50.

ROMANTIC KING'S GAMBIT IN GAMES & ANALYSIS by *Santasiere & Smith* - The most comprehensive collection of theory and games (137) on this adventurous opening is filled with annotations and "color" on the greatest King's Gambits played and the players. Makes you *want* to play! Very readable; packed with great concepts. 233 pages, $17.50.

WHITE TO PLAY 1.E4 AND WIN by *Eric Schiller* - *Shows you how to develop a complete opening system as white beginning 1. e4.* Learn the recommended opening lines to all the major systems as white, and how to handle any defense black throws back. Covers the Sicilian, French, Caro-Kann, Scandinavia; many more. 166 pages, $16.50.

BIG BOOK OF BUSTS by *Schiller & Watson* - Learn how to defend against 70 dangerous and annoying openings which are popular in amateur chess and can lead to defeat if unprepared, but can be refuted when you know how to take opponents off their favorite lines. Greet opponents with your own surprises! Recommended. 293 pages, $22.95.

MIDDLEGAME/TACTICS/WINNING CONCEPTS -

CHESS TACTICS FOR ADVANCED PLAYERS by *Yuri Averbakh* - A great tactical book. Complex combinations are brilliantly simpified into basic, easy-to-understand concepts you can use to win. Learn the underlying structure of piece harmony and fortify skills through numerous exercises. Very instructive, a must read. 328 pages, $17.50.

BIG BOOK OF COMBINATIONS by *Eric Schiller* - Test your tactical ability in 1,000 brilliant combinations from actual games spanning the history of chess. Includes various degrees of difficulty from the easiest to the most difficult combinations. Unlike other combination books, no hints are provided, so you'll have to work! 266 pages, $17.95.

STRATEGY FOR ADVANCED PLAYERS *by Eric Schiller* - For intermediate to advanced players, 45 insightful and very informative lessons illustrate the strategic and positional factors you need to know in middle and endgame play. Recommended highly as a tool to learn strategic chess and become a better player. 135 pages, $14.50.

HOW TO BECOME A CANDIDATE MASTER *by Alex Dunne* -The book that makes you *think* is packed with tips and inspiration; from a wide variety of openings in 50 fully annotated games to in-depth middle and end game discussions, the goal is to take your game up to the Expert level. A perennial favorite. 252 pages, $18.95.

- ENDGAMES -

ESSENTIAL CHESS ENDINGS EXPLAINED VOL. 1 *by Jeremy Silman* - This essential and enjoyable reference tool to mates and stalemates belongs in every chess player's library. Commentary on every move plus quizzes and many diagrams insure complete understanding. All basic positions covered, plus many advanced ones. 221 pages, $16.50.

ESSENTIAL CHESS ENDINGS EXPLAINED VOL. 2 *by Ken Smith* - This book assumes you know the basics of the 1st volume and takes you all the way to Master levels. Work through moves of 275 positions and learn as you go. There are explanations of every White and Black move so you know what's happening from both sides. 298 pages, $17.50.

- ORDER YOUR BOOKS TODAY AND BE A WINNER! -